Palgrave Executive Essentials

Today's complex and changing business environment brings with it a number of pressing challenges. To be successful, business professionals are increasingly required to leverage and spot future trends, be masters of strategy, all while leading responsibly, inspiring others, mastering financial techniques and driving innovation.

Palgrave Executive Essentials empowers you to take your skills to the next level. Offering a suite of resources to support you on your executive journey and written by renowned experts from top business schools, the series is designed to support professionals as they embark on executive education courses, but it is equally applicable to practicing leaders and managers. Each book brings you in-depth case studies, accompanying video resources, reflective questions, practical tools and core concepts that can be easily applied to your organization, all written in an engaging, easy to read style.

Amit Basu • Steve Muylle

Competitive Digital Innovation

Transforming Products, Processes
and Business Models to Win
in the Digital Economy

Amit Basu
Edwin L. Cox School of Business
Southern Methodist University
Dallas, TX, USA

Steve Muylle
Vlerick Business School
Ghent University
Ghent, Belgium

ISSN 2731-5614　　　　　ISSN 2731-5622　(electronic)
Palgrave Executive Essentials
ISBN 978-3-031-23439-2　　　ISBN 978-3-031-23440-8　(eBook)
https://doi.org/10.1007/978-3-031-23440-8

This Palgrave Macmillan imprint is published by the registered company Springer Nature Switzerland AG.
The registered company address is: Gewerbestrasse 11, 6330 Cham, Switzerland

Acknowledgements

The authors would like to thank the many executives they worked with on various executive education sessions and workshops around the world. They would also like to acknowledge the research assistance of Dr Willem Standaert. The authors would also like to thank their families for their invaluable help and support.

Abstract

The focus of digital innovation in business has shifted from internal transformation within firms to their market interface and ecosystems. Business executives and strategic planners need to understand how they can leverage digital technologies to redefine their market-facing business processes, their products and services, and often even their scope and business models, to be competitive in today's hybrid markets. This book provides a coherent and comprehensive approach to address these challenges, to not just survive but rather thrive in the twenty-first-century global marketplace.

Contents

About the Authors

Amit Basu holds the Carr P. Collins Chair in MIS and is a professor at the Cox School of Business at Southern Methodist University in Dallas. He has also been on the faculty of Vanderbilt University and the University of Maryland. His research and teaching interests are in the areas of knowledge and database systems, decision support systems, digital strategy, electronic commerce and workflow management. He has also been a consultant and advisor to a number of private and public sector organizations, both in the USA and in Western Europe, and was the President of the INFORMS Information Systems Society from 2012 to 2014. He holds a PhD from the University of Rochester, an MBA from Southern Illinois University, and a BTech in Electrical Engineering from IIT Delhi.

Steve Muylle is Partner and full professor at Vlerick Business School and Ghent University, Belgium. His research interests are in the areas of digital strategy, electronic commerce and business-to-business marketing. Through his research and teaching, he has worked with many companies across the world, from large multinationals to start-ups and scale-ups on various projects involving digital strategy, marketing, supply management, and innovation. He also serves as an Independent Director on Corporate Boards. He holds a PhD and a degree in business engineering from Solvay Management School, Belgium, and received a doctoral fellowship award from the Intercollegiate Center for Management Science, Belgium. He was a visiting PhD student at the Owen Graduate School of Management, Vanderbilt University.

List of Figures

List of Tables

1

Introduction

So what do we mean by Competitive Digital Innovation and what is this book about? It is about how a business can use digital technology[1] to compete effectively in today's hyperconnected and highly sophisticated markets. It is valuable for business leaders of established companies, providing key insights on how they can use digital technologies to transform their products, market-facing processes, and business models. It is also valuable for leaders of tech and digital companies for planning their future expansion and evolution.

Note that the fuel for digital competition is information. In 2003, in the midst of the dot-com bust after Y2K and the go-go tech explosion triggered by the commercialization of the Internet in 1995, Nicholas Carr wrote a provocative article in the Harvard Business Review entitled "IT Doesn't Matter". While it provoked strong sentiments on both sides from various stakeholders, some of the reactions were based on misunderstandings caused by the provocative title. Carr was not suggesting that information technology had no value. Rather, his key point was that much of the technological innovation enabled by advances in digital technologies were infrastructural changes that provided little sustainable competitive advantages to any specific businesses. He went on to suggest that unwarranted faith in the strategic value of information technology was leading many companies to overspend on computer hardware, software and services. Perhaps coincidentally, many companies downsized their information technology organizations over the next few years,

---

[1] In this book, we use the term "digitalization" to refer to the use of digital technologies such as computers, mobile computing devices, digital communication networks, embedded computing devices and software applications in products, processes and business models.

© The Author(s), under exclusive license to Springer Nature Switzerland AG 2023
A. Basu, S. Muylle, *Competitive Digital Innovation*, Palgrave Executive Essentials,
https://doi.org/10.1007/978-3-031-23440-8_1

outsourcing much of their needs and treating information technology as a utility.

Over the first two decades of the twenty-first century, the role of digital technology in business has only grown. It has led to excitement and speculation about technology trends such as Big Data, Analytics, Artificial Intelligence, the Metaverse, Mobility and IoT. Recognizing the reluctance of many companies to invest in internal information technology resources, a thriving industry of service providers has evolved, to help their clients leverage the benefits of these technologies. Yet the question of whether information technology provides sustainable competitive advantages still remains, as do the concerns raised by Carr in his article.

In our view, that question is the wrong one to ask. Businesses should not be looking for competitive advantages from digital technology, since indeed, technology is infrastructural and replicable at progressively lower costs, and even proprietary technologies are difficult to protect. However, when used effectively, these technologies can yield assets that do provide highly sustainable competitive advantage. These assets are the information and knowledge that can be gained through digitalization. They can reshape the products, processes, and even scope of any business to compete more effectively. We believe that the winning businesses of the future will be those that better use digital technologies to generate, manage and use information for competitive advantage. That is a key premise of this book.

Consider the companies represented in Fig. 1.1. What do all these companies have in common?

Fig. 1.1 Some leading companies

In our view, although they are in different sectors and industries, they share a number of common features, including:

1. They are all global leaders in their primary industry sectors.
2. All of them are facing competitive threats from tech-savvy new entrants.
3. All of them have enormous potential to generate future market value with digital.

One thing that should be very apparent, is that competitive digital innovation is not about technology leadership. Clearly, companies that sell information and information products, such as Google with its search products, Nielsen with its media information business and infomediaries such as Airbnb, LinkedIn and Uber, as well as producers of digital technologies such as Intel, Qualcomm and Nvidia, implicitly fit into the mold of digital competitors. However, it is not necessary for a business to have information or digital devices as a product in order to competitively leverage digital technologies. We are not suggesting that Whole Foods should stop selling groceries, or that General Mills should stop selling cereals.

Rather, we believe that businesses need to focus on information as a strategic asset, and use digital technologies aggressively to maximize the value of this asset; leveraging information for strategic value needs to be part of the corporate DNA and central to its culture; and its products and processes should be designed to capture, manage and leverage information creatively and effectively, to differentiate it from its competition.

Clearly, every business has a variety of critical assets, such as facilities, people, money and materials. What is so special about information versus other assets? We are not claiming that information makes other assets irrelevant, or less valuable. However, there are indeed some significant features of information as an asset:

1. *Cumulative Value*: Much has been said (and written) about the declining value of information technology, due to commoditization, technological advances and falling costs. Spending thousands, or even millions, on technology assets with rapid obsolescence can be a deterrent. However, information can have growing cumulative value, so that the more information you have, the more valuable it can be. This is particularly the case in settings where information has persistent value (for instance, consumer preferences versus news).
2. *Scalability*: Unlike most other assets, information can be reproduced and distributed at virtually no cost. For instance, human advisors or experts are

expensive and hard to replicate, while knowledge and even expertise can be replicated at scale.

3. *Portability*: Information can be easily transmitted almost instantaneously, at virtually no cost and to any place on the globe that is connected to the Internet.

4. *Transmutability*: The form and value of information is "in the eye of the beholder". That is, more than any other asset, information can be easily shaped to suit the needs and expectations of different users and uses.

5. *Securability*: Unlike information technology, which can be hard to keep proprietary, information can be secured and kept private and confidential. At the same time, it can also be one of the most vulnerable assets of a business in today's hyperconnected global economy.

Effective use and management of digital technology to yield high-value information therefore requires different approaches, and a different way of thinking, than other assets.

The power of digital technology for strategically leveraging information is exemplified by Amazon. When it first started selling books online, a common view was that Amazon's primary competitive edge was in its business model, which avoided expensive facilities such as stores, warehouses and trucks. Today, Amazon has stores, warehouses and trucks. So was it the fragmented structure of the bookselling sector? Today, books are just one product line for the company. Another common view was that Amazon's secret sauce was in economies of scale and lower prices. However, there is plenty of evidence that from its inception, Amazon has not had the lowest prices in many of its product categories. Yet another view was that Amazon was successful because it focused on services. Again, today the company sells a variety of tangible products, from Kindles and Echo to Ring and even TVs. However, smart investors looked past the company's lack of profitability, the narrow scope of its initial business (at one point, Amazon's market value was a significant percentage of that of the entire bookselling sector), its later expansion to seemingly diverse sectors, and even its forays into tangible products such as readers and digital appliances, to the company's true asset, its ever-growing treasure-chest of consumer information. The company's founder and first CEO, Jeff Bezos once said that the goal of Amazon was to be the most "customer-centric" company in the world across multiple sectors. Everything that Amazon does is geared towards knowing and understanding its customers better, and then serving them in smarter and more effective ways. This information is its true strategic asset, and the company's relentless pursuit of information leadership through creative digitalization is its greatest competitive weapon.

Clearly, not every business can, or should, try to be another Amazon. Far from it. And neither does a business have to be at the "bleeding edge" of information technology to successfully compete with digital. The goal of this book is to examine the various ways in which *any* business can use digital innovation to redefine its products, processes, and even scope, such that it effectively builds and uses its information assets to make it a more effective competitor in its markets.

So what about tech companies like Google, Airbnb, Uber, PayPal, eBay and Robinhood? In this book, we don't focus on these companies although our ideas apply to them as well. The reason for this is that such tech companies implicitly compete using digital technology and their information assets. However, we have found over the past many years that many business leaders think that competitive digital innovation is not for them and will take them outside their strategic focus and priorities. Many also believe that information technology is a support resource. Our goal in this book is to convince you that regardless of your business type or industry vertical, you can enhance your competitive position and win through judicious and effective use of digital technologies. And we show you how to think about the various possible types of competitive innovation that apply to your business. We believe that this will change your mindset. And then you can use our digitalization framework to identify, prioritize, operationalize, and evaluate appropriate digital innovation initiatives.

Overview of the Book

Digital technologies are forcing companies to rethink how they compete. Opportunities for digital innovation can arise in two contexts, the internal operations and processes of the business, and its interaction with its markets and other external stakeholders. While both contexts are important, the focus of this book is primarily on the second context, namely on the business's market interface. The reason for this is that the opportunities for internal innovation have mostly operational benefits, such as cost efficiency, process efficiency and resource utilization. In other words, they typically do not have strategic implications for management, even though they may sometimes require executive approval and large expenditures, and may yield significant business value. On the other hand, the innovations at the market interface often have significant strategic implications, and our goal is to better connect digital innovation to business strategy.

The book is organized in three parts. In Part I, we discuss how a business can seek to build competitive advantages using digital technologies to transform its market-facing processes and its products and services. In Part II, we examine how a business can reposition itself within its industry ecosystem, by leveraging digital technologies. We look at three issues: first, how businesses can exploit digitalization to directly engage with end consumers and restructure their industry position; second, how businesses can consider opportunities for digital (re)-intermediation; third, how businesses can generate revenues through digital innovation. And in Part III, we discuss how the strategic focus and priorities of a business can impact the choice and prioritization of its market-facing digital innovations, and how management can evaluate such initiatives. Finally, we end by discussing some of the risks of competitive digital innovation and some trending technologies.

Reflection Questions

- Reflecting upon the use of digital technologies in your business, to what extent do these technologies help you compete more effectively in your key markets?

- How are your competitors using digital technologies to change their products?

- How are your competitors using digital technologies to interact with key stakeholders such as customers and suppliers?

- Does your business focus on information as a strategic asset and use digital technology to maximize its value?

Part I

Using Digital Technologies to Transform Processes and Products

The COVID-19 Pandemic that suddenly emerged in early 2020, severely disrupted businesses everywhere and the global economy (as well as society at large) within a matter of a few weeks. Governments had to impose drastic curtailment of the movement and interaction of their citizens with each other, as well as travel. As businesses of all types scrambled to find ways to keep operating, two things quickly became clear:

1. Companies that had digitalized their internal processes could continue to operate more easily than those that relied on physical processes.
2. Companies that had digitalized their products and market-facing processes could continue to serve their markets better than those that relied on physical products and processes.

In the real estate arena, the contrasting experiences of Century 21 and Zillow are good illustrations of these points. Century 21 has a storied legacy as a traditional real estate brokerage company. They have a huge presence in the USA, as well as in many other countries, achieved through a vast network of local offices and realtor networks. While they have made a number of digital innovations, the focus has been on digital transformation and automation of internal processes to support the front-office workforce of realtors and agents. On the other hand, Zillow started as a pure-play info-tech company, providing consumers and businesses with online information about real estate investments. When the COVID-19 Pandemic hit, it severely limited the ability of Century 21's real estate agents to conduct their business. At the same time, these agents did not have the resources in place to pivot to a digital format and channels. However, Zillow was perfectly positioned for the new setting, and was able to add a variety of transaction services to its initial advertising-based business model. This is evidenced by Zillow's financial performance, as illustrated in the figures below. The difference was magnified by the fact that Century 21 had a significant focus on commercial real estate, which ground to a halt during the Pandemic, while Zillow's consumer-first and information-driven business was not affected as significantly—even when consumers didn't buy and sell much as for instance in the early stages of the Pandemic, this did not keep them from doing online research on real estate, which helped Zillow's revenues. And later, in 2021 and 2022, when the level of transactions went up significantly, Zillow was able to get a significant portion of the business.

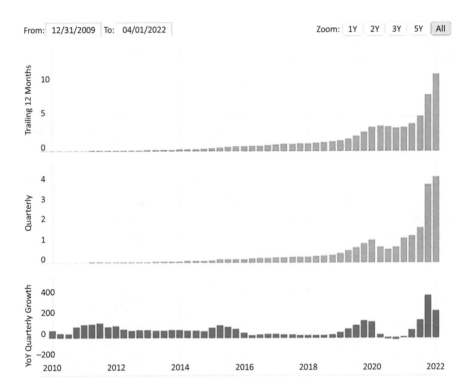

Fig. 1 Zillow Revenue 2010–2022 | ZG | MacroTrends

Of course, that does not mean that digitalization is a panacea for every crisis, and there could be other crises where it would not be a key factor. However, it has certainly sensitized companies all over the World to the merits of business processes that are independent of location or even geography, of virtual work environments, of information flows that are realized through the movement of electrons (or photons) rather than of paper, of e-commerce and of digital products. It is also interesting to note that many traditional businesses viewed the Pandemic as a significant but temporary shock to their markets and looked forward to returning to business as usual once the Pandemic was over. It is already clear that this last view was both incorrect and detrimental. Most traditional companies that used a stop-gap or Band-Aid approach to digitalization are finding that the shock of the Pandemic has a significant hysteresis, and that business is going to be different for the foreseeable future. Ironically, even those that now realize this are finding it very difficult to pivot due to all the economic pressures today, which are leading to highly volatile markets.

Even before 2020, business was already moving in the direction of increased digitalization of processes and products, so the Pandemic served as an accelerator. Unfortunately, such accelerators do not allow business leaders and executives much flexibility, in terms of choices or priorities. In general, business leaders face a variety of choices when it comes to where, when and how to digitalize their businesses. The purpose of this book is to provide them with a way to organize their thinking about these choices and priorities.

Digitalization can be approached from two directions, outside-in and inside-out. The outside-in perspective starts with the realization or discovery of some need or opportunity in the marketplace, and then proceeds to examine how the business can effectively meet that need. On the other hand, the inside-out perspective starts with the discovery of some idea or technological innovation within the business, and then proceeds to examine how this opportunity can lead to significant market value and returns to the business and its stakeholders.

While both approaches are viable and can lead to successful outcomes, the outside-in approach tends to be easier for new ventures and small organic companies than for established companies with legacy businesses. In fact, one of the challenges in pursuing innovation in an existing company is that it already has its value chain and system in place, buying inputs and selling products through established processes and business and revenue models, deploying legacy resources and dynamic capabilities, grounded in an entrenched organizational structure and deep-rooted culture. The legacy of these structural elements creates inertia, as well as strong incentives to focus on innovations that lead to incremental improvements to existing processes. In other words, the tendency is to ask "what can we do with what we have?"

This perspective of executives is analogous to that of a homeowner contemplating changes/improvements to a large house. It is much easier to consider repainting, upgrades to appliances and fixtures, and general maintenance, than structural renovations. To some extent, this may be driven by fear of the unknown, such as the possibility of structural weaknesses caused if load-bearing walls are removed, or disrupting other elements in a complex inter-connected system. When executives consider digitalizing a legacy business, the same attitude can persist, which often leads to initiatives that merely auto-mate existing processes or products. While such changes can yield benefits, they often fail to realize the full benefits of digitalization.

Digitalization, however, can transform the organization's business pro-cesses, resources and capabilities, products and services, and key relationships in its ecosystem. Given this incredible breadth of scope, the inside-out per-spective can be overly limiting. At the same time, it is difficult and even some-times futile to use a "green field" market-driven approach. For one thing, that can have radical change implications that result in divisive organizational and managerial resistance. So it helps to have some way of organizing one's think-ing about the three key dimensions of digitalization, which are the business, the market and digital technology.

The digitalization framework introduced in this part of the book is an effec-tive way to identify and evaluate a business's digitalization choices. It is intended to help executives and planners step back from their traditional mindsets, and think more comprehensively about the opportunities to benefit from digitalization. It provides a structured approach to identify digitalization initiatives that can enhance the business's market performance and support its strategic priorities. It allows managers to think in a progressively broadening context organized in three levels.

The three levels of the digitalization framework are as follows:

1. Digitalizing External Processes
2. Digitally Enhancing Existing Products
3. Creating New Digital Products

As mentioned earlier, this framework does not include digitalization of a business's internal processes, such as manufacturing, workforce development, human resource management and internal accounting and financial processes. While many companies still have work to do in this context, the key chal-lenges are well-understood, and there are a variety of existing frameworks and methods to tackle them. That is because these processes were the focus of the first wave of computerization and business automation. Companies such as IBM, SAP, Microsoft and Oracle excelled in enterprise software applications that helped even large and highly complex organizations automate key opera-tions and functions. However, there is a need for guidance on the digitaliza-tion of the external interface of the business, and its interaction with external stakeholders, which is the focus of this book.

We next briefly describe each of the levels of the framework. They correspond to progressively expanding scope and complexity, rather than a prescription for implementation. In other words, a business can start its digitalization efforts at any of the levels. However, initiatives at each of the levels may require (or imply) consideration of issues relating to lower levels. Thus, while a process digitalization initiative typically would not require consideration of product innovation, many initiatives may require changes to both processes and products.

Level 1: Digitalization of Market-facing Processes. This is a useful starting point for existing businesses that seek to use digital technologies to support or transform the interaction of the business with its external stakeholders in its value system and ecosystem. The value system links the business's value chain to those of upstream suppliers and downstream channels and customers, and can be expanded into an ecosystem when considering how it adjusts to the moves of the business, its competitors, and potential complementors and partners.[1] An existing business can use digital technologies to support the various processes through which it interacts with these vertical and horizontal stakeholders. A framework for such innovation is presented in Chap. 2. In a similar vein, new businesses can pursue digitalization of key business processes for interacting with external stakeholders. As such, they can strongly benefit from using digital technologies to market their products as it levels the playing field and lowers the bar on the required scale and resources. By digitalizing the right set of external processes, a new business can overcome scale issues and rapidly build a customer base.

Level 2: Digital Enhancement of Existing Products. This level of the framework is geared towards digital initiatives that enhance existing products. Traditional products have no or few digital features. A refrigerator, for instance, helps to keep food fresh longer, and its basic features include temperature control (to slow down the activity of bacteria in the food) and size (how much food can be stored). Additional features such as efficient energy consumption, a freezer section, an ice maker, and color and design can also add value to the user. However, digitalization can substantially enhance the functionality of the refrigerator. Samsung's Family Hub™ refrigerator, for example, has a big display on its right door for mirroring TV and streaming content, and playing music. The screen can also be used to share family notes and photos, and sync household members' schedules. Furthermore, it is also known as a "selfie taking fridge." By means of built-in cameras, the inside of

---

[1] A. Brandenburger and B. Nalebuff, Co-opetition: A Revolution Mindset that Combines Competition and Cooperation, Crown Business, 1996.

the refrigerator can be viewed from a smartphone when doing grocery shopping. Finally, the smart fridge also connects with and controls other appliances in the house, such as the smart doorbell, oven, lighting or thermostat, and comes with various mobile apps including recipes, view inside, shopping list, fridge manager, Instacart, GrubHub and Amazon Dash. In Chap. 3, we present different ways to digitally enhance products that can assist businesses in digitally enhancing their existing products.

Level 3: Creating Digital Products. The third level of the digitalization framework deals with the development of entirely new digital products. Rather than digitally enhancing an existing product, new digital products can be developed from the data that is generated in other digitalization initiatives. By going digital, businesses can leverage their digitalization initiatives in levels one and two to create new digital products. In addition, new digital products can be developed that are not based on process digitalization initiatives or digital enhancement of existing products, and are derived from an entirely new digital resource such as data or information that the business has access to (e.g., in its supply chain or through its reporting requirements).

3E, for instance, a global provider of compliance solutions, sells access to its database of over 10 million safety data sheets on its e-commerce portal MSDS.com to any organization that manufactures, distributes, uses, stores, transports or disposes of products containing hazardous substances, which involves regulatory compliance obligations to a variety of agencies and government bodies. In the past, safety data sheets were not products. These sheets were required when companies dealt with chemical, pharmaceutical, or retail products that contained hazardous substances. Now, 3E has built the world's largest database of safety data sheets, which it monetizes through a freemium or enterprise plan. In Chap. 4, guidelines for identifying new digital products are presented.

10.1   Using the Digitalization Framework

The three levels of the framework allow one to gradually expand the scope of the context for identifying new digital initiatives. The digitalization of market-facing business processes does not require changing the product. And new digital products can be developed from a new digital resource or from data that is generated by process or existing product digitalization. It is important to note that while the three levels are progressive, the digitalization framework is not a roadmap. In other words, one does not have to start in Level 1, go on to Level 2 and end in Level 3. The identification of new digital initiatives can be focused on process digitalization without considering product digitalization. Furthermore, one does not always have to start with process digitalization. For instance, an initial focus can be on an existing product rather than a process and can lead to initiatives that digitally enhance that product. Likewise, one can also start by identifying a new digital product.

Because of the breadth of the framework, the identification of digital initiatives in a specific level can stimulate the need for initiatives in prior levels. Product digitalization can lead to changes in the process support for the digitally enhanced product. Likewise, creation of new digital products can lead to digitalization of process support for selling the new digital product.

2

Digitally Enhancing Market-facing Processes

In this chapter, we describe the various ways in which a business can digitalize its interactions with external stakeholders in its value system or ecosystem, within the context of its existing products and services.

Market-facing Processes

Market-facing business processes are those that involve interactions with entities external to the business, such as customers, suppliers and business partners. Such processes can be categorized in various ways, but in the context of digitalization, categorizing them into transaction processes and decision support processes is useful.

Transaction processes are a set of processes that come into play when the business wants to conduct transactions with external stakeholders. The processes are outward-facing and supported through transaction-specific elements in the interface between the business and both upstream and downstream entities that transact with it. The key downstream entities are the business's customers, and the business can set up an e-commerce (electronic commerce) initiative in which it acts as a seller and uses digital technologies in support of its online sales process. Conversely, for upstream entities such as suppliers, the business can develop an e-procurement (electronic procurement) initiative and use digital technologies that support the online buying process. Most businesses have to support both downstream and upstream transactional processes, and therefore can consider digitalization on both fronts.

© The Author(s), under exclusive license to Springer Nature Switzerland AG 2023
A. Basu, S. Muylle, *Competitive Digital Innovation*, Palgrave Executive Essentials,
https://doi.org/10.1007/978-3-031-23440-8_2

Decision support processes deal with non-transactional interactions between the business and its external stakeholders, that can support and enhance the management of both parties. Traditionally, some of these processes were limited to the business itself, for internal support of its managerial decision making. However, through the use of digital technologies, these processes can move to the business's market interface and support interactions with external stakeholders to assist them in their decision making. Furthermore, these processes can interact with the transaction processes, as they build capabilities that may derive from or lead to enhancement of transaction processes. Their value is derived through their resulting impact on the other processes and they can offer significant opportunities that will help the business in its marketing and sales or procurement and supply chain management.

In this chapter, we examine the different ways in which digital technologies can be used to enhance and innovate the processes in each of these categories.

Transaction Processes

At first glance, a business transaction may appear to be atomic, a simple ringing of the till or swapping of product and money. However, at a more detailed level, a number of important and distinct processes have to be undertaken when businesses transact with each other or with consumers. Consider the example of a consumer buying a TV. To begin with, the buyer has to discover the available types, brands and model choices, and where they can be purchased. Then the buyer has to determine which particular TV they should buy, and at what price. Having made that decision, the buyer then has to make the purchase, pay for the TV, and then receive it. Each of these steps is non-trivial, and can influence the buyer's experience and potential outcome. Looking at the transaction from the seller's side is also instructive. Consider an electronics retailer like Best Buy or Amazon. At each step, the seller has an opportunity to impact the buyer's experience, and thereby enhance or deter the chance of "winning the deal".

In an innovative study of online flower auctions in the Netherlands, Kambil and van Heck (1998)[1] broke down the auctions into a set of processes, which can be applied to the broader context of all transactions. Interestingly, each of these processes can be digitalized in various ways to add value to the business.

---

[1] Ajit Kambil, Eric van Heck, (1998) Reengineering the Dutch Flower Auctions: A Framework for Analyzing Exchange Organizations. Information Systems Research 9(1):1–19.

Table 2.1 Transaction processes

Transaction Processes	**Search** for products, buyers and sellers
	Authentication of products, buyers and sellers
	Valuation of products
	Payment and payment clearance
	Logistics including order tracking, delivery and installation
	After Sales Service

The key transaction processes are as shown in Table 2.1 , and we examine each of them in turn.

Search

In traditional (physical) markets, business transactions are conducted in stores and offices. This implies that buyers and sellers have to be in the same location (such as a store). On the positive side, this physical face-to-face interaction enables both parties to evaluate each other, the products being transacted, their prices, etc. However, this approach is also limited by the cost of the transacting parties finding each other, setting up meetings of the relevant people, having all the relevant products (and information about them) available, and also all the resources needed to complete the transaction process. On the other hand, in digital marketplaces each party interacts with digital devices and thus cannot directly observe and examine its trading partners. The search process deals with digital mechanisms that enable sellers to find buyers, and buyers to find sellers and products and services.

Digitalization of search has a number of significant benefits. For a business selling products, traditional commerce requires it to have a point of presence, such as a store or office, in a location where potential buyers will find it. Clearly, this implies both significant geographical limitations as well as significant costs. On the other hand, in digital commerce buyers can find potential sellers and vice versa, without incurring such costs and geographical limits. In fact, the use of digital search mechanisms and online markets enables search for buyers by sellers, and search for sellers and product by buyers, to achieve significant scale in both market size and reach.

Digital search mechanisms rely on various digital technologies. Through its registered URL (Uniform Resource Locator), the business can be located on the World Wide Web on the Internet. Likewise, its product pages can be located through their respective URLs. This feature is interesting in itself. Think of the URL as a digital address. In the traditional setting, the store has a single address where customers can visit. However, in the digital world, the store can have as many addresses as it wants. Each address, whether listed on a Web page, embedded in a banner ad or any other Web content, provides visitors with the ability to visit the store with a single click of their mouse. Furthermore, that click can get them to any part of the store, not just the front door. For instance, it could get them to a single product, or even a single promotion page for that product. This is a powerful and subtle feature, since it provides both great opportunities but also cause for caution. While it vastly expands the search capabilities for the store and its products to be found, it also necessitates consistency and coordination between the different parts of the store's Website, not all of which may be managed by the same person or group.

By optimizing its Website for search engines (aka Search Engine Optimization or SEO), the business can make it easier for external stakeholders to find it and its products online. The business can also engage in online advertising on search engines (aka Search Engine Advertising) and comparison-shopping sites, and sponsor or place banner ads in directories of portals or marketplaces. It can also turn to affiliate programs and reward third parties for generating traffic to its Website. The business can also push commercial messages to its target audience through direct email campaigns and email newsletters. Furthermore, the business can turn to social media services platforms. It can advertise on these platforms and establish a presence such that it can be found. In addition, it can launch mobile applications and make these available on mobile platforms such as the Apple App Store and Google Play. Furthermore, the business can integrate with Amazon Alexa, Google Assistant and other voice assistants to support the search process.

Established businesses already have various conventional mechanisms in place in support of the search process. These include billboard, magazine, newspaper, radio and TV advertising, exhibitions and trade fairs, sponsoring, branches and retail shops, call centers, and sales representatives. Some of the digital mechanisms can interact with these conventional mechanisms. A mobile app, for instance, can include functionality for location awareness and inform the user about a nearby shop that is selling a specific product, in support of the product search process. Furthermore, the smartphone's camera functionality together with AI can be used to support visual search. For instance, Asos.com, a British online fashion and cosmetics retailer, lets consumers upload or snap pictures of clothing they like in Style match, a visual search tool in its mobile app, which analyses the pictures and finds the products or recommends similar products from its collection of over 850 brands.

Also, since search is a process relevant to both buyers and sellers, it can be digitalized for not only the business's sales transactions, but also for its procurement and supply chain transactions. For instance, the business can offer a Web portal where suppliers can register, and where the business can post its procurement and supply requirements. However, in the upstream context, the implementation of digital search mechanisms is more dependent on the efforts of upstream partners such as suppliers in digitalizing their downstream transaction systems with listings and descriptions of themselves and their products.

As new digital search mechanisms keep emerging, the business needs to decide which ones to invest in, bearing in mind that supporting more and perhaps even all of the available mechanisms is not necessarily better. A key starting point is the level of adoption of the digital search mechanisms by the business's target audience. For instance, when using social media services platforms, the business needs to "fish where the fish are" and enable search by buyers on the platforms where they are present. In some cases, search could be best supported offline, if the buyer is not actively using any of the digital mechanisms. Another important consideration is search cost. When setting targets for reach, the business needs to consider the associated costs. Given the cost advantages of digital vis-à-vis conventional mechanisms, the business may also use its offline mechanisms to redirect buyers to online mechanisms. Finally, it is important to consider conversion and track whether the buyer engages with any of the mechanisms that support the subsequent processes.

This challenge of ensuring that the search mechanisms supported by the business are aligned with the mechanisms used by the customers and suppliers it wants to transact with, applies not only to consumer markets but also to industrial, B2B markets. Particularly because the latter setting involves larger and more complex transactions, getting the digitalization right can be even more consequential. It is important to note that the benefits of digitalization of transaction processes can depend significantly on the level of alignment between the approaches to digitalization taken by the business and its transacting partners.

Authentication

In the buying process, even after a buyer has found a possible product, it has to ensure that the product not only meets its needs but also meets its expectations in terms of quality. We refer to this as product authentication. In addition, before committing to a purchase from the product's seller, the buyer would want to ensure that the seller is legitimate, qualified and reliable. This is known as seller authentication. In the traditional physical marketplace, product authentication is achieved by reading relevant research reports and reviews, physically examining the product and by interacting with salespeople. Similarly, the seller can be authenticated also by reading reviews (e.g., Consumer Reports, BBB ratings), and by physically visiting its store or offices.

For their part, sellers too need to ensure that the buyer of a product is legitimate. In the physical marketplace, this occurs most commonly through face-to-face interaction, though in some situations, sellers may be willing to commit to purchases via mail orders or phone orders, usually when buyers authenticate themselves by providing proof of financial soundness through credit card information or checks. This is referred to as buyer authentication.

These authentication processes are mostly familiar and even unobtrusive in the physical marketplace (or brick-and-mortar transactions). However, digital marketplaces and e-commerce are different. As the old adage goes: "On the Internet, nobody knows you are a dog." That is why businesses selling or buying online have to use digital mechanism to ensure the identity and quality of their trading partners and products.

Consider the three types of authentication: the business, the product, and the individual. At the level of the business, Website content can serve to identify and qualify the business as a buyer or a supplier. This content can be enriched with endorsement of trusted third parties (e.g., Verisign to establish the business's web presence with a secure and reliable domain name), social media content including user-generated content, and mobile applications.

At the level of the product, similar mechanisms can be used. Customer testimonials, ratings and reviews can be added, as well as expert opinions. Also, interactive customer testimonials can be facilitated through virtual communities to discuss product quality. While businesses often focus on Website content to authenticate themselves and their products, this mechanism is increasingly being considered to be the least reliable. The strength or the robustness of the other mechanisms derives from the fact that they involve potentially unbiased third parties. Some of these parties charge businesses to help establish online customer trust. For instance, Trustpilot, a customer review site that was started in Denmark in 2007, hosts customer reviews of over 270,000 businesses worldwide. It automates review collection with customizable invitations and reminders that are sent to customers after every purchase, provides an analytics tool to the businesses for tracking reviews and identifying trends, and offers integration services that allow the businesses to display their reviews on their websites, in Google search results, in display and video ads, email campaigns, and on social media. Furthermore, Non-Fungible

Tokens, also known as NFTs, which are digital certificates implemented using blockchain technology (see note), can be used to identify a product and record its ownership (see Chap. 4 for NFTs for digital products).

Finally, at the level of the individual, user IDs and passwords, reliable e-mail accounts, and digital certificates can be used. The individual's public information on social media platforms can also be verified. AI is increasingly being used to authenticate individuals. China's Ping An retail bank, for instance, tests micro expression recognition technology to spot early signs of fraud in loan applicant's facial movements while they are explaining why they need the money using their smartphone's camera. As another example, Nike, launched an algorithm in 2022 to identify and reward its most engaged and loyal consumers by giving them priority access to buying limited-edition sneakers, based on their participation in weekly livestreams and interactions with digital content. Thanks to the algorithm, Nike can counter bots that buy these collector items and resell them at much higher prices (aka scalping), and can reward its most loyal fans by authenticating their identity and quality.

Digital authentication mechanisms can be bolstered by physical ones. For instance, Baunat, an online retailer of diamonds, lists its Antwerp-based telephone number as well as the addresses and opening hours of its showrooms in Amsterdam, Düsseldorf, Geneva, Hong Kong, Knokke, London, Mumbai, München, Paris, Shanghai and Zurich on its Website. Likewise, business schools use pictures of their physical campuses to authenticate their online MBA programs.

Note on blockchain. Blockchain technology is increasingly being used to authenticate trading parties and products. For instance, the two largest diamond producers in the world, De Beers Group and Alrosa, together with other industry stakeholders, collaborate on a pilot program to track diamonds from mine to retail. Through the use of distributed ledger technology, artificial intelligence, Internet of Things, and advanced security and privacy, a digital platform called Tracr™ is implemented such that consumers can be assured about the provenance and authenticity of a diamond gemstone. Likewise, a consortium of diamond and precious metals companies involving Rio Tinto Diamonds, Leach Garner, Asahi Refinery, Helzberg and the Richline Group, partnered with IBM to develop a blockchain network to trace the origin of diamonds, known as TrustChain™.

Clearly, deciding on which mechanisms to use to ensure the identity and quality of trading parties and products is key in the online marketplace. When using digital authentication mechanisms, the business needs to make sure these mechanisms help in establishing its online credibility, while preventing cybercrime. Potentially viable digital authentication mechanisms such as ratings and reviews can still be subject to abuse. Consider the Amazon

Marketplace on which some suppliers manipulate the Amazon Certified ratings for their products by buying the products from the Amazon Marketplace themselves and providing top notch ratings and reviews. Breaches in authentication support not only undermine the business's reputation and credibility, but also jeopardize conversion to the next process.

Valuation

The valuation process is about sellers determining the pricing of products and services, and buyers determining how much they should pay for products and services. In physical marketplaces, valuation is commonly done through posted prices, either in price tags or in catalogs. In some specialized settings, usually limited to high-ticket items such as art, collectibles and real estate, dynamic pricing mechanisms such as auctions are also used. However, the digital environment offers a much broader range of valuation options for all kinds of products, options that include mechanisms for both static and dynamic pricing.

Digital static pricing mechanisms include online price lists (e.g., in a digital catalog on the Web or in a mobile app), claiming to have the lowest prices online, and showing competitor prices online.

Digital dynamic pricing mechanisms include personalized discounts, templates for electronic Requests for Quotations (eRfQ), electronic auctions and reverse auctions (run by buyers), online exchanges, and online price negotiations.

Companies that sell products both offline and online can benefit from using digital dynamic pricing mechanisms in their physical stores. This can be done through the use of digital price tags and electronic shelf labels. Furthermore, dynamic pricing can be integrated in a mobile application such that tags or labels are no longer required and users can scan products to see prices with personalized discounts based on their loyalty status. Amazon started and evolved as an online retailer, but in recent years, has opened a variety of physical stores, including bookstores (though Amazon announced in March 2022 that it will close its 68 bookstores). At the Amazon physical bookstores, for instance, Amazon Prime members could enjoy price deals while non-Prime members paid list prices which were above the prices on the Amazon website or mobile application.

When deciding on the use of digital valuation mechanisms, the business can explore the opportunity for dynamic pricing in order to extract more consumer surplus and enhance its profitability.

Payment

The payment process is about how buyers can pay for products purchased digitally. Unlike the common cash-based physical payment process, digitalization enables a variety of digital payment mechanisms, many of which have already been used for physical marketplaces as well. Digital or online payments can be achieved through debit or credit card payments, online money transfers, trusted third parties where only non-sensitive information is exchanged online (e.g., PayPal), software-based cash payments and wallets (e.g., Bitcoin and Ether on Coinbase Wallet and MetaMask Wallet), electronic invoicing, and online accounts (e.g., credit line, loan).

Digital businesses can work with online payment processing providers that act as intermediaries in the support of the payment process. Stripe, for instance, offers a suite of payment APIs (application programming interfaces) that is used by companies such as Amazon, Booking.com, Instacart, Lyft, Slack and Shopify to accept payment online. It partners with local banks and major card networks, as well as Internet browser providers and industry associations, and its developer platform reduces maintenance of legacy systems and enables the design of better customer experiences. PayPal is considered to be the market leader for such online payment processing provisioning. Furthermore, its mobile payment service Venmo, which partners with GrubHub, Lululemon and Uber, amongst others, lets consumers make and share payments with friends (i.e., share online what they purchase while also checking out what friends got), and make purchases at approved merchants. Klarna, a Swedish payment processing provider founded in 2005, adds a "pay later in full" functionality to its customers' checkout such that their shoppers can see and try products before paying for them. The customers get paid in full upfront by Klarna, while it gets paid over time by the shoppers. Klarna facilitates customer integration through its pre-configured modules and plugins for e-commerce platforms such as Adobe's Magento, IBM WebSphere Commerce, Shopify, and Woocommerce.

As social media platforms start to turn to e-commerce to diversify their revenue streams, they also need to support payment. Instagram, for instance, introduced shoppable posts in its feed in 2018 and launched an in-app shopping feature in 2019 for customers to buy and pay for the shoppable products from partners like Burberry, Nike, and Warby Parker, directly on its platform using debit, credit, or PayPal, rather than on the merchant's mobile Website.

For offline purchases, various online payment systems can be leveraged. Customers can install online payment systems such as Apple Pay and Google

Pay on their smartphones and wearable devices to not only pay online or in-app but also in stores that have compatible readers and software. In response to the "pay later in full" online payment functionality offered by Web shops, H&M, a Swedish multinational fast-fashion company, offers a "buy now, pay later" (BNPL) option in its physical stores, through a collaboration with Klarna. Using a mobile app, store visitors scan a QR code when checking out; the bill is sent to them later. Such BNPL options are also offered for online purchases. For instance, Coach, a global fashion house well-known for its leather handbags, lets online buyers in the UK split their total in three interest-free payments, in a collaboration with Klarna.[2] Other players in this space are Affirm and Afterplay (which was acquired by Block, formerly Square).[3] In March 2023, Apple launched "Apple Pay Later", its BNPL solution for iPhone and Mac users in the US who can pay in four installments over six weeks without fees wherever Apple Pay is supported. Users will also be able to monitor their payments in a dashboard application within their Apple Wallet.

Online payment systems can also hold buyer credentials and payment information. Thus, they provide the buyer with a convenient and seamless payment experience, as well as a choice of authentication mechanisms.

Logistics

The logistics process transfers the product from the seller to the buyer. While this is often a simple physical exchange process for offline transactions conducted in stores, it can be more complex for other transactions, including those conducted online, on the phone or via mail orders, where the buyer does not visit the seller's physical location for the purchase. With regard to this process, a distinction can be made between physical goods, services, and digital products.

For physical goods, the seller can offer online track and trace functionality to the buyer in support of the offline delivery or pick up of the products in a store, locker, or other distribution point. Domino's Pizza, for instance, introduced Delivery Hotspots™ in 2018 such that customers can get their pizzas

---

[2] https://uk.coach.com/klarna-faq.html?hp=text_coach_services_klarna Accessed August, 19, 2022.

[3] BNPL providers make money by charging the retailer a 4% commission, and paying 2% fees to other payment companies, incurring a 0.5% average funding cost, and facing credit losses of 1.2%, leaving them with a 0.3% gross profit (before operating costs). For big transaction volumes, this can be very profitable, but credit losses could be higher (Klarna had credit losses of 1.9% of customer lending in Q1 2022). (Source: Financial Times, Buy now, pay later must be regulated—now, June 6, 2022).

delivered to parks, beaches, stadium lots, and more places that do not have a street address.

The seller can also provide order consolidation options to the buyer online. Conversely, the buyer can offer its suppliers online mechanisms to coordinate pick-up of its physical goods purchases from their locations.

Both postal companies and courier businesses assist digital business with options for offline delivery or pick up of physical goods. Interestingly, the traditional courier delivery market for packages and documents for businesses was organized around office hours, with deliveries occurring between 9 am and 5 pm. This nine-to-five schedule did not match e-commerce customer requirements, who wanted a five-to-nine schedule instead (that is 5 pm–9 pm, when customers are at home), which imposed extra costs for delivery for e-commerce players. Furthermore, startups have emerged that deliver products to consumers in minutes, from early morning until late at night. For example, on-demand grocery delivery startups Getir (founded in 2015 in Turkey) and Gorillas (founded in 2020 in Germany and now part of Getir) engage riders to deliver groceries at retail prices from their neighborhood dark stores in ten minutes to consumers.

Product returns also pose logistical challenges for e-commerce players. Fashion retailers such as Berlin-based Zalando.com face product returns of up to 75% of orders. Happy Returns, a 2015 US start-up, offers retailers and brands a broad range of services to support online product returns and reverse logistics. Their services range from initiating returns through a fully branded online flow with one-click exchanges, accepting returns by mail to a regional returns hub, in person for an immediate refund at a nationwide network of 300+ return locations (called Return Bars), or to store via a mobile app or a self-service kiosk, to processing returns including aggregation and disposition, as well as reporting and analytics with real-time dashboards. In The Netherlands, Re:turnista offers Web shop customers the possibility of having their returns picked up at home or in the office in 1-hour collection windows. In cities, the service is done on bicycles to reduce the carbon footprint of e-commerce logistics.

Picnic, a 2017 start-up, offers consumers in The Netherlands a home delivery service for a full range of supermarket items at the lowest price with no delivery fees. Through the Picnic mobile app, users can order various items (which are being pooled by "shoppers" in the company's distribution center) and track the location of the Picnic small electric vans and get an arrival time estimate for their order. Upon arrival, the items are brought into the customer's home by a friendly delivery person, called a "runner." The service is not only about customer convenience but also about sustainability. Fresh, local produce is offered, and consumers can return packaging such as plastics and glass bottles when the vans stop by their homes.

Many services can be delivered online through Web conferencing technologies. BNP Paribas Fortis, for instance, launched its James service in 2009. Rather than coming to a local branch to discuss their portfolio with a financial advisor, customers that have a minimum of 85,000 Euros of Assets under Management, can interact with their personal advisor online. Proximity is established through matching the customer with an advisor that speaks the same dialect. Through moving the service encounters online, BNP Paribas Fortis not only reduces service delivery cost but also enjoys higher customer satisfaction and increased revenues. In healthcare, patients can consult with doctors online and on mobile through telehealth providers such as American Well, BetterHelp, Doctor on Demand, HealthTap, and MDLive.

Digital products such as music, movies, and games can be offered for download or streaming. Also, various services are increasingly being automated for digital delivery. FinTechs such as Betterment and Wealthfront, for instance, provide so-called "robo-advisors" that provide customers with automated investment advice online with personalized guidance at lower fees.

Clearly, the choice of logistics mechanisms is driven by the type of product: physical goods, services offered by humans, or digital products. The lower cost of delivering digital products at scale prompts businesses to automate human service work, such as financial advisors being replaced by conversational AI. For physical goods, the high costs of delivery and returns need to be balanced against the size of the user base and cumulative profitability.

After-Sales Service

The after-sales service process is about the seller supporting the buyer after the transaction. While such services are often very limited in the case of store-based transactions, and may be limited to customer-service specialists that are available in stores, or support personnel accessible through telephone calls. With digitalized transactions, there are a number of ways in which after-sales service can be enhanced, and can become a significant differentiator in competitive markets.

To start with, after-sales service can be offered by the seller through documents and videos posted on the seller's Website on product use, repair and disposal, and a FAQ (Frequently Asked Questions) list. The seller can also provide interactive online technical support (through e-mail, chat, conferencing, etc.), as well as online dispute resolution services and feedback mechanisms (e.g., complaints, suggestions). In addition, virtual community features can be included for after sales support, and mobile apps released for technical support. Finally, embedded sensors and devices (IoT) in physical products in use by the customer can provide the customer with extra services.

Increasingly, AI is being used in support of after sales service. IPSoft's Amelia, for instance, is an AI technology that serves as a virtual customer agent for customers in various industries such as banking, healthcare, insurance, retail, and telecom. While businesses in these industries can train and use Amelia as an IT operations expert for employees, they can also engage her as a service agent to handle customer inquiries and recognize customer intent. Digital ventures that do not have a large number of employees can tap into their customer base to train an AI. For instance, Liv, a digital bank in the United Arab Emirates, which was spun out of Emirates NBD in 2017, ran a campaign in 2019 for its customers to select one out of five potential chatbots and subsequently engaged its customer base to mentor the winning bot, Olivia, in becoming a skilled virtual customer agent, in return for prices such as an Apple iPad.

Decision Support Processes

In addition to digitalizing transactional processes, the business can also use digital technologies to support the non-transactional decision processes of both the business and its external stakeholders. By moving these processes from the back-end to the front-end, the business can support interactions with external stakeholders to assist them in their decision making. The business can also provide digital decision support to enhance the transaction processes or draw on its digitalization of transaction process to offer decision support.

The key decision support processes are as shown in Table 2.2 below, and we examine each of them in turn.

Table 2.2 Decision support processes

Decision Support Processes	Configuration of buyer needs and product
	Collaboration with external stakeholders
	Business Intelligence

Configuration

The configuration process is about helping the buyer to define its needs and helping the seller determine what it should make or provide. Traditionally, the amount of communication between businesses about the configuration and design of products and services has not been very extensive or rich. In some situations, businesses obtain information about customer preferences and priorities through surveys, questionnaires, focus groups or conversations between salespeople and customers. It is not unusual for producers of products to develop products without any direct knowledge of the needs and preferences of specific customers. However, digital technologies can be enormously helpful in refining and enhancing configuration processes by facilitating interaction between producers and their customers or target markets.

Toward that end, the seller can implement various digital mechanisms such as the digital exchange of attachments or configuration documents, online tools for extracting user preferences such as surveys and games, crowdsourcing (contests), and online configurator tools for customization or co-design. These mechanisms can be made available on the seller's Website, and possibly with links provided in social media platforms and portals as well.

ArcelorMittal, for instance, introduced a 3D Car Configurator in the Fall of 2019, through which Original Equipment Manufacturers can define their needs for steel modules in a 3-step process: 1. Select a module by clicking on a three-dimensional interactive car; 2. explore and select the solution of their choice; and (3) save and share their configuration. The module selection can be done in a realistic view, or in an exploded view in full, body-in-white only, chassis-only, or seat-only. When clicking the fender in the exploded view, the configurator presents various customizable steel solutions that meet stringent technical requirements and constraints, and that underwent numerical validation, in a table, showing the trade-offs between steel grades, designs and processes. When selecting one of the solutions, specific ArcelorMittal steel products are shown, which can be applied to the configuration. The user can then save, download and share the configuration. It is of interest to note that this configurator interacts with a new digital catalog that ArcelorMittal introduced to search for and authenticate its products. This catalog, which can be personalized, allows the user to search by product, strength, product reference, or coatings, and obtain detailed product information. Furthermore, the product catalog also supports the logistics process as it shows availability of the product in the user's region.

When deciding on the use of digital configuration mechanisms, various criteria come into play. An important criterion is the user experience. The ArcelorMittal 3D Configurator, for instance, is also available in a light version to deal with lower bandwidth situations and smaller screen sizes. The availability of generally accepted standards for describing products also supports the use of digital configuration mechanisms. For instance, Blue Nile, an online retailer of diamonds, founded in the US in 1999, uses the 4Cs of Diamond Quality standard created by the Gemological Institute of America (GIA), a non-profit institute dedicated to research and education in the field of gemology and the jewelry arts. Blue Nile's Build Your Own Ring® online configuration tool features sliders for users to indicate their preferences for Carat, Clarity, Color and Cut for specific shapes of diamonds (e.g., round, princess, emerald or heart). Furthermore, a price range can be set in support of the valuation process. When selecting a diamond for the ring, the GIA report can be viewed, detailing the shape and cutting style, measurements, and the grading results for carat, color and clarity, in support of the authentication of the product.

As the above examples illustrate, digitalization of configuration can also benefit from digitalization of transaction processes such as search, authentication and valuation. The interaction between these decision support and transaction processes is facilitated by digitalization. A significant recent trend in the development of information technology solutions is a transition from sequential design and development processes to a more iterative, and even concurrent approach involving different functional areas such as design, production, marketing and after-sales service. The digitalization of configuration and transaction processes enables a further extension of this transition, to include even external stakeholders such as customers into the development process for products and services.

Collaboration

This process is about facilitating interactions between multiple businesses or individuals to support collaborative work. These interactions can be synchronous or asynchronous. In traditional settings, collaboration has happened primarily through co-location and face-to-face interaction. Within businesses, collaboration can be enhanced through a variety of office automation tools, enterprise software systems, email communications and knowledge management systems.

Support of collaboration between businesses is more difficult to enable since the businesses invest in resources and systems independently. In this context, until the evolution of open systems such as Web-based applications, digital telecommunications and mobile apps, inter-firm collaboration was largely limited to offline mechanisms.

Today, a variety of communication technologies as well as information processing and abstraction technologies can be used to support collaboration. Communication technologies include blog, bulletin board, chat, e-mail, voice, video, telepresence, virtual environments, shared digital workspaces (e.g., whiteboards, screen sharing), and application sharing.

Information processing and abstraction technologies include data warehouses, Online Analytical Processing (OLAP), Knowledge Management System (KMS), expert systems, e-voting, and virtual reality (VR).

While email and Web audio and video conferencing (e.g., through Zoom) are widely used for collaboration with external stakeholders in business markets, chat (e.g., on Whatsapp or WeChat) is very popular too. In retail consumer markets, chat is a key collaboration mechanism. Blue Nile, for instance, offers 24/7 live chat functionality through which non-commissioned diamond and jewelry consultants collaborate with Website visitors to support their decision making.

Business Intelligence

Business Intelligence (BI) refers to the provisioning of information about the organization to external stakeholders, as well as analytical tools that allow them to model and analyze their business activities to support their decisions making.

Digital mechanisms that support the business intelligence process include graphical tools for sharing (e.g., reports, dashboards, and data visualization tools), shared databases (e.g., purchase transaction history), software tools for external users to analyze both proprietary and market data, and collaborative filtering and recommendation systems.

Product sales information is widely used to support customer decision making by featuring the products that are viewed and/or sold the most. Baunat, for instance, prominently features its most viewed engagement rings and diamond jewelry on its homepage. Furthermore, such data can be used to direct the customer to related products (cf. Amazon's "Customers who viewed this item also viewed" and "What other items do customers buy after viewing this item?" BI functionalities).

More sophisticated BI tools allow users to analyze the data. Insurer Axa's Give Data Back—Motor initiative in Singapore, for instance, enables customers and non-customers to assess the risks on the roads they frequent and how they can avoid car accidents by analyzing Axa's consolidated claims and policy data for car accidents in Singapore. The tool collects user data on a region in Singapore, the accident type (personal injury or vehicle damage), gender, and age bracket, and produces a heat map with green (low), orange (medium) and red (high) risk zones, as well as location statistics consisting of a risk ranking of the selected region, accident frequency, average and maximum cost, as well as the most risky road. While it does not push a car insurance product to the user, a "BUY ONLINE" button in the header of the webpage offers quick and easy access for interested users.

BI can also be used in direct support of the configuration process. Blue Nile, for instance, has a "Best Selling" tab in its online configurator that features the most commonly purchased diamond characteristics, including the 4Cs, at the best possible price, which users can consult to support their decision making.

Operationalizing Externally Facing Process Support

In this section, we illustrate how the process framework is applicable in a business context. When planning digital initiatives that involve externally facing processes, decisions need to be made on which transaction and decision processes to support, and what mechanisms to implement. Toward that end, the following two maps can be used to design the process support (see Figs. 2.1 and 2.2).

In the Transaction Process Support Map in Fig. 2.1, the transaction processes are represented on the horizontal axis, while the vertical axis distinguishes between the nature of the support mechanisms: digital or physical. The various mechanisms that can be used in support of the transaction processes can then be plotted on the map.

In the Decision Process Support Map in Fig. 2.2, the decision support processes are represented on the horizontal axis, while the vertical axis distinguishes between digital and physical support mechanisms. Again, the various mechanisms that can be used in support of these processes can be plotted on the map.

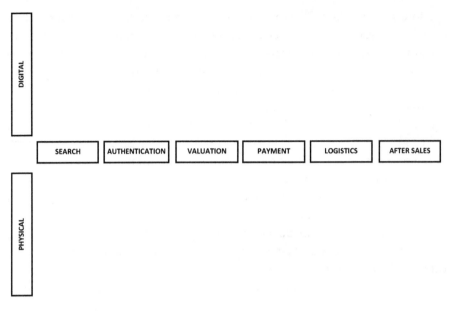

Fig. 2.1 Transaction process support map

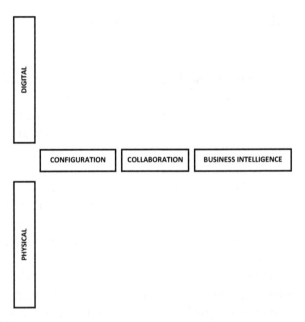

Fig. 2.2 Decision process support map

Both maps can be used to plan the support for both types of processes, and can also show the evolution of the process support. Having established a baseline for process digitalization, the map can be used to envision a to be state. Also, the maps can be used to benchmark the process digitalization of new entrants and competitors.

Example: The Dow Corning Corporation

Dow Corning Corporation (DCC) was originally established in 1943 as a joint venture by The Dow Chemical Company (Dow) and Corning Glass Works (Corning) to explore the potential of silicones. In 2016, Dow completed the restructuring of DCC and became the 100% owner of the silicone business. DCC became part of the Dow Consumer Solutions business unit in the Performance Materials & Coatings Division. Dow Consumer Solutions manufactures, warehouses and sells silicone-based materials to customers worldwide in three businesses: home and personal care for consumer brand owners; performance silicones for use in automotive, high-performance building, pressure sensitive industry and advanced assembly markets; and silicone feedstock and intermediates, which delivers a range of standard silicone materials for established markets.

From its conception, the DCC has been a science-driven company. It has filed thousands of patents for silicone technologies and commercialized its research by selling its leading products worldwide. It typically dealt with large enterprises that face specific challenges and researches and develops solutions for them. The design and delivery of customized solutions for these customers typically involved a relatively long drown out process of high touch service, with strong offline support for business, product and customer authentication, customer service, etc. The DCC was known for its customization, flexibility and expert advice through knowledgeable account managers and technical service staff, as well as its strong R&D capabilities, as demonstrated by its large set of patents.

In 2002, DCC launched Xiameter, a cost-efficient e-commerce model on a Web and SAP infrastructure to cater to price seekers, a growing customer segment of price-driven buyers of mature silicone-based products with an annual spend of at least 50,000 USD. The Xiameter model was radically different from the traditional DCC model, which was focused on delivering innovative, productivity enhancing silicone materials at lower total cost of ownership for customers. The e-commerce initiative focused instead on operational efficiency to sell standardized products online. Initially, a selection of over 350 mature products (out of a portfolio of over 7000 products) was offered online, with certificates of chemical equivalency, as it concerned exact commodities such as silicone fluids, sealants, emulsions, resins and rubber, that were manufactured off-peak in DCC's global manufacturing sites. Over time, more products were offered online, and some products were specifically designed for online sales. The SAP enterprise system automated the ordering process by electronically linking order entry to global production, planning and shipment, while also confirming orders and generating and sending invoices electronically. The Web was used to implement the digitalization of the customer facing transaction processes.

The e-commerce model allowed the DCC to address the so-called long tail (see Fig. 2.3; introduced by Chris Anderson in an article in Wired[4]), the portion of the market that cannot be served using a traditional business approach due to its higher cost. Through the use of digital technologies, the business can reach out to new customers and substantially grow its revenues.

Rather than mostly relying on a specialized sales force, tradeshows, and seminars, a low touch, low engagement digital model was implemented to market the products to a whole range of customers of all sizes, many of which had not dealt with DCC before. Various digital mechanisms were used in support of business, product and customer search and authentication, as described below. Furthermore, valuation was simplified by adopting the digital static pricing mechanism of posting the lowest prices online. Prices were 15% to 20% lower, and to avoid parallel trade, global pricing was established in 6

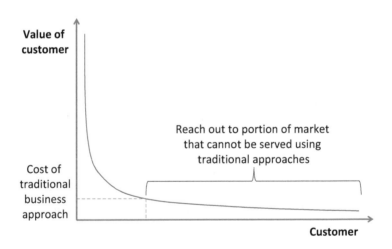

Fig. 2.3 The long tail of business

---

[4] Chris Anderson, "The Long Tail", Wired Magazine, Oct 1, 2004.

currencies. Invoices were sent and traditional payment mechanisms used. As to logistics, shipping dates were 7–20 days from the order date, hence customers needed to plan their material needs 2–4 weeks in advance, and extra charges applied for order changes or cancellations (+5%), or rush orders (+10%). Product returns were not accepted unless the product was damaged, and there was no order-size flexibility as order quantities had to be full truck, train, or ship loads. Also, no technical support was offered.

Given these key differences, Xiameter was incubated outside the DCC and branded differently, while being endorsed by the Dow Corning brand. At the same time, the Dow Corning Corporation was rebranded to the New Dow Corning Corporation to emphasize its unique value proposition and avoid confusion in the market that the Dow Corning Corporation would have been replaced by Xiameter.

The digitalization of Xiameter's customer facing transaction processes was as shown in Fig. 2.4.

To support online search for Xiameter, a URL (Web address) was registered, Search Engine Optimization (SEO) and Search Engine Advertising (SEA) for both the company name and keywords related to its various silicone materials supported, banner ads placed on various industry-specific Web portals, where the company was also listed in the directories and sponsored some content items, and direct email campaigns launched. Product search was not only supported by SEO/SEA but also on the website through an internal search engine and a product catalog. In addition, offline mechanisms were used to support search for Xiameter. A large advertising campaign was

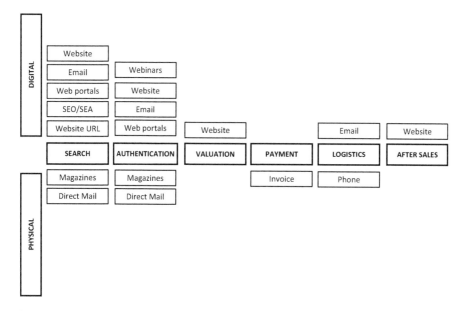

Fig. 2.4 Transaction process support map: Xiameter

launched in business and trade magazines such as Chemical Week with global placement in 9 languages, as well as a direct mail campaign to inform the market about Xiameter. At the same time, both offline and online ads for the New Dow Corning Corporation were also placed to highlight its market relevance and different value proposition.

Many of the above mechanisms were also used to support the authentication of Xiameter and its products. In addition, press releases were displayed on the Website, and webinars offered. Descriptive information on product quality was provided on the Website and in the catalog. Customers were authenticated online through email accounts and passwords, and registered as members before they could transact. A handful of sales representatives, called traders, interacted by email with the members for trust because of the big order volumes.

As Xiameter engaged in spot pricing rather than conventional contract pricing and claimed to have the lowest prices, it supported valuation for customers by showing product names and prices on its homepage. Visitors did not have to log in to see prices, only for ordering. Xiameter provided account-based online sales and stimulated ordering over the Web. Customers could order by email or phone but both had a surcharge of 250 USD. For first-time customers, Xiameter staff called on the customer to confirm the order. Otherwise, the order was confirmed through automated email. The silicone materials were directly delivered by Xiameter on guaranteed shipping dates with reliable global supply. Finally, with respect to after-sales service, Xiameter customers had no access to Dow Corning's technical support services, and thus after-sales service was limited to product details on the Website.

The digitalization of Xiameter's customer facing decision support processes was as shown in Fig. 2.5.

In contrast to the DCC, only customers who could operate under strict business rules could order from Xiameter. In order to keep its prices (and costs) low, Xiameter only offered standard, mature products, which had to be ordered in large, full-load volumes, without an exact delivery date requiring customers to carefully plan their material needs in advance. Hence, configuration and collaboration were not supported at Xiameter. Business intelligence was limited to supporting the transactional processes through a shared database showing the customer's purchase transaction history. It is of interest to note that DCC introduced digital mechanisms to support the decision making of its traditional customer base, by offering live chats and webinars through which customers could engage online with a Dow Corning specialist.

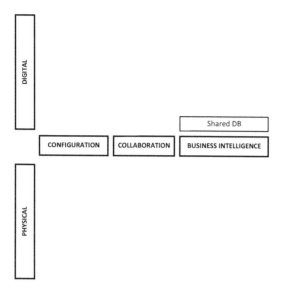

Fig. 2.5 Decision process support map: Xiameter

Xiameter became a significant growth driver for the Dow Corning Corporation. By addressing the long tail and serving the portion of the market that was too costly to serve using its conventional approach, Xiameter generated billions of USD in revenues over time, representing over 30% of total revenues. Moreover, cannibalization was limited. Some customers even bought from both businesses, getting their bulk silicone materials from Xiameter, while turning to the Dow Corning Corporation for customized solutions.

Xiameter's digitalization of customer facing processes not only created value for the growing customer segment of price seekers who could address their needs for standard silicones at lower prices through the e-commerce Website, but also lowered costs for DCC. The cost of the online search and authentication mechanisms was found to be lower than traditional marketing efforts, and response rates were much higher.

When Dow became the owner of Xiameter, it integrated the Xiameter functionality in Dow.com. At the same time, it considered how to expand its trade and decision process support to benefit from further digitalization. As it made its full product portfolio available for sale on its own Web shop by the end of 2019, it enhanced its support for various of the processes through expanded online mechanisms. Product search was enhanced by means of an internal search engine and directories with a large hierarchy of products. In support of product authentication, technical and safety data sheets were made available online. Customer authentication was done through verifiable e-mail addresses and telephone numbers for registering the customer. Spot pricing was replaced by contract pricing for valuation, based on price negotiations over the phone and email, and prices were only shown online to registered customers. Invoices were generated based on purchase orders in the ERP system. For key customers, logistics was direct, while for smaller customers, logistics was done through distributors. Logistics and after sales service were supported over the phone and email. As to decision support, Dow introduced TrendsLab, a formulation configuration tool[5] that used a decision tree model to produce a report with Dow and other ingredient products for potential customers looking for solutions in haircare and skincare. Collaboration was supported through an "Ask an expert" online form, as well as over the phone. Business Intelligence involved recommending which products to view next, based on other customers' prior visits. Dow organized the process digitalization around its definition of a new customer experience, which was in keeping with its addition of customer centricity as a fourth pillar to its mission (the others were innovation, sustainability, and inclusiveness). Rather than having to deal with the joke that Dow stands for "Do it our way," an easy, enjoyable and effective customer journey was put in place that drove customer satisfaction and loyalty.[6]

In addition to enhancing process support on its own Website, Dow further expanded its support for trade processes by engaging online intermediaries. In December 2018, Dow Greater China, a Dow Business Unit that manufactured and marketed chemical products in China, joined Alibaba's 1688.com for selling a selection of its commodity type products online. The products were targeted at business customers in markets such as agrichemicals, automotive, food, home decoration, industrial coatings, personal care, and polyurethanes. It established an online storefront on 1688.com (DowChina.1688.com), as well as a listing on 1688's IMall section and a presence on its Enterprise Procurement Platform.[7]

Dow carefully differentiated its own and its intermediary customer-facing process support. While its product search and authentication support covered the entire product line, including both bulk and custom products, the product range was confined to bulk products on 1688.com. Also, 1688.com

---

[5] https://trendslab.dow.com/

[6] https://www.digitalcommerce360.com/2019/10/03/how-dow-gave-customer-experience-a-makeover/; https://chemicals.bestpracticeconferences.com/event/digital-innovation-powering-customer-experience-transformation-easy-effective-enjoyable/

[7] https://www.digitalcommerce360.com/2018/12/17/dow-chemical-opens-an-online-store-on-alibabas-1688-portal/

product directory hierarchies were not as rich and large as the ones at Dow. com. Likewise, there was less opportunity for rich product authentication as visitors could tap into more refined product features on Dow.com. On the other hand, 1688.com offered tremendous reach, with 150 million daily visitors, giving Dow access to a long tail of Chinese business customers. At the same time, 1688.com hosted over 10 million enterprise storefronts, including some of Dow's competitors, and displayed their products when customers looked for a chemical product category. As to valuation, prices were higher at 1688.com in order not to upset registered Dow.com customers and to account for the higher risks and costs involved in online third-party marketplace transactions. As 1688.com did not offer storage and logistics capabilities, third party providers needed to be involved in support of logistics.

Example: Philips Lighting—Signify[8]

In 2016, Royal Philips, a multinational corporation that was founded in the Netherlands in 1891, spun off its Philips Lighting division in an Initial Public offering. After 125 years, it let go of its signature lighting business, as its LED technology was cannibalizing its traditional light bulb replacement market business model and substantial investments in new technologies would be required to thrive in this market. As the company had its so-called "Kodak-moment," it decided to separate ways and have Philips Lighting, which was rebranded to Signify in 2018, independently focus on meeting the world's need for more, energy efficient, digital light.

In its home market, the BeNeLux (Belgium, the Netherlands and Luxembourg), Philips Lighting started its digital transformation in 2013, and explored how it could use digital technologies to market its products. Traditionally, the company had a two-tiered distribution model for serving business customers, in which a handful of electro-technical wholesalers sell Philips (and competing) products to thousands of installers, who then sell to tens of thousands of business customers. Through the use of the Internet, the company could potentially disintermediate the wholesalers and reach out directly to the installers and end customers. However, given its historical relationships and the revenue at stake at the wholesalers, the company decided to partner with the electro-technical wholesalers to help them serve their customers better, while maintaining their key logistics function. At the same

---

[8] The authors thank Maarten Vernooij for his input. See also: https://www.slideshare.net/WebsNL/dfb2b-2015-maarten-vernooi-go-digital

time, online wholesalers such as Lampdirect operated webshops in the Netherlands and Belgium through which installers and customers could order directly online. In response, Philips Lighting launched digital initiatives to help installers and end users meet their need for product information online, while redirecting them to the electro-technical wholesalers for order taking.

Returning to the long tail, by partitioning customers based on their value, a business can not only use digital technologies to reach out and create value for new customers (cf. the Xiameter initiative at DCC) but also enhance the value of its existing customer base (see Fig. 2.6 below).

In order to enhance the value that electro-technical wholesalers could provide to installers and their customers, and increase the sales of its products, Philips Lighting launched a Partner Conversion Program. Through this program, Philips Lighting offered digital support for the transaction and decision support processes of the electro-technical wholesalers.

Through the use of vertical-specific middleware for classifying and sharing information on electro-technical products in the construction and technical industries (based on the existing, standardized ETIM interface, which stands for European Technical Information Model; see etim-international.com), Philips Lighting gave each of its product a straightforward description, assigned it to a specific article class, and defined it with all of its relevant features, while removing duplicates and outdated records. It made the data available for use in the various ordering systems of the electro-technical wholesalers such that they could present the Philips Lighting products with relevant descriptors (e.g., Philips TLED bulb instead of a product code such as 29XYZ) and descriptions (e.g., product benefits rather than just technical features).

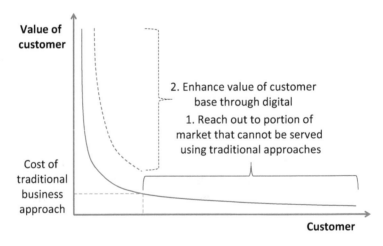

Fig. 2.6 The long tail of business revisited

Thanks to this, the electro-technical wholesalers could more easily convert their traditional order systems to more user-friendly e-commerce portals, accommodating the needs of installers and end customers. Given the increasing adoption of digital technologies by the latter, the electro-technical wholesalers stimulated the adoption of the ETIM standard by the various manufacturers in the industry.

In addition to pushing product information to electro-technical wholesalers, Philips Lighting also exerted a pull on installers and customers by providing them with product information on its own Website and in its own mobile app. As such, it could engage directly with installers and end customers online before they would get exposed to competitor products in the e-commerce portals of the electro-technical wholesalers.

The digitalization of Philips Lighting's customer facing transaction processes was as shown in Fig. 2.7.

Philips Lighting's traditional offline mechanisms for transacting with electro-technical wholesalers were kept in place. Account Managers were responsible for ensuring that Philips Lighting products were featured in the catalogs of the electro-technical wholesalers, supporting the search, authentication, and valuation processes. Furthermore, Philips Lighting participated in key fairs to meet with electro-technical wholesalers, installers, and end users, and supported electro-technical wholesalers by setting up demonstrations, events, and training for installers. Payment was done through traditional invoicing, and products were mostly (over 90%) delivered to stock to the electro-technical wholesalers. Finally, a customer service department provided after sales service to all downstream stakeholders.

In addition to offline support, Philips Lighting leveraged the standard ETIM interface to support online search, authentication and valuation in the e-commerce portals of the electro-technical wholesalers. By using relevant product descriptors and enriching the product descriptions with search keywords, it made it much easier to find its products and improved its keyword ranking by 60% in the internal search engines of the e-commerce portals. The enriched product descriptions also supported product authentication in the e-commerce portals. A noteworthy product authentication initiative was the use of videos on the product detail pages, which generated a 35% uplift in sales conversion vis-à-vis the use of product pictures. Philips Lighting also urged the electro-technical wholesalers to place ads on their e-commerce portals such that it could promote its brand and products to installers.

Philips Lighting also supported the search process for installers and end users by supporting Search Engine Optimization (SEO) and Search Engine Advertising (SEA) for both the company name and keywords related to its various lighting products. It also made information on the company and its

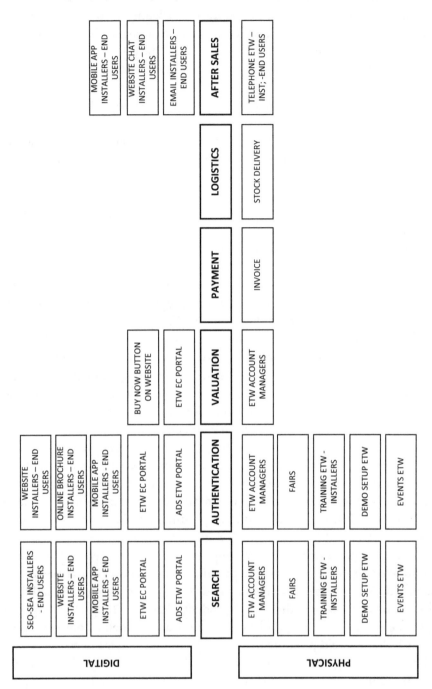

Fig. 2.7 Transaction process support map: Philips Lighting

products available on its Website and in a mobile app. These served as controlled environments in which the installers and end users only dealt with Philips Lighting rather than being presented various vendor and product alternatives in the e-commerce portals of electro-technical wholesalers. The mobile app also served to substantially reduce the use of paper-based marketing collateral, especially the product catalog (the Philips Light Catalog), by providing "app-to-date" product information to installers in a mobile app with a better user experience. In order to support valuation online, the Website featured a "Buy Now" button, which redirected visitors to the product detail pages on the e-commerce portal of the electro-technical wholesaler of their choice. When logging on to the portal, installers then got to see prices that were specific to them. Finally, after sales was supported online through e-mail, a chat function on the Website, and the mobile app. The chat function consisted of a first-line chatbot, which was backed-up by a human customer service representative when needed. The mobile app could also redirect the user to a human customer service representative on the phone.

The digitalization of Philips Lighting's customer facing decision support processes was as shown in Fig. 2.8.

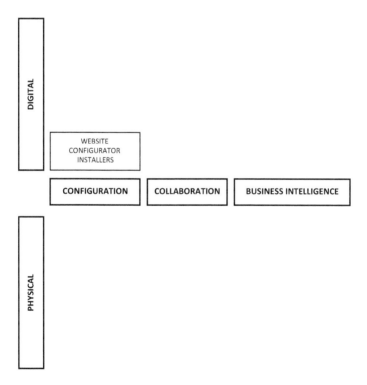

Fig. 2.8   Decision process support map: Philips Lighting

A Website configurator supported installers in configuring a lighting plan by determining the volume and types of Philips Lighting products that are required, as a function of the incidence of light and the surface of the project they are considering. Based on the configuration, an order list is generated. It is important to note that this standard configuration tool substituted the self-service approach for the traditional offline service offered by lighting design specialists at Philips Lighting.

No support for collaboration is provided. While Philips Lighting specialists could collaborate with installers or end users online to discuss lighting plans, no such support is currently offered. As to business intelligence, no overview is provided by Philips Lighting of best-selling products (or so-called high-runners) to support customer decision making. The latter was done, however, by the electro-technical wholesalers, based on their sales data. While initiatives for cross-selling and up-selling have been launched, these were not based on back-end data of Philips Lighting. Instead, simple business rules are used to recommend products to customers based on purchase spend (e.g., if you spend EUR x more, you can buy this product).

The digitalization of market-facing processes by Philips Lighting added value for all stakeholders. Electro-technical wholesalers benefited from the data integration through the vertical-specific middleware in support of the transaction processes in their e-commerce portals for installers. Installers and end users further benefited from the SEO/SEA, Website, and mobile app initiatives of Philips Lighting, while installers could also turn to a convenient, Website configuration tool to design their light plans, rather than having to rely on traditional, slower, service-delivery by human experts. Philips Lighting itself not only strengthened its partnerships with the electro-technical wholesalers, winning various "best digital partner" awards, it also realized efficiency gains through for instance a 50% reduction in the allocated human resources for small light plan design. In addition, it also enjoyed enhanced sales for new products as installers and end customers got better informed.

Reflection Questions

- What opportunities can you identify for enhancing your market-facing processes with digital innovations that would differentiate you from your competition?

- What opportunities can you identify for enhancing your supplier-oriented processes with digital innovations that would strengthen your supplier relationships or the cost-effectiveness of your sourcing and supply chain?

- How does your business use digital technology to enhance and innovate its transaction processes with customers and suppliers?

- How does your business use digital technology to support customer and supplier decision making?

3

Digitally Enhancing Existing Products

Any kind of product can be digitally enhanced. Products can differ in terms of their tangible and intangible attributes and therefore the word 'product' is used here to refer to both a product that has physical form and to a service that lacks physical form. A product that has physical form can be described by physical attributes such as size, shape, color, taste, and smell. A service with intangible attributes can be defined through the experience that is involved in its consumption or use. Also, the opportunity for digitally enhancing an existing product varies by product category. Whereas some product categories such as music and news have been largely digitally transformed, others such as clothing, food, and education still offer ample opportunity for digital enhancement.

Digital enhancement of an existing product not only changes the form of the product but also the way in which the product gets sold, priced, distributed, and experienced by the customer. Furthermore, digital enhancement can broaden and enhance the value for all parties in the ecosystem, going beyond the customer, involving other stakeholders. Hence, the digital enhancement of an existing product can potentially change how the market-facing processes are digitally supported or transformed.

Note on Digitalizing Existing Products: Hilti, a multinational company in Liechtenstein that designs, manufactures, and sells products and services for the professional construction industry, digitally enhances its products with its ON!Track asset management service. Through the combination of rugged, Bluetooth-enabled barcode tags that are put on the equipment with a cloud-based asset management software that runs on mobile or desktop devices, customers can allocate, track, and control their assets. ON!Track provides the customer with information about what

© The Author(s), under exclusive license to Springer Nature Switzerland AG 2023 **47**
A. Basu, S. Muylle, *Competitive Digital Innovation*, Palgrave Executive Essentials,
https://doi.org/10.1007/978-3-031-23440-8_3

equipment they have on the jobsite, where exactly it is on the jobsite, and who is using it. Also, when equipment is in need of maintenance or calibration, it alerts the customer through the ON!Track service. Likewise, the service notifies the customer when it is time to renew training or certification. As a result, the customer maximizes utilization and minimizes productivity losses because of workers wasting a lot of valuable time tracking down missing or forgotten tools on busy and messy jobsites, and the company avoiding the cost of buying or hiring replacements. The services also help the customer in respecting the equipment's service intervals and return dates, and staying compliant with all safety rules and regulations. It is of interest to note that the Hilti ON!Track service works regardless of equipment manufacturer, such that the customer can also track and control the tools and assets of vendors other than Hilti. Given that Hilti runs the service, it can hence obtain valuable insight on the use of its and other equipment and assets on jobsites.

Regardless of the extent of digital enhancement of an existing product, the question of how the product can be (further) digitally enhanced is not easy to answer for many executives. This chapter introduces and illustrates four dimensions of product digitalization that can be used by executives to identify opportunities for digital enhancement of an existing product. Furthermore, the extent to which the product can be digitally enhanced is considered. Also, the resulting impact of the digital enhancement of an existing product on market-facing processes is discussed.

Four Dimensions of Product Digitalization

Product digitalization can be defined as the use of digital technologies to enhance and even transform a product by either partially or completely converting a product into digital form. In order to identify initiatives for product digitalization, executives can turn to the four dimensions of product digitalization that are presented here.

Product digitalization is not limited to specific digital technologies or product categories. It is comprised of four dimensions, which can be referred to as the 4-Cs (or "the force"):

1. Composition
2. Connectivity
3. Capabilities
4. Context

Composition

A product can be viewed as a system, consisting of one or more sub-systems, in multiple layers, which in turn consist of components (see Fig. 3.1). The system lays out the structure of the product, which could be informed by its product architecture or service blueprint.

Product digitalization involves converting an analog (tangible, electromechanical) system to a digital system, which can occur at every level, from the digitalization of a component, to a sub-system (involving all components in that sub-system), and finally to the product itself (covering all sub-systems). While this analog-to-digital conversion can be initiated for existing components or sub-systems, digital components or sub-systems can also be added to the product. In any case, for a physical system and/or user to experience and interact with a digital system, a digital-to-physical interface is required.

Consider Assa Abloy's Yale ENTR® smart locking system as an example of replacing existing product components or sub-systems by electronic ones. The ENTR® smart locking system can be installed on existing locks by removing the traditional mechanical cylinder in the lock and inserting an electronic combination dial that has no physically rotating cogs. The lock can then be automatically controlled through the use of a smartphone, tablet, or other Bluetooth low energy (BLE) enabled device.

An example of adding a digital component to the product is Norway King Crab's addition of Quick Response (QR) codes on its packaging. The company checks every single crab at arrival in its processing plant and logs information about the crab's weight, the time and location of the catch, as well as

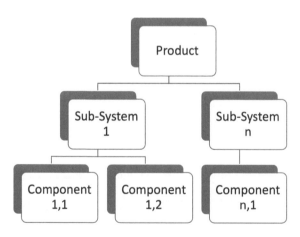

Fig. 3.1 Product composition

information about the fisherman. It then tags this information to the crab with a unique ID number and a QR code. By scanning the QR code with a mobile app or entering the ID number in a website, the consumer then receives unique tracking information about the crab he or she is about to eat. Likewise, specialty steel manufacturer SSAB's SmartSteel application marks a steel product individually before it leaves the mill and stores the data in the SSAB cloud. Upon delivery, the customer uses the SmartSteel mobile app to scan the product to view product data (e.g., thickness and dimensions) and access the product certificates, which can be stored in the customer's own cloud. Also, if needed, a claim can be created.

The use of sensors can also serve to digitally enhance a product. Consider the i-DOS washing machines from Bosch. Through integrated sensors, the load volume in the drum gets measured and the fabric type detected, as well as the degree of soiling. Furthermore, the water hardness gets considered for each wash. Based on this information, the i-DOS dosing system automatically sets the precise amount of detergent and water that is required. Hence, instead of measuring cups, the user simply needs to fill up the 1.3 litres tank for liquid detergent just once (same for another 0.5 litres tank for fabric conditioner) for washing several loads of laundry, and gets an alert from the system on the machine when the tanks need to be refilled. Thanks to this system, the user not only saves on detergent, water, and cups, but also avoids visible residues due to overdosing, which can cause skin irritation, or bad cleaning results because of underdosing.

Another way of adding digital components is through the use of wearables. Health insurer Aetna, for instance, has partnered with Apple to develop Attain by Aetna[SM], a mobile app that combines a user's health history with his or her Apple Watch® activity to set personalized goals, recommend actions (exercise, sleep, nutrition, and medical check-ups through preferred partners for primary care, radiology scans, and lab diagnostics), and offer rewards through points earned for putting in the effort or hitting the personalized daily or weekly goals. These points can then be exchanged by the user for gift cards from popular retailers or a new Apple Watch®. Aetna® commercial medical members that are at least 18 years old and have an iPhone® can bring their own Apple Watch® or be given one if they use the Attain app to earn points (e.g., for meeting their daily active calory goal based on their weight) to cover all or part of their Apple Watch® payment over 24 months (which can be checked in the points history tab in the app). If the user does not hit his or her monthly points, his or her credit card is charged for that month's balance.

Wearables are not just for humans. Animals too can benefit from the use of wearables. Consider MooCall, an Irish agricultural machinery manufacturer that creates hardware and software for beef and dairy farmers. Its calving sensor, which is put on the tail of a pregnant cow, monitors her contractions to determine when she will most likely calf, and about one hour prior to that, issues an advance warning by SMS, email or mobile app notifications to the farmer. A MyMooCall online dashboard is available to monitor alerts and battery status (about 60-day battery life), and control phone numbers associated with the device, as well as free mobile apps for device management, herd management, and community support. There is also an off-tail notification if the device falls off the tail.

Connectivity

Connectivity is about the kind of connections and integration the product enables with other entities in its environment. Three types of connections can be established:

1. With the local user, who has direct access to the product;
2. With the local environment, which can consist of other users, products and systems in the vicinity of the product;
3. Through the cloud, with a remotely located user, producer, or other entities, products and systems, which can make the product part of an ecosystem of entities.

Returning to the Assa Abloy Yale ENTR® smart lock, the local user no longer needs a key to open the lock and can choose between different accessories to directly access the product such as a rechargeable, battery-operated touchpad reader or a finger print reader. These devices support up to 20 personal codes or fingerprints, making it possible for other users to open the lock. Also, up to 20 different remote controls can be added for short distance operation by the user and others. Furthermore, as ENTR® is based on standard protocols it can be integrated with several smart home and home automation systems such that users can control the lock from the same interface that operates the thermostat, lighting, or other devices around the home. Finally, a mobile app enables remote control and access through the Bluetooth low energy (BLE) standard.

Continuing the Bosch washing machine example, users can download the Bosch Home Connect App on their smartphones or tablets from the Apple or Google app stores and create an account. When they connect their appliance to their home WiFi network, they can connect the app to the washing machine, and remotely operate and monitor it. Through the app, users can tell the washing machine what is in the load and it will work out the optimal program and even make suggestions to take out items that need to be washed in a different way. Also, users can start a wash remotely through the app, or pause and hold a wash when they get called away and later trigger the final rinse to make sure their clothes come out clean and smelling fresh rather than being damp and smelling musty. Finally, the Home Connect app can also be connected with other Bosch appliances in the household.

Capabilities

The digitalization of the components, sub-systems or product, generates data. If the product is connected, the data can be used to enhance the product's capabilities and the customer value proposition.

Six capabilities can be distinguished, as shown in Fig. 3.2. At the basic level, the data can be sensed (through sensors) to inform the user. In addition, the data can be processed (through programming logic) and the user informed about the outcome, or the state of the product changed (through actuators). Finally, the data can be used for learning (through machine learning algorithms) and the user informed, the product state changed, or product performance improved.

Continuing the Assa Abloy Yale ENTR® smart lock example, the touchpad reader has LED indications for lock and battery status. Likewise, the fingerprint reader has such LED indications, as well as an OLED screen and navigation panel through which the master user can define schedules for use, edit the defined users and review entry. When using the mobile app, users can

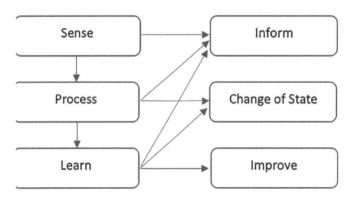

Fig. 3.2 Product capabilities

receive notifications such as locking, settings, and low-battery warning, automatically receive software updates (Firmware Over The Air—FOTA), and access a technical support interface. Also, users can remotely change the state of the lock and open it (through an actuator).

As another example, consider Eight Sleep, a 2014 start-up, that sells sleep trackers and smart bedding systems. Its Smart Bed features a Smart Cover that consists of a layer of sensors that tracks sleep patterns and biometric signals. Through a mobile app, users can view health statistics including REM sleep, deep sleep, heart rate, and respiratory rate. Also, using sleep data and programmable personal preferences, the user's sleep experience can be controlled. For instance, each side of the bed can be warmed independently. Also, when the sensors detect that the user is in a period of light sleep, it uses a smart alarm to wake the user at the optimal point in his or her sleep cycle.

As an example of learning and product performance improvement, consider the Google Nest Learning Thermostat, which adds a memory and learning component to a manual thermostat with a high-resolution color display. In addition to allowing the user to make adjustments for controlling the temperature, either manually or remotely through a mobile app, the system records the user activity and starts recognizing that as a pattern, providing it as a suggestion or autonomously changing the state. As the system learns about user preferences, it improves its performance and become autonomous in controlling the temperature, generating energy savings.

Product composition, connectivity and capabilities are orthogonal to each other, as shown in Fig. 3.3.

For each of the composition elements, different types of connections can be established, and increased levels of capabilities developed. The Assa Abloy Yale ENTR® smart lock, for instance, offers the local user direct access to the product through either a touchpad or fingerprint reader, or remote access through a mobile app, with different capabilities for each.

Context

The product components, connectivity, and capabilities also need to be viewed in their specific context. In that sense, the user experience can be viewed as a key feature of each of the three dimensions. The user experience refers to how the user experiences the product. The user can be anyone that interacts with the product and hence the experience that can change is not just for the customer, but also for the producer, upstream suppliers of partners in the ecosystem. Furthermore, product digitalization not only impacts the user experience,

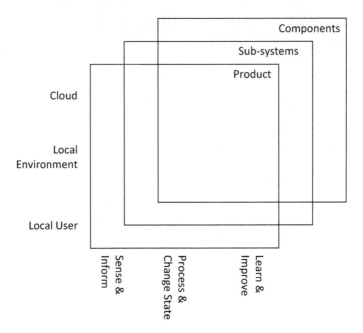

Fig. 3.3 Product composition, connectivity and capabilities

but can also expand it, as new components, connections or capabilities get added. These expansions can also precede and/or succeed the current use of the product.

Revisiting the Attain by Aetna[SM] example, the eligible Aetna commercial medical members change their product experience from being insured by paying monthly premiums for covering specific health-related risks and at some point potentially filing a claim and receiving compensation, to becoming part of a health program through the use of the Apple Watch® and the Attain mobile app. As part of the program, members also experience other entities in the ecosystem such as the physicians and caregivers in the medical centers that are recommended. At the same time, Aetna's experience with its members changes as it can now offer personalized goals at scale and reward its members individually for improving their health. Rather than waiting for claims to be processed, Aetna can now precede this with its digitalized health program, not only expanding the member experience but also potentially reducing the number and cost of claims.

Extent of Product Digitalization

While exploring the opportunities for digitalizing the product's components, connections, capabilities, and context, the business can consider to what extent it seeks to digitalize the product. Four levels can be distinguished:

1. adding information features
2. adding online software capabilities for information processing
3. enabling the customer to personalize the product
4. extending the product with digital add-on features

A basic way for enhancing existing products with digital features is by adding information features to the product. As an example, consider Samsung's Family Hub™ refrigerator's "take a selfie" feature for showing the refrigerator's content in a mobile app, introduced in Part I (in the same way, Bosch Home Connect refrigerators have a "take a shelfie" feature). Likewise, Norway King Crab and SSAB SmartSteel, which were introduced earlier in this Chapter, add information features to their products.

A more advanced way for digitally enhancing products is by adding online software processing capabilities. The Bosch Home Connect refrigerator, for instance, uses object recognition software that suggests the best place in the refrigerator for storing fruits and vegetables, for keeping them fresher for longer. Returning to the Bosch i-DOS washing machine example, software processes the sensor and user data and sets the precise amount of detergent and water that is required.

At the next level, the user can be enabled to personalize the product through the use of digital technology. For instance, a smart fridge's object recognition software could feed the data on what products are in the refrigerator into a recipe application, which can come up with personalized recommendations based on the user's taste preferences. Returning to the Attain by Aetna[SM] example, the mobile app leverages the data to set personalized daily or weekly goals and corresponding recommendations.

Finally, the product can be extended with digital add-on features. The addition of a digital display on the door of a smart refrigerator is an example of that, on which entertainment and family notes can be viewed. The use of digital wearables, implants or ingestibles is another example.

Impact on Market-facing Processes

Product digitalization not only changes the form and functionality of existing products, it also changes how a business interacts with the products it offers to the market. As such, the user relationship with the product changes, as producers, customers, repairers, partners, regulators, and others interact with the product over its useful lifetime.

Thus digital enhancement of existing products can impact the market-facing processes and require their digitalization. As the product's components, connections, and capabilities get digitalized, the way the producer markets the product can change. Also, once a customer has bought the product, the way the product gets serviced, updated and upgraded, can impact process support. Hence a distinction can be made between digital process support for new and existing customers for the digitally enhanced product.

As to the transaction processes, search process support by the producer may be expanded to include keywords to describe its digital features (e.g., "smart" lock). Once the customer has bought the product, support by the producer for the search process shifts from search for the vendor/producer to search for new digital features that can enhance the product. These new features can be pushed by the producer to the customer through updates and upgrades of the product. Likewise, authentication process support can be provided for the product's digital features and vendor authentication can shift to product authentication when the product is in active use. Valuation support goes beyond pricing of the physical product to include pricing for the digital features. Continuing the MooCall example, the producer sells the calving sensor online, pricing it at 329 Euros. Furthermore, 12-months of data, software, updates, and support for the sensor are provided, which are payable after year 1, priced at 150 Euros. New digital features can be included in the product price or free trials offered, or charged extra (see Chap. 4 on New Digital Products). Payment support can also change to reflect the ongoing digital use of the product, as in the Attain by Aetna[SM] example, in which the user pays in monthly installments through reward points or by credit card. Logistics can also be impacted as the digital features of the product need to be activated and the producer can potentially track the product beyond its delivery. Continuing the MooCall calving sensor example, when the customer orders the calving sensor online, the product is shipped un-activated and the farmer needs to activate it upon receipt. Likewise, after sales service can also change as maintenance and servicing can be done remotely. Also, product versioning can be controlled in the market and end of life products recalled and replaced by new ones, when the customer pays a subscription fee for using the product without owning it.

As to the decision support processes, configuration support can be expanded with parameters for the digital features. Once the customer uses the product, new configurations can be pushed to the customer through the product. As to collaboration, the producer and the customer can actively collaborate using the product. Business intelligence can be offered based on product use by the individual or in the aggregate.

Operationalizing Product Digitalization

As a first step, the current state of product digitalization can be assessed by mapping the current product composition, connectivity and capabilities in the context of the key user experience(s). Figure 3.1 can serve to decompose the product in terms of its sub-systems and components, and Fig. 3.3 can be used to distinguish how each product component or sub-system is connected and which capabilities (see also Fig. 3.2) it supports.

Based on this initial understanding, digital enhancement along any of the four dimensions can be considered. This could be motivated by the user experience, by exploring how it can be improved or even transformed by tying it to specific composition, connectivity and capability requirements (e.g., how Aetna changed the health insurance customer experience through the Apple Watch® and Attain by Aetna[SM] app). Alternatively, technological innovation that impacts a specific component or sub-system (e.g., replacing a mechanical cylinder with a digital one in a smart lock), a type of connectivity (e.g., Bluetooth low energy), or a capability (e.g., a new machine learning algorithm), and resulting opportunities in the other dimensions could be analysed. In support of this analysis, the extent of product digitalization can be considered by exploring how information features or information processing software capabilities can be added, personalization enabled, or the product extended with digital add-on features.

Based on the analysis, Fig. 3.1 can be edited to map the projected product composition, and the connectivity and capabilities can be described. Also, the user experience can be mapped in terms of how the product is used, as well as the preceding and succeeding steps.

Example: Eneco Toon

Eneco is a large Dutch utility company, which set up gasworks in the beginning of the nineteenth century and electricity towards the end of that century, and produced and supplied gas and electricity to many households in the Netherlands ever since. In 2007, the company set out to keep energy available and affordable for all through sustainability and digital initiatives in order to prepare itself for the changing energy marketplace. Fierce price competition, high levels of customer churn, alternate sources of energy, consumer energy production and storage, and smart homes, were identified as key market trends, and a potential threat for energy suppliers was that households could become increasingly self-sustaining thanks to solar panels, heat pumps, and batteries, and go off-grid. While Eneco invested in renewable energy installations including wind turbines, solar panels, biomass, and hydropower, it also focused on the use of digital technologies to develop customer-centric energy solutions that give people more control over their energy consumption and production. Rather than selling neutrons, Eneco wanted to offer flexibility to the customer through digital product enhancements and started to develop product digitalization initiatives as of 2010.

A particular initiative was the introduction of a smart thermostat, called Toon (pronounced 'Tone,' which is a familiar Dutch first name, and also means "show") in 2012. The energy product composition is as shown in Fig. 3.4.

The traditional thermostat for controlling energy consumption is replaced by a display which serves as the central home energy control unit. The display is a wall-mounted tablet with a touch screen color display, powered by an OpenTherm (a non-manufacturer dependent system for communication

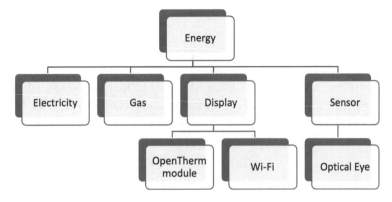

Fig. 3.4 Product composition of Eneco Toon

between a thermostatic controller and a boiler) module through the boiler wires, and WiFi-enabled. Furthermore, a sensor is added to the system when no smart meter is in place, which consists of an optical eye placed on the gas and electricity meters that registers and transfers usage data wirelessly to the display.

In terms of connectivity, the local user has direct access to the display and can interact with it using touch controls for the temperature and programs. Toon connects with the local environment (meter and boiler) in the home through WiFi. Through the cloud, Toon connects with Eneco's back-end systems to access databases and run internal and external applications for energy use, boiler management, Graphical User Interface (GUI), alerts (e.g., boiler failure), advice, and weather and traffic reports. Also, a mobile app to remotely control the smart thermostat is included.

The digital components and the connectivity constantly generate data (on up to 200 variables) that is used to offer various capabilities. Toon senses and informs the user about the time, date, weather and traffic reports, inside temperature, and program selection, as well as actual electricity and gas consumption in volume and Euros, including standby power consumption and peaks in the last few hours. Furthermore, Toon processes that data and reveals the percentage difference between Eneco's annual estimate based on the consumption in the previous year and the household's actual consumption to the user. The data can also be detailed on a daily, weekly, monthly and annual basis, in volume and in euros. A thumbs-up emoticon is shown to the user when on track while an exclamation mark warns the user when actual consumption exceeds estimated consumption. In case of the latter, the display recommends the user to lower consumption or to adjust the monthly instalment amount. Finally, the system also learns how long it takes for the heating system to reach a desired temperature and controls the boiler accordingly.

Toon also changed the user experience. Traditionally, households have one touchpoint per year with their energy supplier, when they receive the overall bill at the end of the year, showing the difference between estimated and actual consumption. Given the increasing cost of energy, the difference between what they have paid through monthly instalments (through automated bank transfer) and the total amount due is typically negative, resulting in an extra charge and an increase in the monthly instalment for the next year. Thanks to Toon, the user now has several touch points per day, and perceives these as positive as he or she gets the feeling of being in control. Given the detailed insight that Toon offers, households can lower their energy consumption and bills. While Eneco potentially sells less energy to the home, it can fight the price competition with a digitalized offer, reduce churn, and help customers gain control their energy consumption.

Further opportunities for the digital enhancement of Toon can be identi-fied in terms of the four dimensions of product digitalization. By aggregating data on household energy consumption, an anonymous benchmark is made available to households that are similar in terms of family composition and size of the house. Other initiatives include adding sensors and software for managing the energy that is produced by the household's solar panels and heat pumps, and the energy that is stored in home battery systems. Another initia-tive involves the addition of smart plugs to integrate household appliances in the system. A power leakage tester for electrical appliances in the home was introduced in October 2017, which can detect energy inefficiencies and waste, based on a patented disaggregation algorithm. One of the potential applica-tions of the algorithm is that it can evaluate whether the house is properly insulated.

The digitalization of the energy product of Eneco, also impacted the digi-talization of the market-facing processes, as shown in Figs. 3.5 and 3.6.

As shown in Fig. 3.5, Eneco supported the search and authentication pro-cesses both offline and online, and door-to-door sales was found to be the most effective in attracting new customers. For customers who had adopted Toon, however, online media were more effective in informing them about further digital enhancement of the product. In support of valuation, a tele-com model was adopted, which involved bundling the hardware and the soft-ware, while giving away the hardware and selling the software. In return for signing a 4-year fixed price energy contract, customers got the Toon thermo-stat and its installation for free (199 Euros and 75 Euros value, respectively), and were charged a monthly fee of 3.50 Euros for the digital service. The thermostat could also be bought at retailers and paid for in cash or card. Payment of the monthly digital service (and energy) was done through wiring the money. Eneco's field technicians installed the smart thermostat at custom-ers' homes, and the digital services were delivered through the home display screen and the mobile app. Various digital after sales mechanisms were sup-ported, and telephone support was also provided.

It is of interest to note that Eneco also made Toon available for sale to non-Eneco customers. Rather than bundling Toon with a fixed price energy con-tract from Eneco, it was sold separately to customers obtaining their gas and electricity from other providers. These non-Eneco customers had to pay for the thermostat and were charged a higher monthly subscription fee (4.50 Euros) for the digital services. This approach enabled Eneco to collect

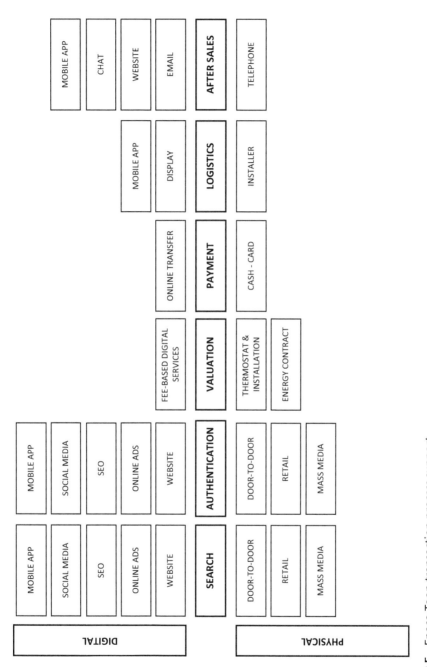

Fig. 3.5 Eneco Toon transaction process support

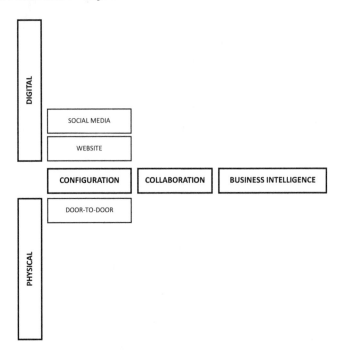

Fig. 3.6 Eneco Toon decision process support

data on the energy consumption of households that chose to get their energy from competing vendors.

As shown in Fig. 3.6, decision support was limited to configuration support on the website and social media services platforms. Offline, door-to-door sales representatives helped new customers define their needs and offered Toon as a solution.

Example: Philips Lighting—Signify InterAct Office[1]

InterAct Office was developed by Philips Lighting as a smart connected lighting system for office buildings, as a digital enhancement of an existing product. In 2013, this digital initiative was implemented together with Deloitte and OGV Real Estate in The Edge, a 40.000 m², 15 stories, multi-tenant office building in Amsterdam's business district, to inspire sustainable building designs around the world.

---

[1] http://www.lighting.philips.com/main/cases/cases/office/edge.html. Philips, 2017. How Deloitte created an intelligent building by harnessing the Internet of Things. https://images.philips.com/is/content/PhilipsConsumer/PDFDownloads/Global/Case-studies/CSLI20180201_001_UPD_en_AA_the_Edge.PDF

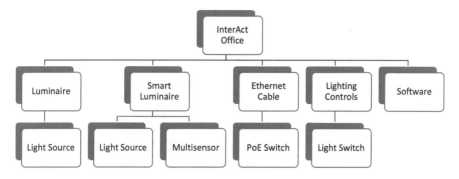

Fig. 3.7 Product composition of InterAct office (on-premise)

The product composition of InterAct Office is as shown in Fig. 3.7.

The on-premise InterAct Office lighting system in The Edge consists of almost 6500 luminaires with LED light sources, of which 3000 are referred to as "smart" as they have multiple sensors for motion detection, daylight control, temperature and noise measurement. Ethernet (instead of traditional electricity) cables power the luminaires and 750 Power over Ethernet (PoE) switches are used to transmit data from the sensors in the luminaire to the building's IT network. The lighting controls have on/off and dimmer switches that control a group of luminaires, and software is added for the management of the lighting system and the building.

In terms of connectivity, every smart luminaire is uniquely identified through an IP address, while one or more non-smart luminaires can be controlled by group controllers that are part of the lighting control system. While physical lighting switches are present for office workers to control the light in their workstation, they can also download a mobile application from the main app stores and digitally control the lighting, as well as the room temperature, of their workspace from their smartphone or tablet. The InterAct Office system connects locally with the building's IT network and Heating, Ventilation and Air Conditioning (HVAC) system. Facility managers can access a Web-based dashboarding application in the cloud to manage the system.

The historical and real-time data of the building's usage that the system generates is leveraged to provide various capabilities. By pointing the camera of the smartphone or tablet upward to the luminaire, the mobile app can detect the modulation of the light frequency of the LED lamp and inform the office worker of the light temperature. Furthermore, as the system senses the presence of the office worker in the workstation (as long as the camera is visible to the light system) and is connected with the HVAC system, it can also inform the user about the temperature of the room he or she is in. Through the mobile app the office worker can change the light temperature (a typical range is between 2700 Kelvin (warm white light) to 4000 Kelvin (colder)), as well as the room temperature. Furthermore, personal settings can be saved and the system can apply these to any workstation the office worker occupies in the building. Facility managers can leverage the anonymous data on building occupancy (e.g., number of workstations and meeting rooms in use; number of people in the restaurant), energy, light, noise, and temperature through the dashboard application to manage the building for space optimization and workplace design, energy efficiency, operations (e.g., only clean workstations and meeting rooms that were used), work productivity, and employee wellbeing. Furthermore, predictive maintenance functionality is supported based on the automated measurement of luminaire usage and behavior (e.g., the electricity flow behavior of the driver). No AI algorithms are being used for learning and improving system performance.

As explained above, InterAct Office changes the user experience, enabling office workers to personalize the room and light temperature of their workstation, while aiding facility managers in operating the building in a cost efficient and environmentally friendly manner. It is of interest to note that The Edge attained a record BREEAM sustainable building score of 98.4% and is hence considered the most sustainable building in the world according to this certification scheme. Part of the score can be attributed to the substantial reduction in energy consumption for lighting (3.9 W/m^2 versus 8 W/m^2).[2] Furthermore, Deloitte, the building's main tenant, claims that InterAct Office has generated 3.6 million Euros of annual savings in office space utilization and 100,000 Euros annual energy cost savings (Philips, 2017).

Further opportunities for the digital enhancement of the product can be identified through the four dimensions of product digitalization. As to product composition, sensors can be added that support new functionalities. In March 2020, Signify announced new IoT sensor bundles for InterAct Office that can measure relative humidity levels, temperature at room and desk level, occupancy, number of people, daylight and noise levels. These bundles are also Bluetooth enabled to support indoor positioning and navigation. Instead of the on-premise wired system that relies on Ethernet cables and PoE switches to transmit data to the building's centrally hosted IT system, a wireless system with gateways to the cloud can be used. While such a system typically has lower data transmission capacity and poses additional security challenges, it

[2] https://www.buildup.eu/en/practices/cases/edge-amsterdam-office-building-highest-breeam-score-date#:~:text=The%20Edge%3A%20Amsterdam%20office%20building%20with%20highest%20BREEAM%20score%20to%20date,-Highlighted%20Case%20January&text=The%20Edge%20is%20located%20in,score%20ever%20awarded%3A%2098.4%25

enables new capabilities such as multi-site comparisons for benchmarking of energy consumption at the level of floors or even rooms.[3]

APIs can be made available to third parties to connect the InterAct Office system with any other system in the building. A such, the system can for instance be connected with the building's fire protection system based on data captured by temperature or smoke detection sensors. Toward that end, Signify launched a developer portal for third parties to leverage various APIs and develop their own applications.[4] As such, Signify not only develops and offers its own applications but also monetizes its data through the APIs on its developer portal. For instance, instead of using Signify's workstation registration app, third parties can use a Signify API to connect occupancy data with a desk booking system and give employees the possibility to locate and join colleagues in the building. Likewise, an application can be developed by an external partner that empowers office workers to monitor their energy savings and stimulates environmentally friendly behavior.

The context of the product can also be extended to the user experience outside the office. For instance, workers can be offered advice on when to come to the office based on the projected occupancy levels and external data on traffic congestion.

The digitalization of the product also impacts the digitalization of the market-facing processes. The product authentication process gets extended with software updates and upgrades that offer new functionality such as office desk booking or indoor navigation. Likewise, valuation and payment support can be extended. Instead of selling light as a service, i.e., charging the customer for light instead of light bulbs, digital light can now be sold as a service in a pay per use model. Thanks to digital measurement, performance-based contracts can be put in place in which customers pay for actual usage (number of hours of lighting) as well as system performance (e.g., quality of light, number of luminaires that break down ahead of scheduled replacement). Furthermore, customer service and decision support are pro-actively offered to contractual customers through remote experts (in an operating service center in India) who monitor customers' systems and provide recommendations.

Finally, the digital enhancement of the lighting system also offers opportunities for creating new digital products. For instance, by aggregating system data across many office buildings, workspace optimization benchmarks for various industry sectors could be sold. This could also impact the business

---

[3] https://www.signify.com/en-gb/our-company/news/press-releases/2020/20200304-signify-raises-bar-for-health-and-wellbeing-in-offices-with-new-iot-sensor-bundles-or-interact-office

[4] https://www.developer.interact-lighting.com/

model as light could be offered for free to the customer and revenue generated on new digital products.

Reflection Questions

- How can you digitally enhance your current products to make them more competitive and differentiate them from those of your competitors?

- How can you digitally enhance your products to increase their appeal to customers even if customers don't change how they use or interact with your products?

- If you digitally enhance your current products, how would you have to change your marketing to customers to realize the benefits of the enhanced features of the products?

- How can you design the market-facing processes of your digitally enhanced products to leverage the information they generate over their useful lifetime?

4

Creating New Digital Products

A digital product is any product that is defined digitally in terms of content or software, and most importantly can be transferred digitally. We start by discussing the different types of digital products a business can create and sell, then describe their characteristics and discuss their implications for market-facing process support. We then discuss hybrid digital products which have both physical and digital features.

Types of Digital Products

Products that are defined digitally in terms of content can consist of data, information, ideas or knowledge. Data refers to a set of details or facts such as observations and measurements that is stored or transmitted. Examples of data include stock prices and flight details. When they are digitized, they can be sold as digital products. Stock exchanges sell stock quotes to portals like Google Finance and Yahoo! Finance, who display them for free. Likewise, ITA sells airfare data to travel portals (e.g., Kayak and Orbitz) and airlines (e.g., American Airlines, Delta Air Lines, United Airlines, US Airways), and was acquired by Google for their flight search engine that provides data on flight routes and airfare for many airlines.

Data becomes information when it is structured and presented in a specific context, involving different methods of data visualization such as sheets, graphs, reports, summaries, and alerts. For instance, 3E, the global provider of compliance solutions introduced in Part I, created a database of over

© The Author(s), under exclusive license to Springer Nature Switzerland AG 2023
A. Basu, S. Muylle, *Competitive Digital Innovation*, Palgrave Executive Essentials,
https://doi.org/10.1007/978-3-031-23440-8_4

7 million safety data sheets which are sold on its e-commerce portal MSDS.com.

Ideas refer to thoughts (e.g., a novel as a collection of ideas in a story). Ideas, information and data that are traditionally captured in books, magazines, and newspapers are usually amenable to storage, access and transmission using digital media and mechanisms. Likewise, products that hold multimedia content such as movies, artwork and music can be released from their physical containers (like DVDs, museums/art galleries and CDs) and offered online. Furthermore, artifacts such as boarding passes, event tickets, and hotel vouchers can also be digitized as they are merely symbols or tokens of value.

In addition to converting physical products into digital products, data assets and intellectual property (which includes information, ideas and knowledge) can serve as a basis for creating new digital products. eHarmony, for instance, offers online matchmaking services for people seeking long lasting relationships and marriage, based on the proprietary algorithms behind its patented Compatibility Matching System®.

Knowledge refers to actual insights and recommendations on how to do things better (e.g., a theory or a set of rules). Firms can create and sell knowledge as a new digital product based on the insight they generate from user data. A case in point is LinkedIn's Economic Graph. LinkedIn, the social network for professional connections, leverages the data it collects from its members (e.g., the changes they make to their profiles, the vacancies they apply for, the skills they learn, etc.) and customers (e.g., posted positions, company profiles, advertisements, etc.), to build a digital representation of the economy, called the Economic Graph, and spot trends like hiring rates, talent migration, and in-demand skills by region. Governments and companies can partner with LinkedIn to obtain this knowledge and support their decision and policy making. The city of Amsterdam, for instance, which seeks to strengthen its position as an attractive hub for digital start-ups in Europe, obtained insight through LinkedIn's Economic Graph on start-up workforce composition, education levels, job functions, and digital skill sets, to develop policies that help the city deliver on its vision.

Data, information and knowledge can be structured in a computer program or software package. Data can be made accessible through a digital database (e.g., an online dictionary), information can be accessed through an application program (e.g., an online encyclopaedia), and knowledge can be programmed as a set of decision rules (in an expert knowledge base) or as a new algorithm (e.g., a way to optimize a process, accessible through artificial intelligence applications and natural language interfaces). Along with content, software can also be transferred over digital networks. Traditional software packages such as computer games, desktop productivity suites, enterprise applications and operating systems can now easily be delivered online. Furthermore, computer programs can be developed that enable users to access, manage, process and share content online. Application programs for e-books, e-magazines and e-newspapers, for instance, enable users to search and filter content. Furthermore, based on user preferences and behavior, the programs can personalize the user experience. This is also true for multimedia digital products such as Spotify and Netflix.

Firms can build new applications into commercial software. In his Wall Street Journal essay entitled "Why software is eating the world",[1] Marc Andreessen introduced the idea that "every company needs to become a software company," pointing to software's vast potential for innovation and economic growth. In the meantime, digital native firms—like Airbedandbreakfast. com (later rebranded to Airbnb) and Uber which were launched in 2008 and 2009, respectively—built global businesses by creating new digital products. Attracted by the opportunities for the agile and faster development cycles of software (vis-à-vis hardware) and using design thinking and user experience and customer collaboration approaches, many traditional firms are now seeking to create new digital products. Volvo Trucks, for instance, monetizes the data its trucks generate through their Global Positioning System (GPS) and various sensors for tracking acceleration, breaking, and curbing, via its Dynafleet Fleet Management System. Volvo Trucks are generally sold through dealers to transport companies, who can monitor the exact location and status of individual trucks and drivers through the service. The hardware is either pre-installed at the factory or retrofitted by a dealer. The software is made available through a mobile application, which has various functionalities. In return for a fixed monthly fee per functionality and per truck (including international roaming services), the user gets instant access to fleet, fuel, and driver information, and obtains insight in where fuel savings can be made and carbon dioxide emissions cut. The software also generates pro-active alerts to ensure compliance with regulation, and shares warnings and alarm lamps in the truck's instrument cluster. Furthermore, messaging functionality is offered, as well as a personal coach who helps cut fuel consumption by up to 5%.

Furthermore, by creating new digital products a business can be truly innovative and introduce products and services that were simply impossible to create in a physical format. Consider Zoom Video Communications, a provider of remote conferencing services through which people can meet across

---

[1] Aug 20, 2011; https://a16z.com/2011/08/20/why-software-is-eating-the-world/.

thousands of miles, which is impossible to do through a physical product. Likewise, StarCraft II, a real-time online strategy game lets customers experience intergalactic warfare through an epic story campaign and digital, cinematic representations, single-player and multi-player competition, and collaborative missions, which a board game simply cannot offer.

Characteristics of Digital Products

Let us start by identifying some distinctive characteristics of digital products that set them apart from traditional physical products. To start with, digital products are amorphous, since they do not have any specific physical form. Partly as a result of this formlessness, they are also unbreakable, and do not suffer wear and tear. In addition, they are transmutable (easy to modify), which in turn enables them to be easily customizable, and even personalizable. And perhaps their most valuable property is that they are infinitely reproducible and little or no variable cost. Let us look at these characteristics in a bit more detail.

Consider the amorphous nature of digital products. At their core, these products are essentially large collections of bits (binary data). These bits do not have any physical form, and take on whatever form the technology used to create, store, transmit and experience them requires. For example, consider the digital form of a song. When the song is recorded, electromechanical devices are used to convert the data in the song's sound waves into a stream of bits stored on storage devices such as magnetic disks, optical disks or solid-state memory chips (semiconductor devices). When the song is transmitted, the bits are converted into electrical signals or pulses of light or radio waves. And finally, they are experienced through a process of conversion into sound waves that a listener can hear. Notice that this implies a related property of digital products, namely *polymorphism*, the assumption of different forms. What is interesting is that this amorphous nature of digital products is both a blessing and a curse. On the one hand, in order to persist, the bits comprising the product have to be stored on physical media, and transmitted through physical channels. Thus its survival is determined by the quality and features of those physical media and channels. For instance, a song stored on a magnetic disk can decay over time, a song transmitted through a noisy channel can degrade in quality and content, and a song heard from audiophonic speakers can degrade as the quality of the speaker worsens over time.

However, it is not the digital content itself, but rather the physical means of storage, transmission and delivery/experience that degrades. This ability to separate the digital entity from its physical container is in itself special. To see this, consider a piece of art. If someone slashes a painting with a knife, the painting is destroyed forever. However, in the case of digital art, the destruction of a physical rendering of that art, whether on a screen or a sheet of canvas, does not destroy the art, merely its physically rendered form. And this leads to the property of reproducibility.

Sidebar on the challenges of making digital products eternal: The indestructible nature of digital products raises a number of challenges. Consider the Titan family of expendable rockets that were developed by the Glenn L. Martin Company as intercontinental ballistic missiles and space launch vehicles for use by the US Air Force, the National Aeronautics and Space Administration (NASA), and the National Oceanic and Atmospheric Administration (NOAA), between the nineteen fifties and the early two-thousands. The software systems for these rockets included an autopilot system, a flight control system, and a missile guidance system, powered by computers such as the IBM ASC-15. Because of the military and civilian significance of the rockets and the associated risk of creating vulnerabilities when making changes, their original hardware and software were kept in place, maintaining for instance their floppy disk systems for continued operations. Notwithstanding the roll-out of a weapons modernization program and the emergence of new digital technologies, the US Air Force stood by the hardware and software systems that were developed in the nineteen fifties. As this example shows, a key challenge is the maintenance of digital products. This is also the case for embeddable technologies such as implants and sensors in humans. For instance, once a patient has a pacemaker, the hardware and software need to be maintained over time and cannot easily be replaced. Furthermore, digital product data needs to be stored, its provenance tracked by recording the origins of the data as well as the inputs, entities, systems and processes that influence the data. A related challenge is the design of repositories that make huge amounts of data easy and fast to access, analyze, and use over time, as the amount of digital product data grows exponentially. Storage media technologies and services (e.g., cloud storage) need to ensure that the customer can access and keep accessing the data, and transfer the data across media and services, as formats and technologies evolve. Consider the National Millennium Time Capsule that was unveiled by President Bill Clinton and First Lady Hillary Clinton on December 31, 1999, and will not be opened before 2100. In the time capsule, the White House sealed various items that represent the US in the twentieth century including an audio recording of Louis Armstrong's trumpet sounds, a CD-ROM of the human genome project, and a film reel showing Neil Armstrong's landing on the Moon. The time capsule was carefully designed to preserve its contents and is vented to allow the contents to benefit from the climate-controlled environment of the National Archives and

Records Administration (NARA), where it is stored. NARA also regularly transfers the data from one technology to another, including the audio and video recordings which are transferred to a new medium every ten years.[2] Clearly, when storing digital content for future use, it is key to address the challenge of preservation, by transferring the content to newer digital technologies or including guidelines for the construction of devices to access that content.

Reproducibility refers to the ease of reproducing, storing and transferring digital products. This is in keeping with Wired founder Kevin Kelly's tweet (April 24, 2016) that "The Internet is the world's largest copy machine. If something can be copied and it touches the internet, it will be copied. #theinevitable." After bearing the initial development cost, the marginal reproduction cost for the business is almost zero, which implies that prices need to be set to cover the initial investment cost. However, copycats can duplicate the digital product and as a digital product is indestructible, sell it to others by undercutting prices. In order for the business to recoup its investment, it can either try to prevent reproduction and reselling of its digital product (e.g., paid walls in e-newspapers) or make duplication less valuable by constantly evolving the product (e.g., dynamic news reporting by a knowledgeable journalist, potentially enriched with reader comments). Given the difficulty in preventing reproduction using technology, the latter option is generally considered to be more viable. If the creator, however, would choose not to change the digital product, robust mechanisms need to be put in place to preserve the product's integrity (in storage and transition), potentially complemented by legal means. When the digital product does constantly evolve, the creator needs to make sure the customer uses the latest version. For instance, every time a user visits a Webpage, he or she downloads a copy of that page on a hard drive, and next time he or she visits, that copy is pulled from the cache of the digital device.

As long as digital products are maintained on robust and reliable media, their quality does not degrade, and thus digital products are considered to be indestructible. As such, the life of the product can exceed the product's usefulness for the customer, which implies that a digital product can only have temporal value and hence be only worth something in a certain time window. Given its digital form, however, the product's life and value can be extended by updating and upgrading the software, introducing new functionality to the customer, and potentially changing the user interface to signal the new version. Likewise, new content can be made available. Both software and content are indeed dynamic, rather than static, making the product future-proof.

---

[2] https://clintonwhitehouse4.archives.gov/textonly/Initiatives/Millennium/capsule/perservation.html.

Consider software for reading e-books. Such software enables users to buy and read books from a large digital content repository. Every time a user wants to read another e-book, no new software is required. However, new software functionality can be added over time, such as the possibility to make annotations in the e-book. Likewise, the content is dynamic. In addition to being able to read an e-book in a traditional, static manner, the reader can now for instance click on hyperlinks in the text and consume extra content, and view annotations by other readers.

Sidebar on the challenge of reproducing digital products: While manufacturers of physical products such as blockbuster drugs or fashion items (e.g., handbags, sports shoes, watches) need to deal with producers, distributors and sellers of counterfeit goods that infringe on their brands, copyrights, patents, or trademarks, most producers of physical products are implicitly protected from counterfeit and do not face that challenge as the investment for reproducing their goods is too high for copycats to earn a return. Digital products, however, can easily be copied, at very low cost. While various mechanisms exist to establish ownership of a digital product, including digital rights management and blockchain technology, it remains difficult to enforce ownership. In order to mitigate the risk of getting copied, sellers of digital products move from ownership-based models to rental-models in which the user can experience the digital product without owning it. A case in point is the use of streaming technology, as a stream generally cannot be reproduced (even though there are workarounds and hacks), rather than enabling downloads, such as the streaming of music and videos to deal with online piracy, the practice of downloading and distributing digital products without permission.

Digital products are also easy to change, which is referred to as transmutability. Thanks to this, businesses can evolve their digital products constantly and make them extremely customizable, driving differentiation. Furthermore, businesses can allow their customers to make changes to their digital products which offers opportunities for co-creation and innovation. On the other hand, businesses can try to preserve the integrity of their digital products by employing technological mechanisms that prevent (e.g., Adobe's Portable Data Format (PDF)) or verify (e.g., through encryption technologies) digital modification.

An interesting development is the creation of unique digital products. CryptoKitties,[3] for instance, offers a blockchain technology-based game that allows users to breed (by signing up for an account and paying a small fee of about 0.008 ether per Kittie) and collect unique (with their own set of traits, called Cattributes), digital cats. These are owned 100% by the user, who can also buy and sell cats with the community. Also, these digital cats cannot be

---

[3] https://www.cryptokitties.co/.

destroyed nor replicated. The latter are based on digital certificates implemented on a blockchain, which are also known as Non-Fungible Tokens (NFTs). They are used to assign and record the ownership of a digital product to the owner of the certificate. These NFTs can be traded to exchange ownership, which has become popular for digital assets such as artwork and music, but also for tweets, as well as the original source code of the World Wide Web by its inventor Tim Berners-Lee, for which the NFT was auctioned by Sotheby's for 5.4 million USD in 2021. Likewise, the establishment of property rights can be done through the creation of unique digital products. Traditionally, notaries serve as trusted third parties to register the transfer of a property from a seller to a buyer, drawing up an authentic deed on paper, ensuring the enforceability of the agreement. However, blockchain technology's smart contracts and ledger abilities can be used to facilitate real estate transactions, making them more efficient and transparent, while ensuring their integrity. An example is Meridio, a 2017 US start-up (formerly Pangea) that has partnered up with ConsenSys Codify, a blockchain company,[4] to facilitate fractional ownership of real estate. Property owners can create, manage and sell digital shares that represent equity or debt in the underlying asset to both institutional and individual investors, and use smart contracts to manage pay-outs from rental income, while managing the portfolio and tracking the current investors, issue dividends to a large number of investors, and recapitalize assets. When investors want to sell their digital shares, they do not have to deal with contracts, lawyers or even the property owner. Instead, they can sell their tokens on the open market in direct peer-to-peer transactions and the smart contract is updated automatically. Also, regulatory compliance with respect to investor Know Your Customer (KYC), Anti Money Laundering (AML), and accreditation verification for platform access are ensured.

Digital products can also be characterized in terms of how their quality can be evaluated. Toward this end, a distinction can be made between search and experience goods. For search goods, the buyer can rely on external measures to judge quality before actually consuming or experiencing the product. Experience goods need to be consumed or experienced by the buyer before their quality can be judged. In fact, the distinction between search and experience goods is not a pure dichotomy but rather a continuum. Whether a product is a search or experience good depends on the buyer. For some buyers, a car is a search good as they feel they can evaluate its quality by learning about its consumption, performance, carbon dioxide emissions, and other features, from information provided by the seller and trusted third parties (e.g., Kelly

---

[4] https://codefi.consensys.net/.

Blue Book). For other buyers, however, a car is an experience good as they want to kick the tires and test drive the car to judge its quality.

Digital products are generally considered to be experience goods as product information on content and software is often the digital product itself. As such, potential buyers cannot simply search for information on the product but need to experience the product digitally through a demo, shareware, or free initial trial to judge its quality.

Another characteristic of digital products is that they can have network externalities. With network externalities, a product has more value if other people also use it. For digital products, network externalities can result from the increasing number of users (like more students in a Massive Open Online Course (MOOC) or participants in a multi-player online game) and/or from the increasing number of external software developers. Network externalities can lead to so-called "winner-take-all" dynamics as users and developers gravitate around the most popular digital product. This typically leads to a natural divergence between the dominant product and the other product as the incremental value of the dominant product for each marginal customer is greater, as well as the positive network externalities to the existing customers of that product. A case in point is Google Search, brought to market by Google in 1998, whose algorithm not only produced better search results than the ones of existing players such as AltaVista (which launched in 1995 and was sold to Overture Services, Inc., which was then acquired by Yahoo! in 2003), but more importantly crawled more websites faster, making its search results much richer over time. As Google Search built momentum by increasing the incremental value of its search results for every additional user while enhancing the value for its existing user base, it gradually became dominant in search.

Market-facing Process Support for Digital Products

Given their specific characteristics, digital products enable and often require different forms of market-facing process support. As a business creates a new digital product, it also needs to plan how it will support the transaction and decision support processes. In this section, we offer guidelines for businesses to support these processes.

Digital technology has enhanced the search process for both physical and digital products. However, new digital products can penetrate the market much more quickly which can raise awareness much faster than for physical products, which in turn can facilitate search. A case in point is the 2016 release of Pokémon Go, a multiplayer smartphone game, by developer Niantic (originally an internal start-up at Google) in collaboration with Nintendo (for the licensing of its characters) and The Pokémon Company, in which players needed to capture and domesticate tiny virtual monsters that could be spotted in augmented reality at specific GPS locations. In addition to it only taking 19 days to hit 50 million users, Pokémon Go became the most downloaded mobile game in its first month (130 million times), as well as the fastest game to gross 100 million USD in revenue (20 days), according to Guinness World Records.[5] Following its record-breaking launch, Pokémon Go was expanded with digital and live events, new features and in-app purchases, which generated over a billion USD in revenue and a net income of 169 million USD in its 2020 fiscal year ending May 30th, 2021.[6]

A key process that is impacted by the characteristics of digital products is product authentication. As digital products are indestructible, businesses typically choose to pursue a strategy of planned obsolescence. In other words, they constantly evolve the digital product by introducing updates and upgrades, making prior versions obsolete. In doing so, they need to be careful not to make new versions of the digital product overly complex by adding unnecessary functionality. Instead, user feedback can serve to improve the product. The latter can also help the business in addressing the challenges posed by the transmutability and reproducibility of digital products, which require customization and personalization (e.g., through user updates) for product differentiation and making reproduction less valuable or irrelevant.

As the digital product constantly evolves, authentication support needs to be frequently adjusted. While this can be done in the product itself for existing customers, it is less obvious for new buyers. Given the digital nature of the product, however, product authentication can be stimulated for new customers through a demo, shareware, or a free trial, for them to experience the product. Quibi, for instance, a mobile app for short-form videos on the go, launched in the US in April 2020, offered its service for free for the first ninety days for users to experience it. As part of this, the value that customers derive from the product needs to be evaluated to assess its viability. Continuing the example of Quibi, as the covid-19 pandemic unfolded and the Quibi on the go streaming service proposition struggled to resonate with consumers, it failed to attract paying subscribers and was shut down after six months.

---

[5] https://www.guinnessworldrecords.com/news/2016/8/pokemon-go-catches-five-world-records-439327.

[6] https://www.statista.com/chart/25833/net-income-of-the-pokemon-company-by-fiscal-year/.

Digital product authentication can also be reinforced through buyer authentication. Buyers who have actually bought and experienced the digital product, can be authenticated and leveraged to share feedback and testimonials in order to convince new customers about product quality. moveUP.care, a Belgian healthcare start-up, for instance, launched digital therapy services in orthopedics in 2018 by providing a digital platform to patients and surgeons, as well as physical therapists and life sciences companies, for digital outpatient monitoring (through messaging, online questionnaires and possibly wearables), coaching, and therapy (through pre-recorded videos with exercises), from pre-surgery assessment until three months post-surgery. In order to authenticate its product, its website features testimonials of patients, surgeons and therapists who have experienced the solution.

Seller authentication can also support product authentication. As many digital products are experience goods, the seller's brand can do the heavy lifting in positively influencing the buyer's perception of digital product quality. By having its reputation precede the product experience, potential customers can be influenced to positively judge product quality before actually using the product. Apple Music, for instance, leverages Apple's reputation for user experience by advertising Apple Music online as being as easy as it sounds.

Another key market-facing process that is impacted by the characteristics of digital products is valuation. The indestructability of digital products implies that there is no second-hand market for the product, that the total addressable market size shrinks with every sale, and that the creator competes with its own past sales. Hence, a digital product needs to be sold at the lowest possible price, as anyone can copy and resell it. Alternatively, the digital product can be licensed over time, charging for usage in every period. Because of the transmutable nature of the product, digital products can be sold as a service and valuation can be dynamic and personalized. If the creator seeks to protect its digital product from being reproducible, it will incur costs for copyrighting the product, as well as for combatting copyright infringement, which will increase the marginal cost per copy, which will need to be included in the pricing. Returning to the example of Quibi, following the ninety-day free trial, users were charged a monthly subscription fee (7.99 USD) to continue experiencing the short-form video service.

As with digital product authentication for experience goods, the seller can authenticate buyers who consumed and reviewed the digital product and share their feedback with potential new buyers, together with price information, which can be used as a basis for valuation. Furthermore, uncertainty about digital product quality can be countered by offering a money-back guarantee. For instance, Rockable Press, a publisher of how-to guides and resources for web and creative professionals and part of Envato, an Australian company that offers a collection of products and marketplaces for creative digital assets, offered a 100% money-back guarantee on any e-book purchase.

In support of valuation, a freemium model can be used. The term Freemium was introduced in 2006 by Jared Lukin. It refers to a contraction of free and premium, providing users with limited free functionality while making additional functionality available for a fee. LinkedIn Premium, for instance, allows users to reach out to anyone on the social media network site through extra InMails (messages within LinkedIn) per month, see who has visited their profile page in the last 90 days, obtain insights on competitors, leads or job applicants, and access LinkedIn Learning courses, on top of its standard functionality. Such a model enables potential buyers to experience some of the features of the digital product before buying the premium version and experience more features.

Given that many digital products are sold as a service, payment process support needs to include mechanisms that support this. Rather than providing payment mechanisms for supporting one-off transactions (e.g., wire transfers), mechanisms for supporting pay-per-use and subscription-based models can be put in place (e.g., online credit card payment).

As to logistics, choices need to be made on making the product available for downloading and/or streaming. Students in Online MBA programs, for instance, not only want to access online learning content through streaming, but also through downloads in order to be able to study in places without (free) Internet access (e.g., on airplanes). As discussed above, making the digital product available for download may pose challenges in terms of enforcing digital product ownership and preventing online piracy.

Given the dynamic nature of digital products, after-sales service support can be expanded with so-called customer success managers who point existing customers to the latest functionality and even demo it online for them to experience the product's benefits and value first hand. A case in point is Salesforce, a US-based provider of Customer Relationship Management (CRM) solutions in the cloud, whose Customer Success Managers (CSMs) support the customer online to help them achieve their desired business outcomes by leveraging the Salesforce solutions.

In addition to transaction processes, decision support processes are also impacted by the characteristics of digital products.

Given the transmutable nature of digital products, the configuration process can be supported through digital tools that help buyers understand which product functionality meets their needs. These configuration tools can be part of the digital product itself and made available before purchase through demos, shareware and free trials. Continuing the Salesforce example, the software can be configured from changing logos, themes and layouts to adapting objects, fields and workflows and creating reports.

The network externalities of digital products can benefit the collaboration process. By making collaboration tools available online and/or integrating them in the digital product for an increasing number of customers, users and/or developers can collaborate to improve the digital product. Returning to the Salesforce example, customers can add features to the CRM solution such as views and dashboards through custom development by coding and testing in a sandbox environment before integrating the features for wider deployment in their organization.

Finally, as digital products tend to be dynamic, customer-revealed information can be leveraged in support of the business intelligence process. Back-end data and learning that occurs on personal preferences (e.g., music, movies, etc.) can help buyers in the front-end to decide on which digital content to consume next.

Pure versus Hybrid Digital Products

Pure digital products are products that consist of software program code that provides functionality to the user. However, digital products can also be enhanced with physical features, and become hybrid digital products, consisting of both digital and physical components. In the previous chapter we discussed how existing physical products can be digitally enhanced. The result of those enhancements is a hybrid digital product as it has both physical and digital features. Our focus in this section is on hybrid digital products that result from adding physical elements to purely digital products.

As human beings cannot sense a digital product, a physical device is needed for experiencing the product. A user can access the functionality on devices that can run the software. These could be traditional computing devices such as desktop, laptop, or tablet computers, as well as smartphones and wearables. Furthermore, other so-called smart devices, including appliances and cars, can run software provided that their sellers allow third-party software to run on their products. By doing so, these sellers could run digital platforms, which are discussed in Chap. 6.

Digital content can be processed and made accessible to the user through the software. Using the razor-and-blade metaphor, software can be viewed as the razor, while content refers to the blades. However, both are now digital, which implies that their characteristics are very different from physical products, as described above. Both the razors and the blades now become dynamic, with new software and content being introduced over time.

An interesting example of dynamic software is a Web browser, which is software that runs on a computing device to access Websites. Initially, browsers provided hypertext with colors, but then got upgraded to enable animations, video rendering, and other new classes of content. A recent feature is Google Chrome ScrollToTextFragment that anticipates in which place a user wants to be on a Webpage when using the browser to go to that Webpage. Rather than opening the Webpage at the top of the page, the user is taken to a specific place in the Webpage that addresses the user's search through deep links.

Hybrid digital products consist of software that is enhanced with physical features. Instead of the user accessing the software on a device sold by others, the producer integrates the digital product into a device of its own. As such, the software can be optimized for use in the product's hardware and performance and security improved. This is in keeping with the traditional notion of a product platform (see Chap. 6), which enables the product to evolve from one traditional form to a new one without having to change everything.

An example of a hybrid digital product is Amazon's Kindle e-book reader. While the Amazon Kindle mobile app allows users to read e-books on their smartphones or tablets and the Kindle Cloud Reader lets users read books in their Web browser, the Amazon Kindle reader augments the reading experience by leveraging its hardware. Not only do the form factor (dimensions and weight), paperwhite screen (e-ink screen and front light LEDs with auto-adjusting light sensors instead of a backlit screen), page turn buttons, and weeks of battery life make for a compelling reading experience, the reader also provides automatic rotating page orientation and direct access to the Kindle store for browsing and buying e-books.

When creating a new hybrid digital product, a company is digitalizing the product in a way that is different from the digital enhancement of an existing product. Consider Barco Demetra[7] (see example), a hybrid digital product for the management of skin cancer by dermatologists and general practitioners (GPs). Instead of digitally enhancing an analog dermatoscope by expanding its components, connectivity, capabilities, and context, Barco recently developed two fully digital components: Demetra Cloud for cloud storage and processing (including algorithms for better visualization and analysis of skin lesions) of images and patient information, third party application integration

---

[7] https://www.barco.com/en/page/healthcare/demetra.

(e.g., electronic medical record integration) and tele-dermatology, and Demetra Web to access the cloud solution from any Internet-connected device with a Web browser. Given its competence in digital light technology, Barco also created Demetra Scope, a hardware device for acquiring high quality skin images, and optimized its software for use in the product's hardware for improved performance and security. As the product's further and future differentiation is geared towards the personalization of the workflow for dermatologists and GPs, AI algorithms for skin lesion analysis,[8] and the tele-dermatology functionality, the physical component becomes a less significant piece of the offering. Moreover, in the future third party solutions could be added to the product, either by having the hardware serve as a gateway for offering third party digital products or expanding the digital product with third party solutions, potentially turning Barco Demetra into a digital platform, and thus a pure digital offering.

The razor-and-blade metaphor can be expanded for hybrid digital products. The hardware can now be viewed as the razor, the software as the blades which can be upgraded (imagine blades that lubricate while shaving), and the content as an additional layer (imagine the razor playing music while shaving). An example is Tesla whose cars have 8 external cameras, a radar, 12 ultrasonic sensors and an onboard computer. When the customer purchases and activates Autopilot and Full Self-Driving Capability, Tesla's software suite of driver assistance features, through his or her Tesla account after the car has been delivered, new functionality such as traffic-aware cruise control, auto-steer, auto lane change, autopark, and summon are enabled. Autopilot and Full Self-Driving Capability can be experienced on a test drive at one of the Tesla store locations.

As a result, when creating a hybrid digital product, the seller needs to decide on the combination of hardware, software, and content. Likewise, it needs to decide on what to charge for, and what to protect for differentiation. For instance, the hardware can serve as an entry point in the user environment and serve as a gateway for offering other digital products to the user, which could also come from third parties, potentially turning the product into a digital platform (see Chap. 6). Moreover, a fourth level can be added as the consumption of the content can itself provide the basis for other digital services. Consider a smart home system that consists of various sensors, software and content, such as the Eneco Toon smart thermostat discussed in Chap. 3, that records what the user is doing in his or her home, providing insight on

---

[8] "Evaluation of multi-class risk scoring AI in dermoscopy using per-class histograms", EADV 2020, October 2020.

potential health issues the user is having (e.g., detect early signs of Alzheimer's disease through pattern recognition), and proposing medical support and services.

Example: Barco Demetra[9]

Barco, a global technology leader in networked visualization solutions for various professional markets, traditionally offers a broad range of high precision medical display systems for radiology, mammography, surgery, dentistry, pathology, point-of-care, and clinical review imaging. In February 2019, Barco expanded its commercial range of high-end healthcare solutions by launching Demetra, a skin imaging platform, for dermatologists and general practitioners (GPs) in Europe.

Dermatologists and GPs traditionally use an analog dermatoscope, which consists of a magnifying glass with a white light, to examine pigmented skin lesions. Based on the examination outcome, an GP can refer the patient to a dermatologist, who can diagnose the skin lesion. If the lesion is considered suspicious, the dermatologist can decide to excise it on the spot. The biopsy is then sent to a lab for histopathological analysis to confirm the clinical diagnosis and start a treatment plan if needed. If the lesion is not considered suspicious, the dermatologist can ask the patient to return in a few months and keep track of changes in the lesion over time.

In addition to analog dermatoscopes, digital systems are available that are typically cart-based and consist of a computer, a large screen, and a hand-held camera, and require a substantial capital outlay (typically around 50,000 Euros per system). Given that these systems are hardly affordable and not very portable, their clinical use is rather limited.

The current tools and systems, however, may not be sufficient to address the increasing problem of skin cancer, as melanoma incidence rates keep growing and treatment costs are high, especially for advanced melanoma. As rapid, accurate diagnosis and treatment are essential for improved patient outcomes and lowered treatment costs, dermatologists can benefit from new solutions to deal with the pressure to examine more and more patients in less time and increase their confidence in diagnosing skin cancer. Likewise, patient anxiety can be reduced by treating them faster, as many patients currently face long waiting lists because of the shortage and uneven distribution of dermatologists in many countries. Furthermore, more accurate diagnosis can avoid

---

[9] The authors thank Dr Tom Kimpe for his input.

many unnecessary excisions of benign lesions and the resultant scars. Finally, GPs can also benefit from new solutions to refer their patients to dermatologists with higher accuracy and more confidence.

In order to address these market challenges, Barco Demetra was designed as a hybrid digital product, which consists of Demetra Scope, Demetra Cloud and Demetra Web.

Demetra Scope (see Fig. 4.1) is a wireless, portable and ergonomic hardware device with a handle and a touch display (the size of a normal smartphone) with two integrated cameras and lenses for multispectral dermoscopic, close-up and clinical overview imaging, leveraging Barco's competence in digital light technology (including image processing, color calibration, multispectral imaging, LED/laser, complex optics). Thanks to the cameras and lenses, specific skin structures such as pigment distribution and blood vessels (vasculature) can be clearly visualized, providing better insight in the inner structures of lesions. Also, lesions can be charted on a mannequin or clinical overview image, facilitating documentation and follow-up. All of this supports efficient decision making on referral, diagnosis, treatment, and follow-up. The device is battery operated (full day battery life), uses a Qualcomm chipset, runs on the android operating system, and has WiFi connectivity built-in, making it traceable.

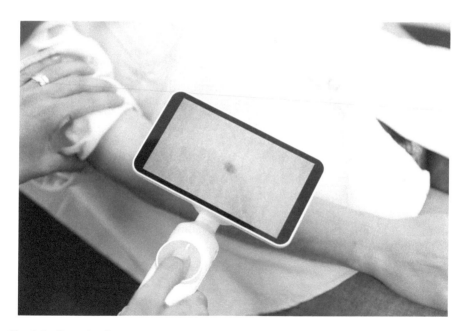

Fig. 4.1 Demetra Scope

Demetra Scope connects with Demetra Cloud, which is used for secure and private storage and processing of images and patient information. Image localization, diagnosis and management strategy can be entered and followed-up over time. Images can be easily compared side to side (e.g., comparing a new lesion image taken now versus the image of 6 months ago, comparing dermoscopic and clinical image). Demetra Cloud is also capable of exchanging information with electronic medical record systems to make patient management easy.

Image annotation and drawing tools in support of (remote) case communication with other healthcare professionals, configurable reports, practice dashboards (e.g., overview of patient numbers, and case types, including peer benchmarks based on anonymous, aggregated patient data) are some of the planned future functionalities.

In support of GP referral and dermatologist diagnosis decision making, an AI algorithm for risk scoring of lesions[10] is under development by Barco data scientists, in collaboration with the Interuniversity Microelectronics Centre (IMEC, an international R&D and innovation hub in nanoelectronics and digital technologies with 4000 researchers) and Ghent University Hospital and University Hospital Leuven in Belgium. Data has been collected from over 3000 patients[11] with their consent. An AI algorithm has been trained on this data after anonymization and aggregation to protect patient privacy, and then tested against new patients. Furthermore, aggregated data from dermatologists is also used to train the algorithm.

Barco Demetra also leverages positive network externalities. As more dermatologists and GPs use Barco Demetra, more skin lesion images can be analyzed and the algorithm improved, increasing the incremental value of its diagnosis for every additional user while enhancing the value for its existing user base.

Demetra Cloud is accessible through Demetra Web, making it available on any device that runs a Web browser, as shown in Fig. 4.2. Thanks to this, Demetra can also be used in a tele-dermatology setting. Images and data can be shared safely and quickly within a hospital or practice, and images acquired by Demetra Scope in a remote setting (e.g., at patient homes or in a local hospital site) are automatically uploaded and immediately accessible via Demetra Web. In the future, this functionality will be expanded to support collaboration with remote external specialists (e.g., dermatologist secondary

---

[10] "Evaluation of multi-class risk scoring AI in dermoscopy using per-class histograms", EADV 2020, October 2020.

[11] https://clinicaltrials.gov/ct2/show/NCT03818620.

Fig. 4.2 Demetra Cloud and Web

opinion). Demetra Web can also be used by the dermatologist to configure his or her preferred workflow, which can also be done on the Demetra Scope touch display. As such, the digital imaging of lesions (scanning, storing, processing, following up) can be configured in keeping with the workflow of dermatologists and GPs. For instance, some dermatologists adopt an image-by-image workflow, while others prefer the images to be uploaded in bulk for subsequent analyses. The ease of use and end-to-end process save time for healthcare professionals, while increasing their diagnostic accuracy and confidence. At the same time, patient satisfaction is enhanced.

The value system for Demetra is fundamentally different from Barco's traditional approach. Rather than selling its healthcare products through integrators (such as GE, Philips or Siemens) and resellers (such as Dell and HP Healthcare) who typically bundle and install fully integrated solutions in hospitals, Demetra is sold directly to end users (dermatologists and GPs). In some regions Barco works with selected partners for both the initial demo and sale, and installation and training for bigger orders, as well as for annual renewals and upselling. Logistical providers ship the product directly to end users. A global Web shop that is integrated with Barco's ERP system with proper tax calculations is being developed.

Barco Demetra uses various digital technologies in its direct interactions with end users to support its market-facing processes. SEO/SEA, social media campaigns, online workshops and courses and a Website support the search process and are leveraged for audience building. At the same time, conventional mechanisms including (physical) conferences and print brochures are still key for generating awareness and interest in some geographical regions.

Product authentication is done through Website content and a downloadable brochure, and new customers can request a demo or sign up for a try-and-buy program, including a free one-month trial, to experience Demetra. Furthermore, buyer authentication is used to reinforce product authentication through video testimonials on the Website (What do your colleagues think of Demetra). Likewise, seller authentication is leveraged in support of product authentication. The Barco brand is made very visible on the device, facing the patient, leveraging Barco's reputation as a highly reliable medical device manufacturer in adjacent domains (radiology, surgical, pathology), as well as Barco's deep understanding of digital light technology. For all customers, software updates are regularly provided, while the number of hardware versions in the market are limited, simplifying regulatory compliance and reducing complexities concerning legacy issues. While Barco chose to constantly evolve the digital product components and extend their life and value by updating and upgrading the software, the hardware device does suffer wear and tear and will need to be replaced over time. Hence, when necessary existing customers can swap old for new devices, by returning the old product upon receipt of a new device from the logistical provider.

As to valuation, Barco Demetra is sold purely as a service and hence end users pay only for what they need, with no capital outlay, when becoming a paid subscriber after the free 1-month trial, generating recurring revenue streams for Barco. Barco Demetra plans to work with Governments to secure patient reimbursement, as well as with private insurers to offer Barco Demetra as a service to their customers.

Payment is supported through traditional invoicing (email with invoice attached) and wire transfer. The Web shop also accepts online credit card payment typically preferred by small practices. Logistics for the devices is done through delivery partners who move the boxes to dermatology practices and hospitals, and deliver Web orders, with online tracking and tracing. Software updates are done through the cloud. Demetra Care Service and Support offers customer service by email and telephone.

The decision support processes are enacted through demos and the try-and-buy program. As explained above, users can configure their preferred workflow and obtain peer benchmark intelligence on Demetra Scope and Demetra

Web. For now, no collaboration tools are made available online or integrated in the digital product for users and/or developers to collaborate to improve the digital product.

It is of interest to note that while Barco Demetra is sold as a hybrid digital product to healthcare professionals such as dermatologists and GPs, new entrants are selling pure digital products to end consumers. SkinVision, for instance, a Dutch start-up, offers a skin cancer melanoma detection mobile app for end consumers to perform regular self-checks for skin cancer with their smartphone, with the goal of increasing skin cancer awareness. SkinVision also engages private insurers in offering the app to its members. While such offerings are complementary to Barco Demetra, an important question is what gives Barco Demetra a competitive edge? Does the Barco Demetra hardware give Barco an edge and can that be protected? Does the software do that? Or both? Today, the combination of the high-quality hardware with the software functionality, especially the optimal work flow, offer a competitive advantage. Over time, this will shift towards the digital component of the product, especially the algorithm and tele-dermatology functionality, as well the integration of the dermatology with the GP offering.

Reflection Questions

- Using the ideas presented in this chapter, can you identify potentially attractive digital products that would appeal to your existing customers? To new market segments?
- If you offered some new digital products, how would they affect the market for your existing products?
- How can you digitally enhance your market-facing processes to effectively sell new digital products?

Part II

Using Digital Technologies to Transform Business Scope

So far, we have focused on the various ways in which a business can leverage digitalization to innovate its products and processes, within its existing scope. In other words, we have assumed that the business's position within its sector's value system remains unchanged. This is important, since too often, businesses shy away from significant innovation out of fear that it will force them to change "who they are". The previous chapters have demonstrated that there are a number of ways in which digitalization can add significant value while the business continues to serve the same markets, deal with the same supply chain and business partners, and use the same business and revenue models as before.

We now step back and examine some ways in which digitalization can create opportunities for redefining the business's scope and market position. As the next three chapters demonstrate, a business can exploit digital technologies to change how it operates, what it does, how it makes money, and who it sells to. As part of this, we show how the business's digitalization strategy needs to factor in its competitive strategy as well, and the factors that impact the choices it makes with regard to digitalization opportunities.

It is worth noting that the use of digital technologies to redefine scope and structure is not a new phenomenon. In fact, computers and networks have played a significant role in some major shifts in business trends in this regard. In the latter half of the twentieth century, we witnessed a dramatic shift away from large, vertically integrated companies that characterized many successful businesses in the previous half-century. Two key trends that became popular towards the end of the twentieth century were globalization and outsourcing/offshoring. The ability to out-source different "non-core" functions and processes to distant suppliers and serve global rather than regional or national markets was significantly enabled by the availability of computing and communication technologies that allowed businesses to coordinate with globally distributed suppliers and customers. What we see today with regard to the evolution of business ecosystems, and the ability of even small businesses to thrive in a global marketplace is the evolving form of those same trends, even though off-shoring has lost its appeal, mostly for a variety of reasons not related to digitalization.

10.1   Redefining Business Scope

When considering the impact of digitalization on industry dynamics in terms of business interactions with suppliers and buyers, it is also useful to consider the business's value system beyond direct suppliers and buyers. By considering how upstream suppliers and downstream buyers are impacted by digitalization, the business can decide to revisit its scope. For example, as discussed in Chap. 5, the business can consider its position in the B2B2C value system and engage with end consumers, either directly by disintermediating its traditional customers, or indirectly by supporting its direct customers to offer digitalized solutions to the end consumer.

In order to see how digitalization can lead to changes in a business's scope and structure, consider the following effects of digitalization on a business and its value system:

1. Significantly lowering the operating costs of a process
2. Redefining scale economies of processes so that they can be cost-effective at lower scale
3. Lowering the costs and complexities of establishing business ties with partners such as customers and suppliers
4. Reducing the transaction costs associated with market-based transactions, so that the business can leverage market efficiencies rather than having to vertically integrate.

All these effects help a business limit its scope to the processes and activities that it can perform better than other players. In other words, digitalization can enable a business to carve out processes and activities that it cannot do as well as other businesses in the market, so that the business can instead partner with those businesses for those processes and activities. This in turn moves businesses from vertically integrated monoliths to specialized members of eco-systems.

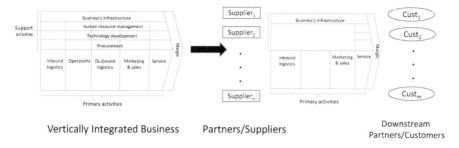

Fig. 1   Slicing up the business's value chain

To some extent, such changes can be caused by digitalization of internal processes, and as we mentioned at the outset, our focus in this book is on external-facing processes. So we will not discuss the specific internal processes that might be outsourced. However, note that outsourcing in effect makes a process that may have been internal into an external-facing process, of the types discussed in Chap. 2.

In addition to the above changes in scope, in some cases a business can also consider the option of moving from being an enterprise offering its own products and services to becoming an intermediary, or even a two-sided platform. This change in scope and structure implies significant changes in not only the business's external interfaces and processes (both upstream with suppliers/providers and downstream with customers/consumers), but also its business model and revenue models. As discussed in Chap. 6, this decision depends upon the opportunities for various network effects and the core functionality that the business could provide as a platform.

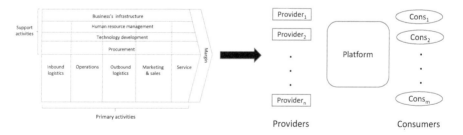

Fig. 2   From enterprise to platform

Some authors[1] argue that Porter's 5-forces, while still relevant, are considered to behave differently for digital platforms. Rather than being considered as threats that the business needs to build barriers against, the external forces are viewed as adding value to the platform business, as they drive network effects (e.g., more customers add more value to the existing customer base, and can attract more suppliers). As the boundaries separating providers, consumers, competitors and complementors can shift rapidly, digital platform operators need constantly stimulate positive network effects while monitoring participant activity that can decrease value. Amazon and Facebook, for instance, need to develop the ability to deal with bad actors such as suppliers of inferior quality products buying and rating their own products to enhance their search ranking on Amazon Marketplace, and users that post offensive content on Facebook.

While digitalization motivates businesses to become less vertically integrated, the ability to process information more efficiently and manage more complexity also enables firms to grow effectively. However, this growth may occur horizontally, rather than vertically. To see this, consider a firm like Apple. When Apple was relatively integrated, making its own devices and their major components, its product line was relatively small. Today, while Apple makes very few of its products itself, it offers a broad and diversified product line, with all its products leveraging the company's design expertise with respect to both aesthetics and functionality.

---

[1] M. van Alstyne, G. Parker and S. Choudary, Pipelines, Platforms and the New Rules of Strategy, Harvard Business Review, April 2016.

5

Engaging Consumers

The use of digital technologies can change the business's market scope. In addition to pursuing digitalization with its traditional supplier and customer base, the business can use digital technologies to interact with other organizations that are further upstream or downstream in its value system, and potentially engage end consumers. In this chapter, we describe how the use of digital technologies can broaden the business's market scope and present and illustrate an approach for businesses to organize and structure their thinking around the use of digital technologies for engaging end consumers. We also discuss how the business can move from a linear to a triangular approach to consumer engagement, in which downstream business customers remain significant for engaging with consumers. Furthermore, we examine how social media mechanisms can be used to engage with consumers.

Market Scope

Traditionally, businesses are categorized as either Business-to-Business (B2B) or Business-to-Consumer (B2C). B2B businesses sell to organizations, including other businesses, institution and governments, while B2C businesses sell to retail consumers.

B2B businesses typically develop long lasting relationships with a smaller set of bigger business customers that are more professional in their acquisition of products and services, which is done through so-called decision-making units that are more rational, focusing on technical features, product benefits, and monetary value versus price. B2B businesses also stimulate collaboration and

A. Basu, S. Muylle, *Competitive Digital Innovation*, Palgrave Executive Essentials,
https://doi.org/10.1007/978-3-031-23440-8_5

innovation with their customers, adapting and customizing their products for specific customers. Conversely, B2C businesses are typically transactional in their dealings with many individual or household retail consumers, who are more emotional in their decision making and buying and more sensitive to advertising and price promotions for mostly standard products and services.

While B2C businesses deal with consumer demand by retail customers for consumer products and services, B2B businesses deals with derived demand by business customers for business products. The latter refers to demand for a factor of production or an intermediate good that results from the demand for another intermediate or final good. Hence, a consumer product is a product or service consumed by a retail customer, while a business product refers to a product or service consumed by a business customer, as either a component in another product (e.g., DuPont non-stick coatings for cookware products) or as a resource in the production of another product (e.g., strategic consultancy services for a client). While resources are not part of the final consumer product, components can be part of a consumer product (like for DuPont non-stick coatings in cookware sold to retail customers). If the component, however, is part of a business product that becomes a resource later on (e.g., a fibre for industrial gloves that are used as a resource by operators in a car manufacturing plant), it does not become part of the final consumer product (e.g., the car).

Digitalization can reshape consumers' interactions with B2B businesses in two ways: First, by making B2C more relational, i.e. more like B2B, and second, by connecting B2B businesses with end consumers.

B2C businesses can leverage digital technologies to develop close relationships with their consumers, much like B2B businesses do with their customers in a personal manner. B2B, also referred to as "Belly-to-Belly," is typically characterized by close relationships between members of the customer's decision making unit and their counterparts at the supplier. As these professionals interact over time through visits, meetings, emails, telephone calls, negotiations, workshops, and possibly lunches, dinners, and other events, relationships are forged, which are solidified as both parties deliver on their promises and take corrective action when needed. Such a personal approach is only feasible when interacting with a relatively small set of (bigger) customers, which is much more typical of B2B than B2C, as the cost of personal interaction with many customers is prohibitive. Digitalization, however, offers B2C businesses the opportunity to develop individual relationships with their many consumers, without the need for close personal interactions. Thanks to the long tail, as discussed in Chap. 2, B2C businesses can lower the cost of their traditional business approach and reach out to a larger portion of the market. As B2C businesses digitally innovate their market facing processes, also as described in Chap. 2, they can leverage the transactional and decision support process data to customize and even personalize their digital process support for every single consumer. Likewise, when B2C businesses digitally enhance their physical products (see Chap. 3) or create and sell new digital products (see Chap. 4), they again can leverage the data to customize and personalize the product for every single consumer, and also customize or personalize the corresponding market-facing process support. As such, digital technologies can substitute for personal interactions to develop close consumer relationships. Furthermore, personalized loyalty programs can be designed for rewarding the consumer for his or her patronage. A case in point is Amazon Prime, which offers various loyalty benefits in return for a monthly fee. These benefits include shipping, promotions, cloud services, and access to Amazon's repository of e-books, music, movies and series.

Note on Consumerization. While digitalization can support B2C firms in becoming more relational, much like B2B firms, B2B businesses can benefit from digitalization by making their online transactional experiences more like those of B2C businesses. By engaging in consumerization, a term coined by global research and advisory firm Gartner that refers to the reorientation of product and service designs by businesses to focus on the end user as an individual consumer rather than as a user of an enterprise IT system, B2B businesses can design user experiences that are easy, convenient, and require no training, much like an online B2C user experience. For instance, rather than having industrial buying agents use traditional Enterprise Resource Planning systems and Buyer Portals for procuring industrial goods, consumer-like online user experiences can be designed and implemented that offer the buyer the convenience and appeal of well-established B2C online buying experiences. Furthermore, some B2C e-commerce players expanded into B2B e-commerce, leveraging their well-established online user experiences. A case in point is Amazon, which expanded its B2C e-commerce and e-marketplace (see Chap. 6 on digital intermediaries) offerings into Amazon Business, which combines the convenience, selection, and value of Amazon with features that help improve business purchasing. These features include account management for adding multiple users, manage permissions and create buying groups for added efficiency, integrated workflows for maintaining compliance with organizational policies by setting guidelines, spending limits, and approvals, and Amazon Business analytics for tracking and reporting individual, group, and company spend. Amazon Business also offers systems integration as it can be set up as a punch-out option with various e-procurement systems. Finally, Amazon also extends its loyalty program to B2B, where Business Prime members get extra features such as compliance guiderails for steering employees to the right products or suppliers with guided buying, and advanced spend analytics for making better decisions with spend visibility.

Digitalization can also connect B2B businesses with consumers, putting the "C" of the consumer in B2B, and hence broaden the B2B business's market scope to B2B2C. Here, the connection between the B2B business and the organizations that are upstream and downstream in the business's value system are made explicit, as well as the end consumer. Hence, the B in the middle can refer to one or multiple businesses.

Consider the example of the core brassiere wire B2B2C value system for Bekaert, a global steel wire transformation and coatings company, headquartered in Belgium, as shown in Fig. 5.1.

Bekaert produces core brassiere wire in a wide variety of tensile strengths and shapes to meet the requirements for any type of bra and provide the right support for its wearer, while preserving the bra's original shape, even after numerous washings. The zinc and the PET (polyethylene terephthalate; also known by the brand name Dacron in the US) coating on the wire increases the lifetime of the wire and prevents it from breaching the fabric, while also preserving the bra's original form for a longer time.

Bekaert transforms wire rod that it acquires from steel manufacturers into bra wire, and also uses zinc and PET coatings, which it sources from chemical companies. It also uses consumables such as dyes and lubricants. Bekaert sells its core brassiere wire globally to producers of underwire, who convert the wire into underwire, and sell to companies that design and produce bras. These companies then sell bras through wholesale and retail to end consumers. Designers of bras typically work with some consumers and inform their suppliers about the requirements for their designs.

Traditionally, companies such as Bekaert would focus their market scope on their direct suppliers and customers, which are B2B, without hardly or ever interacting with end consumers, having only indirect or no insight on consumer markets and preferences. However, digital technologies offer businesses operating in B2B markets direct access to consumers, broadening their market scope to B2B2C. A key question then arises: How can a B2B business identify the key opportunity areas for engaging with consumers and leveraging consumer information through the use of digital

Fig. 5.1 Brassiere wire value system

technologies? In the next section, we present an approach for answering that question in a structured way.

From B2B to B2B2C

Engaging consumers can deliver significant benefits to B2B businesses. Armed with a better understanding of consumer markets and preferences, a B2B business can enhance its revenues and margins by stimulating consumer demand and charging price premiums driven by preference insight and higher customer switching costs. At the same time, it can also reduce its costs through improved production planning, inventory management and logistics.

Toward that end, the approach presented in Table 5.1 can be used by B2B businesses to structure their thinking about how to engage consumers through the use of digital technologies.

Consumer engagement has two dimensions: the market scope, and the focus of digitalization.

The market scope refers to the B2B business's position in the B2B2C value system. It can leverage consumer insight to strengthen its B2B position vis-à-vis its business customers, and/or market a consumer version of its product directly to consumers, becoming B2C oriented. If the B2B business's offering is not part of a consumer product, a B2B2B perspective can be adopted, as discussed in the note on B2B2B customer engagement.

Note on B2B customer engagement: As stated earlier in this chapter, some business products, such as resources as well as components that become resources for downstream business customers, are not part of an end consumer product and hence can only be sold to business customers. Businesses operating in such a B2B2B setting, however, can benefit from digitally engaging downstream business customers. Let us revisit the example of Philips Lighting—Signify, introduced in Chap. 2. In addition to its Partner Conversion Program, which offered digital support to the electro-technical wholesalers, Philips Lighting launched digital initiatives to engage installers and their business customers to generate derived demand for its products. It launched a digital campaign on social media that incentivized

Table 5.1 Consumer engagement

	Existing product	Digitally enhanced product	Digital product
B2B	Process improvement	Digitally enhanced business product	Digital business product
B2C	Consumer sales	Digitally enhanced consumer product	Digital consumer product

installers to showcase a project they were proud of, by giving them a chance to win a promotion campaign worth 10,000 Euros. The installer typically engaged with the business customer to co-promote and document the project by means of user generated content. Both the installer and business customer then tapped into their social networks to have people vote on their co-promoted project, which was featured on a dedicated Website. The installer that got the most votes was then awarded the prize. By having installers and their customers act as ambassadors, the digital initiative created a lot of buzz on social media. What is more, it also drove demand for Philips products at the electro-technical wholesalers. The sales target of 10% for the period was beaten as sales shot up 44%. Because of its success, the campaign was repeated in a later period, and again considered successful. Another double-digit sales increase was realized, while the project that got the least votes still had more votes than the winning project of the previous campaign. This time the prize was a 10,000 Euros value advertising campaign in the soccer stadium of PSV Eindhoven, also known as the Philips Stadium.[1]

The second dimension refers to the focus of the digital innovation. For both the B2B and B2C market scope, the B2B business can leverage consumer access and insight to digitalize its market-facing process support (see Chap. 2), digitally enhance its product (see Chap. 3), and create new digital products (see Chap. 4).

B2B businesses can use digital technologies to access consumer markets and leverage consumer insight in six distinct ways, which are discussed next.

1. Process Improvement for an Existing Product

A B2B business can improve various of its processes for an existing product by leveraging insight about the end consumer market in the following ways:

(a) Develop internal business intelligence from consumer data to improve internal operations
(b) Analyse consumer product preferences for product configuration and discovery of new applications
(c) Optimize pricing
(d) Generate derived demand
(e) Generate and qualify leads

---

[1] https://www.slideshare.net/WebsNL/dfb2b-2015-maarten-vernooi-go-digital;   https://www.lighting.philips.nl/campagnes/project-spotlight.

Bekaert, for instance, probed various social media services platforms for end consumer mentions and discussions of the product. As its business product is a component (core brassiere wire) of another business product (bra underwire), which again is a component of a final consumer product (bra), it monitored social media for the term "underwire," which consumers also use to refer to the product. By developing internal business intelligence from consumer data on perceived product quality and performance, it could improve its internal operations. The intelligence revealed that end consumers faced quality issues with underwire that was breaking, which dissatisfied them as it tore the fabric of the bra, or underwire that made disturbing, squeaking noises. As such, Bekaert could improve the quality assurance process and start an R&D project to strengthen its position and product range in the core brassiere wire market. The analysis of consumer product perceptions led to the development and commercialization of a new non-squeaking solution in its product portfolio. Furthermore, the consumer insights helped Bekaert to optimize its pricing when promoting this attribute in the value proposition for its business customers.

As stated above, B2B businesses deals with derived demand by business customers for business products, while B2C businesses deal with consumer demand by retail customers for consumer products. By engaging the end consumer, a B2B business can generate derived demand for its products by influencing consumer demand. DuPont, for instance, leveraged social media services platforms to educate end consumers about the benefits of its Teflon™ non-stick coatings in cookware. Toward that end, it organized a contest on Facebook for end consumers to share their secret to great grilled cheese and share that with their social networks to be entered for a chance to win a Flip-It Pan with Teflon™ non-stick coatings. In doing so, it stimulated end consumers to ask retailers about cookware with Teflon™ non-stick coatings, which further generated derived demand for the product by cookware makers. Moreover, when probing social media services platforms, cookware makers could see the end consumer discussions on non-stick coatings and get motivated to contact DuPont for more information. As such, DuPont restructured the traditional information flow in its B2B2C value system by breaking the sequential constraint and engaging with end consumers directly. Rather than instructing its business customers about its products and relying on them to promote its value to downstream customers, DuPont can influence its business customers with information about what end consumers want.

Another example is Solvay, an advanced materials and specialty chemicals group, who used social media services platforms to educate end consumers about its Emana® yarn in apparel. Owing to the bioactive minerals embedded in the yarn, Emana® absorbs the body heat and emanates infrared rays back to the human skin, which improves blood micro-circulation and offers thermo-regulation properties. The latter enhance the wellbeing and comfort of the end consumer, improving skin elasticity and reducing the appearance of cellulite, as well as sports performance by reducing muscle fatigue with less oxygen consumption and fast recovery. As Solvay sells Emana® to fashion, lingerie, shapewear, hosiery, socks, and jeans and sportswear manufacturers, who sell their apparel through wholesale and retail to end consumers, it traditionally did not connect with the end consumers. By establishing a presence on various social media services platforms, it informed end consumers about different customer products that feature Emana® and encouraged consumers to share their experiences wearing such products in sporting events, using hashtags that refer to the product. By providing end consumers with hyperlinks to the online shops of its business customers on its social media outposts, it could increase the derived demand for Emana®.

Finally, a B2B firm can engage end consumers through the use of digital technologies to generate and qualify business customer leads. Continuing the Emana® example, fashion, lingerie, shapewear, hosiery, socks, and jeans and sportswear manufacturers, who do not use Emana® can be made aware of the product and informed about its value proposition by consumers who engage with Solvay's social media outposts, which can trigger these potential business customers to reach out to Solvay to inquire about the product.

2. Digitally Enhanced Business Product

In addition to process improvement for existing products, a B2B business can leverage consumer insight to digitally enhance its business product. As discussed in Chap. 3, a business can increase the extent to which it digitally enhances its existing products, ranging from the addition of information features and online software capabilities for information processing to enabling the customer to personalize the product and extending the product with digital add-on features.

A case in point is AB InBev, which, through its acquisition of beverage analytics company WeissBeerger, digitally enhances its product (beer) with analytics tools for bars to obtain better insights into their operations and sales. By attaching sensors to kegs and beer taps, the flow of beer on tap can be measured. Analysis not only shows the volume of each beer brand on tap that was served at each point in time (which can lead to recommendations for bars such as serving a Bud with a vodka at 2 a.m., when beer consumption drops as patrons typically switch to vodka), but also reveals the cleanliness of the pipes (the beer flow is slower if pipes are dirty) and how well the tap beers are poured (creating the proper amount of head).

3. Digital Business Product

By engaging end consumers, new digital business products can be created and sold to business customers. As discussed in Chap. 4, these products can consist of content (data, information, ideas or knowledge) or software.

Continuing the AB InBev example, WeissBeerger created Trayz, a software solution for the food and beverage industry that allows its business customers to run their business better by tracking their performance over time and against other businesses like theirs, based on end consumer data. As the software securely connects with various Point Of Sale (POS) systems such as TouchBistro, lightspeed, Square, toast, and clover, it can measure average consumer transaction size, number of transactions, and top selling brands. In addition, the data is anonymized and aggregated across business customers in the same area for benchmarking purposes. Also, it not only tracks the consumption of beer but also that of food, wine, spirits, and non-alcoholic beverages. Using the consumer insight, the software offers customized sales insights and trend recognition that can be used by the business customer to optimize its product portfolio and menu pricing.

4. Consumer Sales

When altering its market scope to B2C, the B2B business can market a consumer version of its product directly to consumers, through a model known as D2C (see note on D2C). As such, the firm can sell its consumer products online, both directly through its proper online shop and indirectly through online marketplaces such as Amazon (see Chap. 6 on digital intermediaries). PepsiCo, for instance, launched two Web shops in May 2020, to sell snacks and pantry items directly to consumers in the US. While snacks.com lets consumers create a snack pack with their favorite Frito-Lay products, pantryshop.com offers pantry kits for various occasions such as breakfast ("Rise & Shine") and sports ("Workout & Recovery"), in both a standard size and a family size.

Consumer sales are not limited to traditional consumer packaged goods manufacturers. Consider the mattress industry. The traditional value system consists of suppliers of mattress components including pocket coils, PET, foam, latex, gel and wool, which are sold to manufacturers of mattresses, who produce and sell fully finished mattresses to retailers, who then market the consumer products to end consumers. As new "mattress-in-a-box" players such as Casper emerged, which sell a limited assortment of affordable mattresses, compressed in a box for easy delivery, with a 100-night risk-free trial and a 10-year warranty directly to consumers over the Internet, traditional manufacturers as well as suppliers who also sell finished mattresses, started to sell their products to these D2C players. However, as these D2C players develop their brands and direct relationships with end consumers, the incumbent players can also consider reaching out to the end consumer themselves. While a DC2 player can be acquired (cf. the acquisition in 2018 of Tuft & Needle by Serta Simmons Bedding, a US bedding manufacturer that was established in the 1870ies), manufacturers can also sell branded consumer versions of their products to end consumers directly through their own Web shops or indirectly through marketplaces like Amazon and Wayfair. Tempur Sealy International Inc., a manufacturer of mattresses and other sleep and relaxation products, for instance, sells compressed mattresses for consumers at various price points, including the Sealy® and Cocoon by Sealy® mattresses available at Sealy.com and CocoonbySealy.com. It also introduced TEMPUR-Cloud®, a premium mattress-in-a-box offering, in Dallas, Los Angeles, Miami, New York City, San Francisco and Seattle, in early 2020.[2] Furthermore, suppliers can also offer consumer products online. Purple, for instance, which has a background in creating high-tech carbon fiber sporting goods and wheelchairs as of 1989, and invented Hyper-Elastic Polymer™ in 1996, which it licensed to consumer mattress manufacturers in Europe, Japan, and Australia, developed Mattress Max™, a machine for producing Hyper-Elastic Polymer™ king-sized mattresses, in 2013. Using its machine, it could produce premium quality mattresses at lower cost, and started selling these as consumer products directly online, branded as the Purple Mattress, as of 2016.

Note on D2C. *Direct-to-Consumer business models, referred to as D2C, have become popular thanks to the availability of the digital infrastructure in the marketplace. Rather than adhering to the traditional value system, new entrants ignore incumbent distributors such as wholesalers and retailers and sell to end consumers directly online. D2C models have emerged across a wide range of industries including food (e.g., Blue Apron, HelloFresh), glasses (e.g., Warby Parker), mattresses (e.g., Casper, Tuft & Needle, Tediber), menswear (e.g., Bonobos) and razors and grooming products (e.g., Dollar Shave Club). As D2C players upset the value*

---

[2] https://www.prnewswire.com/news-releases/tempur-sealy-announces-direct-channel-expansion-update-300985483.html.

system and business model, traditional retailers have responded by acquiring such players (e.g., Walmart's acquisition of Bonobos in 2017) and selling retailer owned brands though such a model (e.g., Walmart's Allswell Bed-in-a-Box Mattress). Conversely, D2C players experiment with physical retail models to reach out to the portion of the market that does not buy their products online. For instance, Tediber, a French mattress-in-a-box player, founded in 2015, launched shop-in-shops in Carrefour hypermarkets and a Printemps Haussmann department store, in addition to its own concept store in Paris.

5. Digitally Enhanced Consumer Product

If the business decides to sell a consumer version of its product online, it can also consider to digitally enhance the consumer product by adding information features or online software capabilities for information processing, or enabling the consumer to personalize the product, or extend the product with digital add-on features.

Continuing the example of the mattress industry; Eightsleep.com, the 2015 start-up introduced in Chap. 3, sells its sleep trackers and smart bedding systems directly to consumers within the continental US, while having a retail store in New York City. In keeping with the digitalization initiatives of such new entrants, incumbent manufacturers could also digitally enhance their consumer products and sell smart mattresses directly online.

The digital enhancement of consumer products can also lead businesses that traditionally do not sell directly to end consumers to leverage digital technologies to do so. As an example, consider how the producers of self-dosing washing machines are manufacturing the detergent cartridges, and selling those directly to the end consumer, disrupting the traditional detergent producers. The washing machines, which are WiFi connected, can automatically reorder detergent at online retailers such as Amazon.com when the cartridge is detected to be empty. Miele, for instance, developed its own detergent cartridges for TwinDos, its automatic dispenser system for washing machines. A two component detergent is built into the appliance, consisting of UltraPhase1 for protecting colors and removing the bulk of soiling, and UltraPhase2 for removing persistent stains, which has oxygen bleach in it, an ingredient that is not found in any regular liquid detergents. UltraPhase 1 and 2 can be bought directly online in a Miele Web shop or through online retail.

Businesses operating in traditional B2B industries such as construction can also benefit from introducing and digitally enhancing a consumer product. Consider BESIX Group, an international contractor that was established in

1909 in Belgium and has built airport terminals, bridges, car parks, convention centers, dams, hospitals, hotels, marine works, offices, ports, power stations, stadiums, theme parks, tunnels, warehouses, wastewater treatment plants, and skyscrapers. Over time, the company has evolved from its core contracting business into property development and concessions in the public and private sectors. While the company is operating in traditional B2B markets, it has also launched a strategic digitalization initiative that engages the end consumer. A-Stay[3] is a new hospitality concept launched in November 2019 in Antwerp, Belgium. The 192-room hotel offers guests the opportunity to create their own stay. Guest can stay for a short while or a very long time, use self-serve spots for laundry services and grab-and-go food and drinks, and enjoy a joint lounge or use co-working areas. Rather than focus on the traditional build stage of the asset, BESIX, together with a partner, sells A-Stay to end consumers online, generating recurring revenue over the lifetime of the asset. Furthermore, it digitally enhances the hospitality service by adding features such as kiosks for check-in and check-out, and palm vein recognition as a biometric authentication method for room access and payment (linked to a credit card) for extra services or drinks in the self-serve bar. By scanning their personal QR code on their room TV, guests can use their smartphone to control all room features, including mood lighting, and setting the frequency of cleaning the room and changing the sheets, with high-speed Wi-Fi being available in every room. Furthermore, the breakfast area is equipped with Apple iPads on which guests can configure their favorite cappuccino or fruit juice. As new hotels will be opened, A-Stay guests will be able to enjoy personalized services based on their idiosyncratic preferences set during their past stays in any of the other hotels.

6. Digital Consumer Product

Finally, the business can introduce a digital consumer product and sell data, information, ideas, knowledge, or software applications based on consumer data to consumers online.

Continuing the example of the mattress industry, incumbent manufacturers could create and sell a software application that provides sleep advice to the consumer based on data that is generated by the smart mattress. Likewise, in the hospitality industry, A-Stay could leverage consumer data from its guests, combining its data with that of its guests (e.g., health data from their

---

[3] https://www.a-stay.com/.

wearables) and recommend and sell other coffee blends and fruit juice mixes that match their tastes and optimal energy and health levels. As these guests have already grown accustomed to paying with their hand palms, this payment method could be used to facilitate sales.

From Linear to Triangular Consumer Engagement

As businesses introduce new digital initiatives to engage with consumers in their B2B2C value system, the business customers that traditionally market their products and services to the end consumers, referred to as the "B" in the middle, may perceive these initiatives as conflicting and disruptive. Especially when the business starts selling a consumer version of its product directly to end consumers, traditional business customers may object and try to thwart this form of digital disintermediation. The business, however, can engage with end consumers and manage potential conflict by moving from a linear to a triangular model of consumer engagement.

The traditional B2B2C value system can be described as a linear model, connecting the business with the business customer, which in turn connects with the end consumer, as shown in Fig. 5.2. In this linear model, the business customer typically maintains the face to the end consumer, promoting its brand, and leveraging its deep understanding of consumer needs and preferences to bolster its position. By using digital technology, the business can interact in six distinct ways with end consumers and leverage consumer insight, as discussed above, and strengthen its position in its value system.

In order to manage potential conflict with the business customer, a triangular view can be adopted, as shown in Fig. 5.3. Rather than having the business customer own the relationship with the end consumer, the business involves the business customer in its consumer engagement initiatives.

Consider the insurance industry as an example. At its core, insurance is an information service, and therefore highly amenable to digitalization. However, insurers typically rely on intermediaries such as agents, banks and brokers, to market their products, in a linear B2B2C value system. In Belgium, for instance, the majority of consumers trust these intermediaries for addressing their insurance needs. Given the potential for digitalization, AG Insurance,

Fig. 5.2 Linear B2B2C model

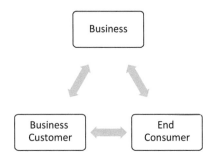

Fig. 5.3   Triangular B2B2C model

the market leader in Belgium, founded in 1824 and part of the international Ageas Group, opted for a triangular model that aligns the interest of the end consumers with those of the intermediaries and the business. In addition, it included non-conventional parties to support its digitalization initiatives, in a broader ecosystem.

As part of digital process improvement for existing products, AG Insurance launched WeActivate, a set of opt-in services for intermediaries to support online search and social media campaigning, as well as templates for customized Websites that feature multiple insurers, and a mobile app for engaging with consumers. As such, it not only assists intermediaries with their digital go-to-market approach, but also obtains valuable end consumer insight. AG Insurance also introduced Video Expertise, in collaboration with a technology partner, a service through which consumers can use their smartphone to have a remote AG Insurance expert assess water or fire damage to their house in real-time, while intermediaries can participate in the video call for assistance or reassure the consumer onsite. This service not only substantially reduces the claims handling process cycle time (from three weeks to a day), but also yields valuable consumer data (e.g., images) that can be used to improve claim valuation models and fraud reduction.

As to digital enhancement of existing products, AG Insurance launched several services, including Mobility Assist, a mobile app for consumers to report a car breakdown, sharing location data and a detailed description of the car with a towing company, while notifying family and friends through social media services. AG Insurance can more quickly start the claims processing and involve the intermediary for follow up and reassuring the consumer, benefitting all parties.

Regarding the sales of new digital products, AG Insurance introduced Yongo, as shown in Fig. 5.4. Yongo consists of a selection of life insurance products that are presented in a more accessible format to consumers (e.g.,

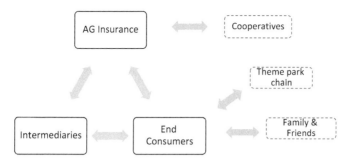

Fig. 5.4 AG Insurance Yongo

Yongo Moon, Star and Dreams, in lieu of conventional Branch 21, 23, and 26 life insurance products). Yongo supports parents in educating their children on saving and investing money for realizing short and long term financial objectives, and partners with two family-oriented cooperatives and a theme park chain to promote the products. Furthermore, family and friends can contribute financially and support the child's save and invest objectives. While the products are sold directly online to end consumers, intermediaries can also propose the Yongo product range to their own clientele and maintain their relationship with the consumer.

Another example of digital process improvement for existing products is that of Nike, the sporting goods maker. While traditionally a B2B company that sold its products through various types of retailers, Nike has been a pioneer in engaging consumers through a variety of digital initiatives, that include rich content on its Web site, a very active and multifaceted social media presence and mobile apps. These initiatives have enabled the company to have extensive and dynamic insights into consumer preferences and tastes, thereby enhancing its marketing efforts and its brand image. As yet another example, AT&T, the telecommunications giant, has leveraged social media extensively, including building a highly sophisticated social media monitoring center at its Dallas headquarters. This enables the company to not only track consumer sentiment, but also to detect problems with its services much earlier and begin responding to outages often even before any consumers have reported those outages.

In conclusion, businesses can leverage digital technologies to engage with end consumers while involving their business customers for adding value. The traditional B2B2C linear value system can be shifted towards a triangular model from which all parties benefit. Moreover, the B2B2C value system can be expanded with partners that can add to the business's proposition to end consumers.

Leveraging Social Media

Social media services are peer-to-peer technology-enabled mechanisms that allow individuals and groups to connect, and to generate and distribute content in an online social network. Features include user ability to construct a profile and view and connect with other users, create and exchange user generated content, and form online social networks based on family ties, friendships, acquaintances, interest groups, or professional relationships. The technology-enabled mechanisms are typically built into software applications that we refer to as social media services, that are typically accessed through Web browsers or mobile apps. Social media services are most commonly offered by specialized companies such as Facebook, Twitter, YouTube, and LinkedIn, that are commonly called **social media services platforms** (SMSPs).[4]

A key distinction between social media services and other Web content and services is that social media services are (at least initially) geared primarily towards interactions among individuals, rather than to facilitate communications between businesses and their customers. Furthermore, what distinguishes them from other peer-to-peer services such as email is that they facilitate broadcast messages to the sender's social network, in addition to directed messages to specific individuals or groups. The resulting ability for individuals to update their entire social network, and conversely, to stay up to date with their entire social network, is a strong motivator for such services. While this has interesting implications for social discourse, it also has implications for businesses, for instance through the potential for viral marketing and communications. Used effectively, such services can be a powerful business resource. At the same time, because of the highly public and information-rich environment in which these services are used, they can also pose significant challenges if misused.

An important implication of these features is that unlike most other technologies used for digitalization by businesses, SMSPs shift the locus of control from the business to the social network. For instance, the content on a business's Website is determined almost entirely by the business itself. However, the content on the same business's SMSP presence is often mostly user-generated content (UGC), which the business cannot control by itself. This makes the SMSP a powerful and yet risky forum for any business. While the business can post positive messages and content on the SMSP that promote its products and services, this can easily be overshadowed by critical and negative

---

[4] We will examine digital platforms in greater detail later, in Chap. 6 of this book.

content from the participants in the social network, which can include suppliers, partners, customers and even end-consumers. This double-edged aspect of SMSPs makes it vital for businesses to manage their role and presence there very carefully.

Before delving into the questions of how and for what purposes a business should leverage SMSPs, there is also the question of which SMSP(s) it should consider. This choice depends on the characteristics of these platforms, which can be categorized in various ways. The following three key dimensions are useful in categorizing SMSPs:

- **Peer-to-peer versus aspirational:** Peer-to-peer SMSPs are geared towards the creation and support of social networks of equals, or networks in which there are no explicit or implicit hierarchies between members. Examples of such an SMSP are Facebook and Youtube. On the other hand, other SMSPs are geared towards social connections that are aspirational, in which individuals seek connections with people and/or institutions that they admire and value. Twitter is a popular aspirational SMSP. Another way of thinking about this dimension is in terms of the directionality of the links they support. For instance, the connections in Peer-to-peer SMSPs are undirected, while the connections in aspirational SMSPs are directional.
- **Social versus professional:** Some SMSPs are positioned to embrace social connections, such as friendship and family (e.g., Facebook). These differ from SMSPs designed to support professional connections and relationships (e.g., LinkedIn).
- **Open versus Closed:** An open SMSP is one that any interested individual can join. Thus, the membership of an open SMSP can be very diverse, and hard to limit, even by the company running the SMSP. Examples of open SMSPs are Facebook, Twitter and YouTube.[5] On the other hand, a closed SMSP limits participation to specific sets of qualified individuals, who have to be authenticated and approved by the SPSP. An example of such a SMSP is Slack, which supports communities within specific businesses.

While the above dimensions can be used to classify most SMSPs, there are some that have hybrid features. For instance, LinkedIn is structurally an open Peer-to-peer professional SMSP. However, it limits access to the information of a participant to only those participants who are accepted by that participant. And while Facebook started out as a social SMSP, it has evolved into a

---

[5] It should be noted that Facebook initially was a closed SMSP, limited to registered students at colleges and schools.

broad-spectrum platform that supports both social and professional links and interactions.

The immense popularity of SMSPs is challenging businesses to seek ways to derive business value from them. In the next section, we discuss how businesses can decide how they can engage with networks of individuals using SMSPs.

Levels of Social Media Engagement

A business can engage with consumers by pursuing four types of progressive engagement on SMSPs. These engagement levels are:

1. Probing social media activity;
2. Pushing content and applications to the business's social network;
3. Priming content by using mechanisms to stimulate the business's social network to distribute messages and applications to its social networks; and
4. Participating with the social network in rich bilateral and multilateral interactions.

These four levels of social media engagement are shown in Fig. 5.5.

Level 1: Probing Social Media Activity

To start with, whether or not a business actively participates in any SMSP, it can probe social network activity and user generated content on the SMSP to obtain an understanding of the scope and extent of discussion about the business. Bekaert's probing of SMSPs for end consumer mentions and discussions of its underwire product is a case in point. Clearly, such probing can benefit the business's initiatives for engaging with end consumers, such as Bekaert's enhancement of its quality assurance, R&D, and marketing processes and the ensuing successful launch of a new product based on the consumer insight it gathered.

Typically, businesses can deploy SMSP monitoring tools to keep track of the number of company and product mentions and the associated consumer sentiment, as well as competitive and market intelligence. While these probing efforts can be conducted through social media management providers such as Hootsuite or Engagor (part of Clarabridge), businesses can also establish internal mechanisms and procedures to operationalize the probing

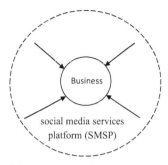

Level 1: Business probes user generated content on SMSP

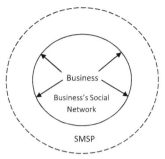

Level 2: Business pushes content to its social network on a SMSP

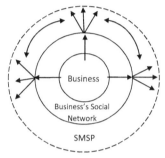

Level 3: Business primes content that users are likely to distribute

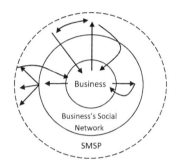

Level 4: Business and its social network participate in meaningful dialog

Fig. 5.5 The four levels of social media engagement

process. Walmart' Social Genome, for instance, is a vast, constantly changing, up-to-date knowledge base that integrates public data from the Web, proprietary data such as customer purchasing habits and contact information, and social media posts. In addition to its potential value for engaging with consumers on SMSPs, the knowledge base also serves to optimize its offline operations. For instance, through its probing efforts, the retailer found that a spicy chip called Takis was very popular with consumers in California and the Southwest. Based on that insight, Walmart introduced a similar spicy chip with its private-label brand in these regions.

Consider SWIFT, the Society for Worldwide Interbank Financial Telecommunication, that operates a financial telecommunication network between more than 9700 banking and financial institutions in 209 countries, while also offering services and solutions. Through probing, SWIFT learned that about half of its target audience, which mostly consists of financial executives, had a LinkedIn profile, and that a substantial amount of them were concentrated in 4 LinkedIn groups. Armed with that insight, SWIFT representatives joined these groups, sharing content on solutions (e.g., a slide deck on Slideshare and a video on YouTube showcasing an innovative authentication device from SWIFT), and participating in the discussions on the platform. The professional focus of the Linked-In platform provided a more relevant audience for its efforts, and it could also leverage the influence of key members of its network. Linked-In supports both aspirational and peer links, which are both relevant for the firm. On the one hand, the views of influential financial executives in its network are extended to the aspirational members of their networks. At the same time, SWIFT is accepted in these groups as a peer that can participate in the discussions and offer innovative solutions.

Level 2: Pushing Content and Applications

Beyond probing, a business can initiate a presence on one or more SMSPs and build out its social network to which it can push content and applications to engage consumers. Likewise, the business can respond to user generated content in its social network (e.g., by answering a question or thanking for a comment). As introduced earlier in this chapter, Solvay connected with end consumers by pushing content on its Emana® yarn in apparel and the different customer products that feature Emana® on various SMSPs. It also informed consumers on these platforms about where they could buy these products online, stimulating end demand at its business customers and derived demand for its product.

Consider Corning Incorporated, the world leader in specialty glass and ceramics that are used in a variety of applications such as consumer electronics, mobile emissions control, telecommunications, and life sciences. Corning does not sell products to consumers. However, it informs potential customers on its technologies and products through its corporate Website, and also operates a separate Website for Corning® Gorilla® Glass, which is featured in various smartphones, tablets, and notebooks. In order to enhance brand awareness and build favorable brand associations for Corning and its products, the business extends its online support for search and authentication by maintaining profile pages on Facebook, Twitter and YouTube, to which it pushes content. Its posts on Facebook reveal Corning's history and promote its cause initiatives (e.g., blood donation), and include promotion codes for free samples of its life sciences products. Its videos on YouTube show how its various glass technologies withstand scratch, bend, and ball drop tests, and display its technological prowess (its most popular video "A Day Made of Glass... Made possible by Corning", has been viewed more than 20 million times since its launch in February 2011). Corning also extends its online support for customer service by pushing how-to videos with instructions on installation and use of its products (e.g., a YouTube video demonstrating installation procedures for end span access of loose tube cables).

Level 3: Priming Content

At the priming level, the business purposefully creates mechanisms to motivate distribution of its content by members of its social network. Traditionally, these efforts are organized around marketing campaigns that feature compelling content or employ incentives such as discounts or user recognition to stimulate word-of-mouth communication and make the message go viral. Consider Corning® Gorilla® Glass, the strengthened glass developed by Corning Incorporated, which is featured in various smartphones, wearables, tablets, and laptops. Corning does not sell its Gorilla® Glass to consumers. However, it informs potential customers on its technologies and products through its Website. In addition, it has established a presence for Corning® Gorilla® Glass on various SMSPs, to which it pushes content. Corning also engages consumers on SMSPs through priming to build product awareness for Corning® Gorilla® Glass by means of a series of compelling viral videos, such as its "An Indian Tribute to Imagine Dragons' Believer" video which invited viewers to enter a chance to attend a special fan event in Las Vegas.[6]

Level 4: Participating in Dialog

The highest level of engaging the business's target audience is by participating with and/or through the business's social network. This level of engagement goes beyond traditional customer service to the business's social network, and harnesses the power of SMSPs to insert feedback loops and foster meaningful dialog with consumers. Toward this end, businesses can dedicate human resources to engage in a dialog with consumers on SMSPs and can offer guidelines or issue policies to other employees to interact with consumers on these platforms. JetBlue Airways, for instance, developed a reputation for interacting with consumers, attracting a large following of fans that it converts into customers on its Website.

---

[6] https://www.youtube.com/watch?v=oHvCAOBHY44.

The level of engagement of a business can also be influenced by its market positioning and industry. For instance, consumer-facing companies, in industries such as consumer packaged goods manufacturers, consumer durables, entertainment, financial services, healthcare, media, retail and travel are likely to have a substantial social network of consumers, with whom the businesses can directly engage, across all the levels. On the other hand, companies in the business-to-business space are less likely to have direct engagement. Thus, their direct engagement may initially be limited to just probing the customer segment of their social networks on platforms such as Facebook, or key influencers on platforms like Twitter. However, they can also benefit from probing the social networks of their downstream customers who do interact with consumers. Even for such companies, sharing innovations and brand-building initiatives with their social network as well as their partners' networks can be useful. We next discuss ways in which both B2C and B2B businesses can leverage SMSPs.

Leveraging Social Media to Engage Consumers

While various digital technologies can be used to engage end consumers, social media services platforms are particularly useful toward this end, as already indicated in some of the examples discussed earlier.

A business that does not have any existing social media efforts and is looking to enter that space, first has to decide which market-facing processes are most critical for such efforts. This choice depends on a number of factors, including the state of the business's current Web initiatives as well as its strategic priorities and IT resource base. Probing user-generated content on SMSPs can also help the business in identifying processes that should be enhanced. However, it needs to establish internal mechanisms and procedures to operationalize the probing process, as Walmart did with its Social Genome project.

Once it decides which processes to support using social media, the business needs to establish a presence on the appropriate SMSPs and then build a social network. This latter step typically requires a proactive effort by the company, even though some customers and even other businesses may become aware of the business's presence on the SMSPs and connect to it anyway, due to either the business's brand equity or word-of-mouth. By establishing the social network, the business implicitly acquires the ability to also probe that network. As the business develops familiarity with the platform and the social media space, it can progressively engage with customers at higher levels. A key consideration in this process however, is that the business needs to dedicate resources and formalize mechanisms and procedures for each initiative and higher level of engagement. While social media services can enhance the business's reputation and competitiveness, poor execution and management of social media efforts can also have a negative impact on reputation and performance. It should also be noted that the resource requirements increase as the level of engagement escalates. To continue the Walmart example, the retailer not only maintains profile pages on various SMSPs to push content, it also runs various campaigns to prime content, and participates in SMSPs to interact with its social network. Walmart's Social Genome uses dedicated and skilled business representatives to identify and reach out to individuals who have mentioned a category or product on a SMSP, for instance to inform them about where to find it in Walmart stores.

If the business decides to extend its online support for e-commerce to SMSPs, it can implement the transactional processes of its e-commerce Website to an online store on a SMSP that supports digital transactions. Similarly, if a business wants to sell online on a SMSP, it would have to support all transactional processes on that SMSP. On the other hand, a business that does not actually sell its products or services online, can still implement some of these processes to support and enhance its offline transaction processes. For instance, while Walmart supports e-commerce and sells products via its Website walmart.com, it does not operate a store on any of the SMSPs. It has been very innovative, however, in engaging its target audience in support of various trade processes on SMSPs. In support of product valuation, for instance, Walmart not only pushes product prices, discounts and coupons (exclusively) via SMSPs, it also primes content that sets prices for specific products. For several weeks during the holiday season, Walmart empowered its social network to vote for which one of two toys to go on Rollback—to be offered at a lower price—via an application on its local Walmart Facebook pages. Users of the application could see who of their friends had voted for what toy, and could invite friends "to help vote". Every Tuesday, Walmart then announced on Facebook what toy was at Rollback and at what price. Likewise, Walmart pushes content to promote its MoneyCard, a reloadable prepaid credit card that can be used by customers as a payment instrument on its Website and in-store, with various advantages. Also, Walmart pushes a Christmas layaway program, an installment payment system that allows customers to set aside a product, and pay for it over time, interest free.

An example of a company that has exploited online payment functionality on a SMSP is Mercedes-Benz, the German car maker. Through WeiboPay, an online payment mechanism offered by Sina Weibo, a Chinese SMSP with close to 300 million active users, Mercedes-Benz allowed consumers to order and make a down-payment on its limited edition "Year of the Snake" Smart car. Mercedes-Benz managed to sell out the 666 cars on Weibo in just under eight hours. Likewise, the Chinese smartphone maker Xiaomi sold its RMB 1999 Mi2 smartphone directly on Sina Weibo. In addition to selling a first batch of 50,000 handsets in about five minutes and taking in 1.3 million reservations, Xiaomi received 810,000 comments, and saw its offer being forwarded 2.33 million times on Weibo. While Xiaomi typically sells its products through its Website, and also through operator stores, its experiment with the Mi2 revealed the potential benefit from engaging with users on a SMSP. A business that explicitly taps into user social networks for payment is 1–800 Flowers, which supports group payment through a Facebook application, allowing friends to each give a little that adds up to a group gift for a mutual connection.

In addition to leveraging SMSPs to enhance online support for transactional processes, businesses can also engage with users on SMSPs to facilitate decision processes for customers. Nike, a world leader in athletic footwear, apparel, equipment and accessories, engages visitors of NikeiD, a Nike Website that allows customers to configure shoes, clothing or gear, to share their designs with peers on SMSPs and solicit feedback. In order to stimulate word-of-mouth communication for its configuration tool, Nike organizes design contests on Twitter where it asks users to post sportswear product designs for an athlete who endorses Nike. The fan who configures the winning design wins the product and Nike also has the celebrity athlete wear the item. For instance, Kobe Bryant, the NBA player, wore the winning design of the Nike Kobe 8 System iD basketball shoe contest in a home game. Nike also engages the Facebook platform through participation with users in the configuration process, regularly requesting users to share pictures of customized products with their design inspirations, and showcasing a selection of submitted designs. Likewise, the company engages its social network on SMSPs to collaborate on specific tasks. Through probing, Nike had learnt that fans of the U.S. National Soccer Team were demanding a red jersey for the team, whereas the team had traditionally only sported white or blue kits. Based on that insight, Nike started to collaborate with its fans on SMSPs and launched a contest to develop a new motto for the team, to be embroidered on the sleeve of the new jerseys. Nike also engaged in interactive participation with its network, providing real-time feedback on submissions and sharing pictures and videos throughout the contest week. Out of 6000 submissions, "Indivisible" was chosen as the new motto, and the winner was awarded with the new kit. Nike also leverages SMSPs for business intelligence on user preferences or suggestions by using polls on Facebook or designated hashtags on Twitter. Nike shares this intelligence with its fans, showing both aggregate results and preferences of the user's connections.

Similarly, at Corning Incorporated, which does not sell to end consumers, representatives still interactively participate with end consumers by responding to user comments and questions regarding product quality on SMSPs and pointing users to relevant content, such as product quality tests and the sequel to the "A Day Made of Glass" video. Corning also engages SMSPs through priming to build product awareness for Corning® Gorilla® Glass. It launched "Gorilla Run", a trivia puzzle game on Facebook, in which players get a chance to win a 100 USD gift card to spend on a laptop featuring Corning® Gorilla® Glass. Corning further extends the reach of the game to the social networks of the players by giving players hints for the game puzzles when they invite their friends to enter the game.

Leveraging Social Media in B2B Settings

Businesses that operate in purely commercial markets and whose products are not part of consumer goods can still benefit from engaging with their user bases on SMSPs. Consider Cisco, a worldwide leader in information technology. The company probes SMSPs to identify and profile Cisco partner accounts who resell and distribute its products, and tracks partner mentions and dialogs in their social networks of Cisco, its products, its competitors, as well as posts on partner events, product launches, offers, campaigns, tools, and Websites. Cisco also maintains dedicated Cisco Channel accounts and groups on various SMSPs. Through these platforms, Cisco promotes its Cisco channels blog, which contains content from technology centers relevant for partners, as well as thought leadership posts by key Cisco executives in the worldwide partner organizations. In addition to partners, Cisco probes SMSPs for user posts on product configurations and comments on the competition to identify emerging themes and trends, find fans and advocates, uncover influencers, discover product issues, manage crises and risk, capture product development feedback and regional popularity, generate sales leads, and obtain competitive intelligence. Beyond monitoring and lead follow-up, Cisco pushes content on SMSPs to authenticate its brand and products, and Cisco representatives respond to any support type question or product question. To prime its content, Cisco launches campaigns that leverage SMSPs in support of brand and product search and authentication. For example, to launch its ASR 9000 Series Router, Cisco highlighted the fun and human side of Cisco, and created a special Valentine's Day video that asked viewers to share the love.[7] The video went viral quickly and generated over 20,000 views, which is substantial given the target audience of IT network engineers. Finally, Cisco als participates in user dialog on SMSPs, both with its channels and (prospective) customers.

Social Media and System Integration

Some businesses have also started leveraging SMSPs for data and application integration with their systems. Consider KLM Royal Dutch Airlines, which allows visitors of the KLM Website to use their Facebook, Twitter, or LinkedIn credentials to sign up and check in for a flight online. In addition, KLM offers 'Social seating', an application that integrates SMSP user profile data with the airline's internal seating system. Passengers checking in online for a flight can choose a seating partner based on their Facebook or LinkedIn profiles. In an innovative example of priming through integration, KLM engages the social network of its passengers through KLM Trip Planner, an application that allows users to suggest up to 5 different options for a trip (including destination and time); it then invites the person's Facebook friends to indicate their preferences. The company also enables passengers to interact with their co-passengers online to set up plans to have a coffee together before the flight, or share a taxi after they landed.

Other examples of businesses that are innovative in the integration of their applications with those on the SMSPs, are General Electric and Nike. GE probes specific key words on SMSPs to identify power outages quickly, and by aggregating the data, visualizes the affected geographic area. Furthermore, by integrating data on the SMSPs with data of smart meters, sensors, and weather reports, GE tries to predict and even prevent power outages. To continue the Nike example above, Nike also leverages SMSPs for integration. Once a jogger has enabled the Cheer Me On feature on the Nike PLUS_SPI Running app, a status update is automatically posted in Facebook and/or Path notifying the social network every time the jogger is on the move (and connected to a wireless data network). Each time a friend likes the activity on Facebook, smiles on Path, or posts a comment to the status update, the jogger will hear stadium crowd cheering as part of the in-run feedback.

By progressing through the four levels, a business can increase its engagement with consumers and the social networks it forms. For any business,

---

[7] https://www.youtube.com/watch?v=Z1xKpm0nURk.

assessing its current social media efforts can be a useful basis for identifying how these efforts can be both reinforced and supplemented to enhance the scope and impact of the business's engagement with consumers.

In summary, although initially dismissed as a consumer fad, SMSPs have emerged as a powerful resource for businesses to understand and interact with consumers and the marketplace. However, effective engagement with SMSPs takes a different approach than traditional digital initiatives, since the dynamics of social media interactions are very different from the interactions supported by Websites. The four levels of social media engagement provide a useful basis for both assessing a business's current initiatives on SMSPs, as well as identifying potentially valuable initiatives to enhance the business's digitalization efforts. While we have focused here on the business's engagement with consumers, this approach can also be used to identify promising initiatives to engage with other stakeholders as well, including investors, suppliers and business partners.

Reflection Questions

- If your business is a purely B2B business, can you identify any opportunities for engaging with end consumers? If so, how would it benefit you, your customers and/or your suppliers?
- If you sell your products to consumers through intermediaries, can you disintermediate your marketing channels to reach consumers directly? Can you do so without disrupting your existing channel partnerships?
- How can you leverage social media to engage with consumers? How would that add value?

6

Digital Intermediaries

While some digitalization initiatives have helped businesses disintermediate key business processes by interacting directly with their suppliers and customers, other initiatives have motivated the evolution of new types of intermediaries in digitalized value systems. As a result, digital intermediaries have become a significant sector of the economy. Companies like Amazon, eBay and Google have become household names and major players in financial markets. In addition to these poster children, numerous digital intermediaries in the business-to-business (B2B) environment have evolved.

The emergence of such digital intermediaries affects the way business is done across industries by increasing businesses access to new customers, expanding supply choices available to businesses, and lowering transaction costs for all participants. As a result, the importance of digital intermediaries is increasing considerably, either as Internet-based platforms for market-facing process support or as gateways to connect and integrate through digital channels such as the Internet.

In this Chapter, we describe various types of digital intermediaries and discuss two key factors that influence the choice of activities they support. We then distinguish between digital intermediaries and digital platforms, and focus on the specific attributes of the latter. As part of this, we discuss how a firm can reconstruct its business as a digital platform.

© The Author(s), under exclusive license to Springer Nature Switzerland AG 2023
A. Basu, S. Muylle, *Competitive Digital Innovation*, Palgrave Executive Essentials,
https://doi.org/10.1007/978-3-031-23440-8_6

Types of Digital Intermediaries

Digital intermediaries can serve in a variety of roles in the network of organizations that they interact with. A useful basis for defining these roles is the set of market-facing processes discussed in Chap. 2. In other words, digital intermediaries can be characterized in terms of the specific transaction and decision support processes that they support and facilitate for their participants. In addition, digital intermediaries can support the integration of databases and applications between the participants. Table 6.1 below shows how the particular process types and the integration supported by a digital intermediary can be used to define seven distinct types of digital intermediaries.

We next examine each of these types of digital intermediaries, to identify their key features and functionalities, and provide examples of existing companies that fall into each type.

e-Commerce Exchange: This is an intermediary that brings together companies that want to sell products and services online and connects them with companies and individuals looking to buy online. The functionalities of the intermediary almost always include some aspects of search, but beyond that can extend through any and even all of the transaction processes discussed in Chap. 2. For instance, the intermediary can facilitate authentication of both buyers and sellers, in the form of third-party validation and verification, product testing, rating and review services, etc., valuation of products through dynamic pricing mechanisms such as auctions, payment services and even logistics and customer service support. An example of such an intermediary is Etsy.com, which enables small businesses, craftsmen and artisans to access a broad online marketplace of buyers. On Etsy, buyers can search products and authenticate sellers and products based on information on the number of transactions by the seller, the year since when the seller has been on Etsy, and its star quality rating. Buyers can also message sellers about the product descriptions they provide, and consult customer reviews. Prices are posted on

Table 6.1 Classification of digital intermediaries

Type of Digital Intermediary	Transactions	Decision Support	Integration
e-Commerce exchange	X		
Collaboration hub		X	
System integrator			X
Value-added exchange	X	X	
Business process integrator		X	X
e-Commerce portal	X		X
Full-service portal	X	X	X

the marketplace and logistical information provided on readiness and cost to ship the product directly from the seller to the buyer as Etsy does not have a warehouse. A FAQ is provided in support of customer service.

Some e-commerce exchanges are focused on price comparison to support the valuation process. In the insurance industry in the UK, for instance, price comparison Websites such as Compare the Market, GoCompare, Confused. com and MoneySuperMarket have become popular e-commerce exchanges as they enable buyers to compare prices and features side-by-side, across a wide range of providers. In response, insurers are launching new ventures that offer dynamically priced products on price comparison Websites. Direct Line Insurance Group plc, for instance, launched Darwin in 2019, a stand-alone digital business that targets customers that mainly buy motor insurance through price comparison Websites and uses a machine learning pricing system to provide a price based on the individual.

Collaboration Hub: This is a digital intermediary that does not support online transactions, but instead provides a variety of decision support services to its participants. Recall that the key decision support processes include configuration, collaboration and business intelligence. A good example of collaboration hubs are the Websites of many trade associations and similar cooperative organizations. The non-competitive nature of such organizations enables them to facilitate collaboration among their members across a wide range, from sharing of technology and domain knowledge to compilation and sharing of sector-specific business intelligence that can be beneficial to all member organizations. The American Chamber of Commerce (AmCham) in Belgium, for instance, is an independent non-profit organization that brings together US companies and local and other international businesses to improve business and investment opportunities (http://www.amcham.be/about-us). As part of its activities, AmCham Belgium provides a platform for members to share knowledge and discuss industry issues.

System Integrator: This type of digital intermediary is focused on enabling interacting participants to establish system-level integration with each other. System integrators leverage their information and communications technology expertise and resources to help participants who may lack such expertise and resources to interconnect their systems with those of other entities. This includes downstream vertical integration between a firm and its customers/distributors, upstream vertical integration between a firm and its suppliers, and horizontal integration between a firm and its partners (e.g., integrated product catalogs or consolidated procurement systems). An example of a system integrator is eBaoTech, a Chinese provider of cloud solutions that connect insurance carriers, channels, InsurTechs, and ecosystem partners to run insurance applications through an open API platform, in over 30 countries.

So far, we have identified digital intermediaries that are limited to supporting a single category of processes and/or services. However, in order to be an essential partner for its participants, particularly in competitive markets where participants have a choice of digital intermediaries, it helps a digital intermediary to reinforce its market position by broadening its capabilities to multiple categories, as in the case of the next four types of digital intermediaries.

Value-added exchange: This is a digital intermediary that provides not only transaction support for e-Commerce, but also decision support services. An example of this is Amazon Marketplaces, which allows sellers to create and operate online stores using Amazon's resources and Website. These sellers are also able to get rich information from the marketplace about the performance of their online stores. On the other hand, consumers purchasing from Amazon Marketplaces can also get advice and information about their transactions there. Value-added exchanges can also focus on specific industries for providing both transaction and specialized decision support. A case in point is UL Prospector®, which provides a raw materials and ingredients search engine for product formulators and engineers across ten industries including adhesives and sealants, lubricants, metals, paint and coatings, and plastics. Through the search engine, daily updated technical data on tens of thousands of products can be accessed, samples can be requested, and vendors can be contacted directly. Furthermore, advanced tools provide industry-specific information (e.g., regulatory and natural product certification information for personal care products), resources to identify alternative products (e.g., resins and OEM-approved automotive plastics for plastics engineers), and a portal (myUL™) to view quotes, orders, documents, payments, samples, locations, inspection reports and variation notices, and receive notifications. Through its knowledge center, UL Prospector® provides industry education and trend information by means of community polls, product announcements, supplier news, articles, videos, white papers, and webinars on specific industry topics.

Business Process Integrator: This is a digital intermediary that supports both decision support processes and integration, but does not support online transactions. Such digital intermediaries can be quite effective in the industrial or B2B sector, where companies may have established offline transactions processes and channels that they do not want to disrupt, but can still benefit from an intermediary that enables them to integrate with their business partners for valuable interactions relating to configuration of products and services, and interfirm collaboration. An example of this is Covisint, which provides valuable supply-chain information and integration services to auto-motive companies and their suppliers. In 2017, Covisint was acquired by OpenText™, an Enterprise Information Management company, whose Business Network cloud platform provides collaboration and business intel-ligence support, as well as streamlined connectivity across the internal and external information systems of its 65,000 customers and their 800,000 trad-ing partners in over 130 countries across various industries including automo-tive and industrial manufacturing.

e-Commerce Portal: Unlike an e-Commerce Exchange, which enables multiple parties to interact, but without any mechanisms for their respective IT resources and systems to interact directly, an e-Commerce Portal provides both transaction and integration services. One way in which the digital inter-mediary can facilitate end-to-end integration between participants is through APIs that are available to both suppliers and buyers, for instance. In this respect, the digital intermediary in effect enables integration through EDI and ERP systems when buyer and supplier firms directly coordinate their integration efforts with each other. An example of such a digital intermediary is SAP SCM, which enables companies to integrate with their business cus-tomers and suppliers to support supply-chain transactions and processes.

Full Service Provider: This is the most comprehensive type of digital inter-mediary, which supports both transaction and decision support processes, as well as integration services. Some digital intermediaries, for instance travel sector sites such as SAP's Concur service are moving in this direction. In the chemical industry, Knowde provides full service support for sellers and buyers of chemicals, polymers, and ingredients worldwide. Sellers such as Dow Chemical, DuPont, DSM, Sabic and Solvay, have established storefronts on knowde.com[1] where buyers can search their products and request documents, samples and quotations, and access support from engineers, scientists and researchers on technical questions. Buyers can also use a messaging app to interact with the seller's sales team, negotiate terms and place orders online. Business intelligence is provided on the use of the seller's products and brands in specific industries (e.g., plastics, elastomers and composites), and buyers can download thousands of starter formulations linked to their ingredients and products. Sellers can access digital marketing (e.g., SEO, analytics, social media campaigning, marketing automation for sending automated notifica-tions and emails to buyers visiting their store), content management (e.g., adding and editing product information) and e-commerce (price negotiation and online ordering) capabilities, and can integrate their storefront through

---

[1] e.g., https://www.knowde.com/companies/dupont

APIs with their Customer Relationship Management (CRM), Product Information Management (PIM), and ERP systems (for pushing online orders directly into their ERP).

Selecting a Digital Intermediary Role

How does a firm that sets out to be a digital intermediary select its role? While various factors come into play (see Chap. 8 on Considering Strategic Priorities), two factors are specific to being a digital intermediary: its resource base and its evolutionary context.

Resource Base

In addition to financial and human resources, computer resources and partnerships are important to digital intermediaries.

Computer resources refer to the hardware and software that are relevant to digital intermediaries for supporting transaction processes, decision support processes, and/or integration services. These can include search engines and digital advertising functionality, product catalog organizers and integrators, auction and exchange software, digital certificate management systems and certificate authority servers, database management systems, CAD functionality, groupware, and tools for online conferencing and collaboration, business analytics, and Application Programming Interfaces (APIs) design, as well as middleware for Electronic Document Interchange (EDI) and XML-based application integration, and Web service configuration and support tools. As digital technology evolves, digital intermediaries do not necessarily need to develop these resources themselves but can also turn to software packages and acquire many of these functionalities.

Instead of building or buying resources, digital intermediaries can also access resources through partnerships. Digital intermediaries usually partner with payment processors and financial institutions, third-party authentication providers and trustees, shipping and delivery partners, market and industry- specific information providers, software support providers, and system integrators. As competing digital intermediaries can typically also access these resources through partnerships, the digital intermediary needs to carefully identify and develop the resources that are key to its competitive advantage. Furthermore, it needs to ensure that the resources that are put in place for process support and integration services all meet customer expectations, as these resources are customer-facing and changes to them may hamper the customer experience. Finally, the digital intermediary may choose not to support certain processes or services, even if it has all the resources available for doing so, because of its evolutionary context, which is discussed next.

Evolutionary Context

While digital intermediaries are often characterized as independent, born on the Internet middlemen that operate fully online, firms that were established in offline markets can also become digital intermediaries as they use digital technology to support specific transaction processes, decision support processes, and integration services between them and their business relationships. As a digital intermediary can start out and develop in various ways, it needs to decide on its evolutionary context by considering one of the three contexts below:

1. **Pure-play**: This is a digital intermediary that is considered an independent or pure intermediary as it does not have any ownership interests in any participating firm. Examples of such digital intermediaries include Amazon Marketplaces, eBay, Etsy, and Knowde, whom typically do not participate in the activities of the participants on their intermediary sites.
2. **Closed online extension**: Unlike a pure-play, this digital intermediary is not independent as one or more of its principals (i.e., firms that have ownership interests in the digital intermediary, potentially as a consortium) participate in its activities, moving pre-existing offline business relationships online. The impetus of such a digital intermediary is to realize online process efficiencies with a closed set of participants. While the digital intermediary can be extended to new participants, this is not an open process and new participants are generally vetted offline prior to joining. Covisint, the business process integrator digital intermediary, introduced earlier in this Chapter, and now part of OpenText™, is an example. Its goal is not to add new participants but to generate supply chain process efficiencies for automotive companies and their suppliers. While new entrants are allowed into the digital intermediary, they are selected and authenticated offline prior to participating.
3. **Open online extension**: This digital intermediary is a hybrid of a pure-play and a closed online extension. It is initiated by one or more principals, but the participant firms change frequently as new entrants are added online. SAP Ariba is a case in point. Through its digital marketplace, Ariba

Network, buyers can digitally connect with millions of suppliers and trading partners across the globe in support of their procurement and supply chain processes. Likewise, suppliers can register and authenticate themselves online to reach out to buyers and simplify their selling and fulfillment processes. Thanks to its acquisition of Ariba in 2012, which had acquired FreeMarkets in 2004, SAP Ariba claims it has the largest B2B network in the world, boasting USD3.2 trillion in business with more than 4.6 million companies and 180 million transactions per year.[2]

The evolutionary context influences the process and integration services support the digital intermediary needs to provide. For instance, authentication process support can differ substantially between a pure-play and a closed online extension digital intermediary. A pure-play digital intermediary that adopts the e-Commerce exchange role needs to support the supplier, buyer, and product authentication processes to be effective. A closed online extension digital intermediary, however, does not need to support buyer or supplier authentication, and can focus on product identity authentication support, with little or no product quality authentication support.

A digital intermediary that selects its role and supports the processes and/or integration services that are consistent with that role can be expected to enhance business performance. At the same time, resource base and evolutionary context influence the extent of support.

Business performance for a digital intermediary is typically defined in financial terms (i.e., profits, revenues, transaction volume), and/or organizational growth (expansion in terms of offices, customers, employees, partners, geography, and industry). Yet, these perspectives are not always appropriate. Indeed, a digital intermediary can also be evaluated in terms of value added for the participant firms that invest in it. This value-add may entail member revenue increases, cost savings, and better decision making (see Chap. 10 on Evaluating Digitalization Initiatives).

---

[2] https://www.ariba.com/

Leveraging Digital Platforms[3]

Companies such as Airbnb, Alphabet (Google), Apple, Meta (Facebook), Netflix, and Uber are some of the most exciting companies today. While each of them has unique features and scope, they all operate one or more digital platforms. The platform structure has enabled these companies to achieve market dominance at a rate that is well beyond the capabilities of established incumbents in their industry sectors. In recent years, a wide variety of established companies in different sectors have considered creating digital platforms as a way to grow their businesses.

What Is a Digital Platform

A digital platform facilitates interactions between and among multiple sets of participants such as consumers, application providers and partners. These features are not unique to digital platforms, and are shared by most of the digital intermediaries we have discussed earlier in this chapter. Furthermore, product platforms have been around for several decades, and have proved to be useful for many companies (see Note on Product Platforms). However, platforms have a key distinguishing feature, the facilitation of interactions among participants from the same stakeholder set, something that is missing in other digital intermediaries. These interactions lead to "same-side" network effects that increase the value proposition of digital platforms.

Note on Product Platforms. The term "platform" first gained visibility in the business lexicon in the 1970s and '80 s, as a basis for organizing product lines within companies. Among the earliest adopters were automotive companies; faced with rising demand among car buyers for distinctive and differentiating features, companies such as General Motors, Ford and Chrysler began offering their models with broad ranges of customization options—in fact, General Motors bragged about offering over a million different configurations of their cars. The idea was to create a base configuration of each model, and then offering a multitude of custom features and accessories that could be added at relatively low cost, but for significantly higher profits. Over time, the notion of the base model extended to multiple models across multiple brands that could share the same chassis and other core features. On the one hand, this approach yielded cost efficiencies, by allowing the companies to design accessories that could be produced at larger scale since they

---

[3] The material in this section is substantially based on Muylle et al., "Digital Platforms", KPMG Point Of View, March 2022.

could be applied to multiple model lines, and even across model years. It also helped third party makers of parts and accessories in the same way. However, it also backfired in some cases. A notable example of this was when Chrysler tried to leverage the idea across both their own brands as well as cars by Mercedez Benz, with which they had established strategic partnerships. While the common platforms helped Chrysler a bit, they hurt Mercedes Benz significantly by tarnishing the luxury positioning of that brand.

In the 1980s and '90 s, the concept of product platforms was very successfully adopted by technology companies like Hewlett Packard, particularly in their printer product lines. While initially directed towards accelerating new product development and greater production efficiencies, HP took the concept further, disaggregating their printers by modularizing the ink delivery systems through printer ink cartridges. The immense success of these ink cartridges enabled HP to keep its printer prices very competitive, while the company could also introduce new models more frequently, leveraging the use of standard ink cartridges. Similar approaches were adopted at many different companies, ranging from computer chips to appliances to even furniture.

The value of the platform approach to product design and production can be analyzed in terms of three entities in a company's value system—the company itself, upstream players such as suppliers and downstream players such as customers, as shown in Fig. 6.1 *below.*

Within a company, the adoption of platform concepts in product development provides benefits to multiple internal entities, from research and development groups who can focus on innovation surrounding a platform in the short term while innovation of a platform is longer term focused, to manufacturing plants that achieve production efficiencies (production setups and training, sourcing of components, etc.), to marketing and branding, and even sales training and support. At the same time, suppliers benefit from the perception that their business with the company is secured across individual product models and lines. Even customers realize benefits, from knowing that their investments in understanding and utilizing the company's products can have returns over longer periods and multiple product innovation cycles.

Fig. 6.1 Value System Components Leveraging Product Platforms

Digital platforms are characterized by four key features, which we discuss next.

First, it is important to recognize that a digital platform is an intermediary between disparate sets of participants. This means that rather than focusing on the value proposition of its own products, the platform provides value through the resources and products of its participants. Thus, the capabilities of the platform have to be geared primarily towards making the interactions among its participants more useful and effective. A digital platform has a common set of rules and processes comprising an open architecture that enables external participants to join the platform and interact with each other. Each type of platform has built-in mechanisms—based on data and algorithms—that enable participants to find, and then interact, collaborate and/or transact with each other more effectively on the platform than without it.

Furthermore, the assets of the business should be complementary to the assets of the providers it supports, rather than competitors or substitutes. To see this, compare a firm like Marriott International, that owns and operates hotels worldwide, to Booking.com, which provides travellers access to thousands of hotels worldwide, but doesn't own any hotels itself. In fact, if Booking.com were to own any hotels, that would hurt its ability to be a digital platform, since its hotel providers would see it as a competitor. In general, platforms do not own the assets that its participants seek to access and use, but rather draw upon a community of providers who provide access to the assets they own. Good examples of this are ride-sharing platforms such as Uber and Lyft, and lodging platforms such as Airbnb.

Second, a digital platform can serve one or more sets of participants, and it is said to be one-sided or multi-sided respectively. Furthermore, its market is not just downstream consumers but also upstream producers. In some settings, there could be multiple types of producers, such as advertisers, developers and merchants, and the platform can derive revenues from participants on any or even all of the sides. Also, while it may not always be optimal for a platform to derive revenues from all sides, it has to organize its activities so that it has that option. As an example, consider Apple's iOS App Store platform, which recently decided to start charging developers of iOS apps for their participation.

Third, a platform should interact with each side through generic interfaces that are standardized for all participants of a particular type/side. In other words, if the digital intermediary sets up customized interfaces with individual participants, this can detract from its ability to easily expand its participant base, and also to support same-side network effects. For example, in the travel lodging sector, platforms like Orbitz and Booking.com have complex interfaces with hotel chains, but are unable to tap into the huge base of individual hosts that Airbnb can access (without going through additional platforms such as VRBO.com, for instance).

Fourth, a platform should reorient the focus of interaction from being between itself and individual participants, to also being among different participants. On the consumer side, this includes features such as content sharing, shared reviews/ratings, discussion groups, etc., while on the provider side, useful features include repositories of shared tools and knowledge bases. In addition, community interaction features can be leveraged on both sides. These features motivate significant network effects (see below), which are a key driver of platform power.

To illustrate these points, consider a traditional intermediary such as a beer distributor. Traditionally, distribution of alcoholic beverages has been a highly regulated business, with distributors often having exclusive distribution rights for any single brand in a given region. However, innovative distributors can use digital technologies to redefine the market potential of their products and services. For instance, distributors have rich data on the sales of different brands and types of beer in their markets, across different types of customers, ranging from upscale restaurants and pubs to convenience stores and supermarkets. Leveraging this data to provide business intelligence to beer makers can provide opportunities for large producers and small craft brands to cooperate even while they compete for market share. Similarly, on the downstream customer side, by sharing information on beer sales of different types at different types of customers (e.g., what's trending upward in Irish pubs in North Dallas can help Irish and English-themed establishments in other areas to learn and benefit). This in turn can encourage new craft brands that are looking for distributors to gravitate towards the distributor that provides such platform features.

Network Effects

Consider a telephone system. A telephone is of no value if you are the only person having one. If one other person has a telephone, then two people can connect. However, if four people have telephones, then six communication paths are made possible. In effect, each additional person adds more than one possible path (and therefore value), and furthermore, the marginal value increases as the size of the network grows. This nonlinear growth in the value potential of a network is very powerful. In effect, the addition of a single entity/node to an N-node network could potentially benefit all N current entities.

In the language of economics, these effects are known as *externalities* (An externality is a side effect of an activity or event that affects other parties that are uninvolved in the activity or event). Unlike linear value systems in which the value elements of any process are often limited to the parties directly involved in the process, the additional network effects and externalities that arise in a network can be significant sources of value. As an example of this, consider a helpful tweet from a Twitter user. It is communicated to all members of the Twitter network who are following that user; and the larger the user's following, the greater is the impact of that tweet.

Same-Side Network Effects

When a platform facilitates interactions among a collection of participants, they can benefit from positive network externalities. A good example of this is a social media platform such as Twitter or Facebook. Consider the effect of a person posting an item on their Facebook wall, or a tweet. While they might be intending to communicate with one person, the effect may be that a potentially large number of individuals receive the information in the post. This is an externality, since many of the beneficiaries of the information may not have been involved in the primary action, the online post. Similarly, when a member of a social network responds to a question raised by another member, a number of other people also benefit from that exchange.

Positive same-side network externalities can arise among a set of providers as well. For instance, the creation of an API by a platform to support interaction with a particular provider may end up benefitting a number of other providers as well that can also use that API. Or consider the effect of a FinTech company that offers tools for payment processing joining the platform. All the existing providers on the platform can benefit from this added resource.

Same-side network externalities can be negative as well. For instance, on the consumer side, each additional participant in a network can potentially use up network bandwidth and channel capacity that increases congestion and thereby negatively impacts other participants in that network. And on the provider side, each incremental provider has a negative competitive effect on existing providers of similar products and services.

Cross-Side Network Effects

A significant aspect of the attraction of platforms is that they support not only same-side network effects, but also cross-side effects. For instance, each participant on the consumer side makes the platform more attractive to many, and potentially even all participants on the provider side, since the new consumer increases the potential market that can be served by all providers. Similarly, each new provider adds value to the platform as perceived by many, and possibly all participants on the consumer side, since they all can avail of the additional products and services offered by the new provider.

Cross-side network effects can be negative as well. For consumers, the addition of a new provider can imply the need for adjustments, including learning new tools and methods in some cases, to accommodate the requirements of the new provider. For instance, consider the addition of Postscript documents from a provider on an information-sharing platform that may have supported only PDF documents in the past. While that may bring in more documents, it also requires consumers who want to read the Postscript documents to have readers and editors that are compatible with Postscript. Another negative impact on consumers may be that they have to deal with advertisements from an additional source as well. As for providers, they typically do not incur significant negative cross-side effects from additional consumers. However, the need to support a larger consumer base can potentially require the commitment of more resources, customer-facing personnel, etc., which may imply additional costs that comprise a negative effect.

Types of Digital Platforms

At a general level, a digital platform can be characterized by two attributes, (1) the number of sides (participant sets) it supports, and (2) its primary focus.

1. **The Sides of a Platform**: As mentioned earlier, a business could be a digital platform even with just one set of participants. Two examples of one-sided platforms are data/tech platforms such as cloud service providers and social media service providers. A cloud service platform such as Amazon Web Services (AWS) can support a variety of technology services involving computation, data storage and communications for a potentially large customer base. Similarly, a social network platform such as Facebook, LinkedIn and Twitter can enable a community of individuals to interact with one another. Such one-sided platforms can still benefit from positive

same-side network effects by facilitating user generated content from their participants.

In multisided platforms, typical participant sets are developers, merchants, advertisers and consumers/users. The potential power of a platform is exponentially greater when it supports multiple sides. An example of a two-sided platform is Etsy, which has artisans and creative merchants on one side, and consumers on the other. It is also not unusual for a one-sided platform to expand by adding new types of participants. For instance, AWS has started offering capabilities developed by companies within its ecosystem, and these are immediately accessible to hundreds and even thousands of other companies on the platform. Similarly, Facebook has added businesses and also advertisers onto its platform, in addition to individuals engaging with their social networks.

2. **The Primary Focus of a Platform**: While digital platforms can be created for a variety of purposes, there are three canonical types of platforms:

- **Transaction Platform**: This is a platform that brings together producers/sellers of goods and services and consumers interested in those goods and services. They are the platform equivalent of a digital marketplace or mall.
- **Innovation Platform**: This is a platform that leverages the "wisdom of crowds". It facilitates intellectual input on problems and issues from potentially many participants, and enables them to collaborate and realize valuable synergies. An online bulletin board for a special interest group is a simple example of such a platform.
- **Engagement Platform**: This is a platform that enables potentially large numbers of participants to mutually interact and share common interests. A social network is an example of a participant set for such a platform.

While a platform could have features and capabilities of more than one of these canonical types, understanding each type can help a business focus on the right structure and development plan for a prospective platform. We illustrate this through some examples.

Amazon Marketplaces is a good example of a transaction platform. When Amazon.com first started its online retail business, it quickly became a highly successful transactional intermediary. However, it quickly developed key features of a platform, such as:

- It started enabling third party sellers to set up shop and collaborate with other merchants and technology providers

- It enabled consumers to interact with each other through features such as online reviews, Q&A/FAQ Lists and peer validation through opinions of reviews, and
- It expanded its portfolio of core services to not only facilitating online stores, but also digital payments, digitally enhanced fulfilment and reverse logistics and even business intelligence services.

These innovations enabled Amazon Marketplaces to progressively become more of a transactional digital platform, and one that has quickly achieved market dominance. In the Netherlands, a similar approach was used by bol.com.

Twitter is an example of an engagement platform. The company clearly recognizes itself as an aspirational platform for social engagement, and has consistently focused on features that facilitate participation by influential people and their followers. In doing so, it has stayed away from transactional features, as well as staying within the short messaging format rather than the richer content that is essential for driving innovation. This has created interesting challenges for the company with respect to revenue and profit generation, but at the same time, has enabled it to defend its market against a variety of competing platforms.

Finally, Kaggle is an example of a company that could become a powerful innovation platform. Much of its initial efforts have been to bring together companies that have analytics problems and match them with individuals who take on those problems as intellectual challenges through contests. It can quickly expand beyond this basic intermediary role, by facilitating same-side interactions of different types. For instance, it could facilitate collaboration among contest participants and peer learning, while also facilitating learning among participating firms, who can learn from each other's challenges and experiences.

Note that a platform can be characterized in both the above ways. For instance, a technology platform can be a multisided innovation platform (e.g., Adobe Creative Cloud), and as mentioned above, a social media platform like Twitter can be a multisided engagement platform. In fact, a platform can also have broader scope that spans multiple categories (e.g., Facebook, which now allows merchants to set up online stores).

Competitive Effects of Digital Platforms

The multiplicative power of the two sides of a digital platform can provide such overwhelming market power that once a platform becomes successful enough, it can drive out competitors from the market in a winner-take-all process. The feasibility of such an outcome, and its likelihood, also relates to the type of network effects created by the platform, as well as some other factors, that we discuss next.

When the network effects created by a platform are significant, they can act as powerful attractors for potential participants, and for market-share growth. This is starkly evident in the market for social media services platforms and exemplified by the comparison between Myspace and Facebook.

Myspace was one of the earliest social media services platforms, and quickly became a market-share leader in that space. So much so that when Facebook was created as a specialized platform focused on high school and college students to connect with their classmates, few people in the field thought of it as even serious competition for Myspace. However, behind the explosive initial growth of Myspace was a fundamental flaw in its model. In order to facilitate growth without any "friction", Myspace required little or no authentication from its participants. While the power of the social network attracted lots of participants, many of them quickly realized that without reliable authentication and assurance of the identity and veracity of member's credentials, it was really not a safe and reliable social forum. The proliferation of sexual and criminal predators on the platform further exacerbated the concerns of participants, who gradually reduced their presence there. On the other hand, Facebook rooted its credibility on robust authentication, starting as a closed forum for authenticated college students and alumni. This made Facebook a desirable place to be in the virtual social context, and enabled it to grow steadily, even when it opened up participation to the general public. However, it was not until Facebook truly adopted the two-sided platform model, by opening up to companies and service providers, that the true value of that robust and largely reliable member base became evident. On the other hand, Myspace failed to develop the provider side of its platform, which only further stymied its growth and long-term prospects.

At the same time, despite the dominant position of Facebook in the market, it is by no means the only viable social media platform today, and a number of other smaller, specialized platforms have managed to do quite well. The reason for this is that in the social networking space, the cost of "multi-homing", which is the participation in multiple platforms, is relatively low. So for instance, people are comfortable using Facebook for family and friends, Slack for at-work interactions, and yet other discipline-specific platforms for other social and professional interactions (e.g., ResearchGate for scientists and researchers). In that sense, social network platforms are like digital payment platforms. Many people are comfortable having multiple credit-card accounts for instance. So in markets where multi-homing is feasible and not expensive, it is unlikely that a single platform will emerge as the winner and corner the whole market.

On the other hand, some platforms operate in spaces where there are strong pressures for "single-homing", which happens when participants perceive significant costs to using multiple platforms. One example of this is the market for Operating Systems software. To some extent because consumers face incremental costs for each software application that they purchase and use, most people tend to gravitate towards a single OS platform, and often stick with it even as they change and update their computers. This is what enabled Microsoft to achieve near monopolistic market share and power, to the point of triggering anti-trust litigation against it. The power of single-homing is also evident in the market for online search, where Google has become the clear and dominant leader. It is interesting to note that in neither of these two example settings have the dominant players become the only players, even though they have come close enough to trigger the attention of anti-trust regulators.

When to Use Digital Platforms

Most of our examples above are technology companies without significant legacy businesses and/or assets. However, platform opportunities can be relevant to any business. A business seeking to leverage platform opportunities needs to consider two key factors:

- The potential to add substantial value to participants on multiple sides of a platform; and
- The potential to create substantial network effects on multiple sides.

Customers value a business primarily based on its products and don't really see or interact with other sides of the company. Similarly, suppliers value the company as a customer, and may not see or interact with any of the company's customers.

The value of the company as a platform shifts the value proposition of the company from the inside to the outside. In other words, the value proposition of the company to each side is a combination of what it offers by itself and what it enables the other sides to provide. In the extreme case, the company's value proposition shifts entirely to the latter component.

So rather than focusing on the value proposition of its products for downstream customers, the business must provide value in terms of the resources and capabilities of its participants. Furthermore, the assets of the company should be complementary to the assets of the providers it supports, rather than competitors or substitutes. For instance, Booking.com provides access to providers such as airlines, hotels and car rental companies, which dont compete with Booking.com but add complementary capabilities. On the other hand, while the Marriott hotel group does allow access to complementary services such as tourist activity companies and events on its online platform, it avoids connecting its customers with hotels owned by competing chains. Similarly, when American Airlines created its Sabre flight reservation system, which also enables reservations at competing airlines, concerns about anti-competitive business practices forced it to spin off Sabre as an independent company. These examples illustrate some of the challenges faced by traditional businesses in transitioning to a platform model.

Due to different network effects, the value proposition of a digital platform can also evolve much faster than that of a traditional business. Rather than being late to market with an offering that no longer matches customers' evolving preferences, the platform can constantly update and upgrade its value propositions with new elements from and for each side.

To operate a digital platform model, the core activity of the company can be communication (e.g., telco networks or payment infrastructure), software or hardware, and can shift over time. When it introduced the iPhone, Apple positioned this hardware product atthe core of its digital platform, and soon after launched the App Store as aresource that broadened the platform, generating strong, positive cross-sidenetwork effects between app developers and iPhone users.

However, when Apple introduced other devices, such as the iPad and Watch,[4] it shifted the core of the platform to software, namely the operating system iOS. Down the road, it could be expected that Apple will integrate

---

[4] iPadOS and watchOS, the operating systems of the Apple iPad and Apple Watch, respectively, are based on iOS.

iOS with the operating systems of its Mac computers (e.g., macOS Big Sur). In contrast, while Google came in with the operating system (cf. its acquisitionof Android) as the basis of its platform to create cross-side networkeffects between app developers and users of Android operated handsets, itis now moving in the opposite direction, putting smart devices (e.g., itsNest and FitBit acquisitions, or its Pixel smartphone with Chrome OS) atthe centre of the network.

While Apple and Google have been very successful in developing and monetising their digital platform models, they still have ample opportunity to leverage cross-side network effects.

Identifying Digital Platform Opportunities

The settings in which platforms are most promising are characterized by what we call the three 'Ns'—Numbers, Networks and Needs:

- **Numbers**—The greater the number of current and potential participants on each side of the platform, the more promising is a platform. For instance, a transaction platform can be successful in a market consisting of a relatively large number of customers, a large set of suppliers, a large number of technology providers and/or a large number of advertisers. In other words, the more fragmented each side is, the greater the potential value of a platform-type intermediary. And it is even greater when the players are all (or mostly) relatively small, with limited resources to do everything themselves.
- **Networks**—Market processes and information flows in traditional businesses are mostly vertical through the linear value system. Suppliers interact with producers, who interact with consumers. However, when there is potential value in facilitating network interactions on each side of an intermediary, platforms become more attractive.
- **Needs**—A defining feature of a platform is the set of core capabilities it offers to each side. The larger this set of core capabilities for each side, the greater is the potential for the platform to attract participation from that side. So if a firm is operating in a sector where the needs of different customers/consumers are very different, building a platform that can serve the entire set of customers/consumers can become difficult. Similarly, if different suppliers and other partners require very different mechanisms and processes to integrate with the platform, it can be difficult to define the core functionality and capabilities needed by the platform to succeed. This

does not mean that the platform cannot provide personalized services, just that it helps if the services offered across each market are based on a substantial common core. In addition, it helps to be digital. So the greater the quantity, complexity and richness of data that has to be exchanged between participants, the greater is the potential value of a digital intermediary such as a platform.

Consider GE's approach to leveraging IoT and sensor-based systems. As GE was seeking to innovate with these technologies within its diversified product line, a traditional linear value chain model was certainly a possibility. However, GE's businesses have large numbers of customers and suppliers, and both constituencies could benefit from IoT capabilities. Furthermore, IoT not only enabled rich interactions between GE and its customers and suppliers, but also within the network of customers and suppliers to serve needs such as product support for suppliers and enhanced product features for customers. By building the Predix platform, GE was able to not only stimulate IoT-based innovation among both its customers and suppliers, but also bring other companies in different sectors that could leverage the platform to either add IoT to their products or leverage IoT capabilities in the products they used.

Digital Platform Development

As with many strategic initiatives, there are many ways to work towards successful platforms. Unlike many other initiatives however, platforms involve juggling multiple balls at once. For instance, there is a fundamental chicken-and-egg problem when developing a platform—the value proposition for each side of a multisided platform depends on the presence and participation of the other side. Consumers are attracted to platforms that support many providers, and providers are attracted to platforms that offer access to large numbers of consumers. One way to solve this problem is to build a strong value-added network in at least one side, which would benefit from same-side network effects. For instance, you could start by leveraging your brand, technology, etc. to build a strong community of participants on one side who value some product(s) or services that your firm can provide or facilitate. This includes services that motivate interactions among the community. Then build the capabilities to invite providers to join in. In order to do that, build upstream capabilities to onboard suppliers, and over time create a basis to generate same-side network effects on that side. For instance, Facebook started as a social media site (a one-sided platform). Once it had a large user community with strong same-side network effects, it started to build its other sides, including advertisers, developers and merchants. Similarly, Apple first built a large consumer customer base for its iPhone and then developed the AppStore to attract developers. On the other hand, Google started by building a community of developers and then provided a broad array of services to consumers.

Another approach is to start essentially as a digital intermediary that brings together buyers and sellers. The initial value of this intermediary would be to enable and maximize cross-side network effects to build both sides. Once established, it can then enhance its platform capabilities by introducing features that motivate same-side interactions. For instance, a healthcare portal can introduce patient community features such as special interest forums on the consumer side and tools to facilitate regulatory compliance for healthcare providers to participate, such as HIPAA-compliance support and electronic patient record protocols and systems.

There are also a variety of choices with regard to the business scope of platform initiatives. At one extreme, you could completely restructure your firm as a platform company. And at the other extreme, you can participate in an existing platform on one or more sides, for instance by becoming a technology partner, a supplier, a customer or an advertiser. Chances are, if you are running an established enterprise in one or more industry sectors, you are not doing the former, and already doing the latter. And there are many options in between.

Two broad strategies for making a digital intermediary a successful platform are "coring" and "enveloping".[5] Coring refers to the process of developing a platform by progressively reinforcing and expanding its core capabilities and functionalities. Recall that the basis for any digital intermediary is the development and support of a significant set of capabilities that are valued by its various participants, and that justify these participants using the intermediary to reach important stakeholders rather than directly interacting with those stakeholders (remember that digitalization facilitates dis-intermediation). Many successful platforms have reinforced their market position by developing strong cores. This includes Apple's iOS operating system platform and Google's online search platform. These core strengths attract both providers and consumers who value the differentiated products and services they can access and use.

---

[5] Annabelle Gawer and Michael A. Cusumano, "How Companies Become Platform Leaders", MIT Sloan Management Review, Winter 2008.

On the other hand, envelopment is the strategy of a platform growing by leveraging complementarities between its core strengths and the capabilities and functionalities of other entities with which the platform can form strategic partnerships. Two excellent examples of platform envelopment are the combination of Google and YouTube, and the combination of Facebook and WhatsApp. Google's strengths and primary business lay in online search and paid advertising. On the other hand, YouTube was a video repository and portal. While seemingly very different, they have been spectacularly successful in complementing each other. YouTube adds a rich dimension to Google searches by enhancing search results with informative and relevant multimedia content, and Google in turn drives searchers to YouTube content, which YouTube can leverage for advertising effectiveness. In the case of Facebook and WhatsApp, that partnership is still being developed, but significant in that Facebook realized the strengths of WhatsApp in the messaging space, and decided to envelop it (by acquiring the company) rather than expanding its own core messaging resources through Facebook Messenger. Note that making such strategic changes have to be done carefully. For instance, Facebook has to consider the impact on the millions of current users of Facebook Messenger, and ensure that they remain under the Facebook umbrella, rather than leaving the platform and moving to a different platform.

Example. Eneco Toon Revisited

Toon, the smart thermostat introduced by Eneco in the Netherlands in 2012 (see Chap. 3), was reconstructed as a digital platform in 2014. Rather than Eneco offering Toon as a digitally enhanced product (electricity and gas with a smart thermostat) to customers, it set out to become a digital platform operator connecting its customer base with external providers that reinforced Toon's value proposition. Its vision was to move from being an energy provider to being an energy services and smart home company that offers health (e.g., assisted living), lighting, mobility (e.g., battery charging), safety (e.g., smoke detection), security (e.g., burglary detection), and possibly other solutions. In support of this, Eneco launched Toon API, a developer portal[6] for accessing and using historical and recent electricity and gas usage data, and setting the Toon thermostat, with quality assurance guidelines and application reviews.

---

[6] https://developer.toon.eu/

The first provider on the platform was Philips Hue (philips-hue.com) enabling Toon customers to use the Toon display and mobile app to personalize their Philips Hue home lighting system. Eneco also worked with Jedlix (www.jedlix.com), a venture that develops smart charging solutions for electric cars, named after Anyos Jedlik, a Hungarian inventor who built the first motorized version of an electric car in 1828. In a partnership with Eneco, Jedlix and Tesla Motors, using the Tesla platform for data exchange, Tesla drivers could charge their vehicles both at home and in public when energy prices are low (this functionality was later expanded to drivers of Jaguar and Renault electric cars). Toon also partnered with Interpolis, a Dutch insurer, to secure the Toon customer's home and reduce home insurance claims and premiums by expanding the system with badges, door and window sensors, and a camera with a siren.

While Toon provided its customers with benchmark insight into gas and electricity consumption of similar households, its focus was not so much on supporting positive same-side network effects through customer interaction. Instead, positive cross-side network effects were stimulated by adding complementary providers that expanded Toons smart energy solution into a smart home solution, which was made available to all Toon customers. Toon's monthly subscription model was sustained to incur revenues from the customer side of the platform, while the provider side of the model was made free to expand the value of the platform to customers. As the platform developed, new providers could be charged to access the customer side of the platform.

It is of interest to note that the cost of "multi-homing" was high for users of smart thermostats. Instead of installing several smart thermostat systems, users typically engaged in "single-homing," using one system only. Given that Toon had progressively reinforced and expanded its core capabilities and functionalities, it had established itself as the leading smart home platform in the Netherlands. When Essent, the Dutch market leader and part of a large German energy group, announced a partnership with Google Nest to introduce the Nest Learning Thermostat in the Netherlands in 2014, Toon could rely on its core to protect its lead position. Toon's capabilities in installation and integration with Eneco billing and other back-end systems for showing users their real-time energy consumption in volume and value, its cybersecurity, and its expanding set of functionalities offered through complementary providers on the Toon platform all shielded it from this fierce competitive attack. Eneco continued to develop its Toon platform and user base until March 2020, when a Mitsubishi-led consortium completed its 4.1 billion Euro acquisition of Eneco, outbidding Royal Dutch Shell and global investment firm KKR, in an all-cash deal that provided the consortium with a platform for future growth.

Reflection Questions

- If your business is an intermediary, such as a distributor, wholesaler or retailer, how can you use digital innovation to strengthen your position in your sector?
- Do you see any opportunities to become a digital intermediary in your sector's value system?
- How can you create a digital platform by enabling upstream providers and suppliers to offer innovative products and services through your business?

7

Digital Revenue Models

A typical business derives revenues primarily from its customers. Some business can also derive additional revenues from advertisers. This is particularly true of businesses that digitalize their transaction processes. Furthermore, businesses that are digital platforms can derive revenues from additional sources as well, such as suppliers, merchants and application developers. We start by looking at models based on revenues from a single constituency. We then discuss opportunities for generating revenues from multiple constituencies and the implications of this approach.

Consumer-Based Revenue Models

Businesses typically sell products and services to consumers, which can be retail or business customers. A business can digitalize its transaction processes to engage in electronic commerce, and use various mechanisms for supporting the valuation and payment processes (see Chap. 2).

Valuation can be digitalized through static pricing mechanisms (e.g., online price lists) or dynamic pricing mechanisms (e.g., online price negotiations). In traditional physical market settings, a Posted Price revenue model is predominant, though some sectors, such as auto sales and many B2B settings, prices can be negotiated, but the processes are time-consuming and expensive. The digital marketplace offers a business a more viable setting for dynamic pricing, whether through price negotiations, auctions or reverse auctions. These approaches can enable the business to extract more consumer surplus and enhance its profitability. For instance, ArcelorMittal's SteelUser online

© The Author(s), under exclusive license to Springer Nature Switzerland AG 2023
A. Basu, S. Muylle, *Competitive Digital Innovation*, Palgrave Executive Essentials,
https://doi.org/10.1007/978-3-031-23440-8_7

auction system provides customers with visibility into the latest offers of available steel materials and enables them to submit bids to buy these materials.

For digitally enhanced and new digital products, the business can exploit the digital features of the product to generate revenues in new ways. A particularly interesting approach to support the valuation process is the Freemium model (which was discussed in Chap. 4), in which basic functionality is offered for free, while a premium is charged for additional functionality, such as in the case of LinkedIn Premium. This model enables the business to exact consumer surplus in a variety of markets. First, in a differentiated (by demand) market, the free portion of the product offering serves as an attractor for a large potential market of customers who find sufficient value to justify their engagement and use of the product. This enables the business to reach consumers who receive positive but relatively low value from the product. The premium version(s) of the product then enable the business to exact the consumer surplus for the segment of consumers who drive greater value from the product's full functionality. Second, the freemium model can be used to tap into a temporal dimension of demand as well. For instance with a new product, the lack of awareness of the product or its value elements makes it hard to sell without extensive and expensive marketing efforts. By offering a free version for an initial period, the business can expose a possibly large market to the product and enable them to recognize its value to them. By introducing a premium offering at a later point, the business is able to serve a high-value segment of the market that was created through the initial free phase. In other words, potential buyers can experience some of the digital product features before buying the expanded functionality of the premium version. Note that by continuing the free offering, the business can continue to leverage the larger "tail" of the market distribution as described above. Likewise, a business that provides a (free) mobile app can support in-app purchases through which the user can buy digital products (e.g., a virtual outfit in a game) within the app. Third, a try-before-you-buy variety of the freemium model can be leveraged to stimulate existing customers to buy the expanded functionality of the premium product. Toward this end, the business can appoint so-called customer success managers in after-sales service, who provide customers with online demos to experience the product's latest functionality first-hand before upgrading, such as in the case of the CRM solutions offered by SalesForce (see Chap. 4).

A related consumer-based revenue model is Buy Now Pay Later (BNPL). This is also a variant of the traditional credit-based revenue model, with the difference that the seller receives deferred payment as well. The business can digitalize payment through a variety of mechanisms, while working with online payment processing providers to support the payment process (see Chap 2). An example of this is the BNPL option offered by Web retailers through specialized providers such as Klarna.

Yet another consumer-based revenue model that is well-suited to digitalized settings is Product as a Service. Essentially, this involves converting the product into a service. A traditional manifestation of this approach is the leasing model. However, when selling digitally enhanced or new digital products, key features of digital products such as transmutability and reproducibility (see Chap. 4) make this approach very cost-effective. An early application of this approach was with software, in the form of Software as a Service (SaaS). By converting capital expenses into operating costs, this approach has significant benefits for consumers. It also keeps the product itself within the control of the seller/maker, which makes it far easier and cost-effective to manage over the product's lifetime, particularly for products that evolve significantly, such as software. The MooCall calving sensor example from Chap. 3 is a case in point, where the farmer pays a subscription for using the digitally enhanced product, without owning it. Clearly, the revenue model for this approach is typically a subscription model. The general notion of a subscription model is a natural fit with many digitalized services. An example of this is Amazon Prime, which bundles basic market access with shipping, shopping, streaming, reading, gaming and other services.

The business can also develop new revenue streams by reshaping its business scope. It can derive revenues by digitally enhancing its business product or selling new digital business products based on end-consumer information, or even sell its products, or its digitally enhanced or new digital consumer products to end consumers directly (see Chap. 5). Alternatively, it can assume the role of a digital intermediary and also tap into potential supplier revenue streams in a digital platform model (see Chap. 6), which we discuss below.

Advertiser-Based Revenue Models

In digital marketplaces and digital channels, advertisers are another key constituency for generating revenues. The business can monetize its consumer base by charging advertisers to promote their products to them online. Digital advertising differs from traditional advertising in a variety of ways. First, digital ads are created digitally, potentially in an automated manner using standard templates, which makes them relatively fast to produce, place, optimize (change when they are already online), personalize, and scale up with a pay-as-you-go budget. Second, they can be targeted for relevance, based on data about the user (see Chap. 11 on privacy concerns), the online content where the ad is placed, or other contextual input. Third, it is easier to measure and track performance of digital ads, which changes what the business can price. Rather than simply using a traditional performance metric like Cost Per Mille (CPM), where the advertiser is charged a price for a thousand exposures or "eyeballs," more advanced metrics can be used. One such a metric is Cost Per Click, where the advertiser only pays when a user clicks on the ad, while another is Cost Per Conversion, where the advertiser only pays when there is a specific action, preferably a sale. The "cost" side of the metrics can be set using fixed (e.g., set fees) or dynamic (e.g., auctions such as on Google AdWords) pricing models. Furthermore, these metrics can be used progressively to guide customers through the various transaction processes, along an awareness-consideration-conversion marketing and sales funnel.

The business can provide advertisers with an inventory of places where they can publish their ads, such as on their Website or in their mobile app, for example a news Website offering advertisers to pay for banner ads on its homepage. Alternatively, the business can automate the selling (and buying) of digital advertising inventory, which is referred to as programmatic advertising. Through a so-called sell-side platform, the business can automate the sale and management of its inventory, while advertisers, typically through an agency, can use a demand-side platform to automate the buying of ad places at certain prices from multiple publishers, which are then matched with the inventory. Through programmatic advertising, advertisers can be more dynamic in serving ads in various media to reach more specific target audiences. Examples of businesses that build advertising media networks are Amazon, Carrefour and Walmart, through which consumer packaged goods companies can reach their retail customers, with the potential for closed-loop attribution from online advertising to online sales.

The business can also consider using ad consumption as a currency. Rather than selling its products for money, it can offer the product for free if the customer agrees to consume ads. American Airlines, for instance, offers 30 minutes of complimentary high-speed satellite Internet access on its domestic flights, if the customer watches an ad for its new loyalty program. The business can also adapt a Freemium model with such an ad consumption approach, in a hybrid model. To continue the American Airlines example, after 30 minutes of free, high-speed, in-flight Internet access, the customer can pay for more.

While a revenue model based on a single constituency is simpler and allows the business to focus on that constituency, a business can choose a hybrid model based on multiple constituencies. An example of this is the traditional newspaper and magazine publishing business, in which publishers charged consumers for their products (using both single-copy purchases and subscriptions), while also charging advertisers for advertisements places in the publications. While this approach worked for many years, it became increasingly difficult as digital media evolved. As the subscriber base shrank, publishers had to increasingly rely on advertisers, who in turn shied away since they saw decreasing value from those traditional media.

Digitalization can facilitate more complex or multi-faceted revenue models. For instance, the business can choose to allow advertising on its digital storefront, while also charging customers for their purchases. Examples of this include Netflix and Disney+ launching cheaper, ad-supported versions of their streaming services, to grow their user bases (note that players such as Hulu (majority owned by The Walt Disney Company) and HBO Max (owned by Warner Bros. Discovery) already offer ad-supported streaming tiers). The business still has to be careful not to alienate customers, who may resent the distraction and intrusiveness of advertising by third parties. In fact, depending on the media and technology used, advertising may compete with products for digital real estate. For example, advertisements on the business's Web page take away space that the business could use to provide product information, and in settings like mobile devices, the digital real estate (screen space) can be very limited. With the increasing use of mobile commerce, revenue models based on combining advertising with transactions are becoming more challenging. The business can also exploit the digital real estate of other businesses through online affiliate marketing, in which it rewards these third parties for supporting the search and authentication processes and referring customers to it (see Chap. 2).

In the physical marketplace, location matters, and a new business can leverage its location to successfully sell products and services to the local market. In virtual settings however, a new business may have much greater difficulty establishing its presence and building awareness in its target market. One approach that many digitalized businesses have used is to start by offering an array of valuable services or content for free, perhaps supported by a variety of search mechanisms. Once the traffic to the business reaches a critical mass, the business can start generating revenues through sales of some products. This approach has been used by some digital media services such as online newspapers and magazines. However, the business has to keep in mind that pricing products that were hitherto free can lead to significant attrition in the customer base. Alternatively, once the traffic reaches a critical mass, the business can choose to introduce an advertising-based revenue model instead, as has been done by

Google and Facebook on their Websites. In either case, this transition can be structured as a form of the Freemium approach, with the business continuing to offer certain basic products or services, but charging for others.

In addition to consumers and advertisers, a business can also adopt a revenue model based on its suppliers. This is a model that is mostly limited to businesses that are intermediaries that enable their suppliers to reach a potential market. For example, consider a shopping mall. The owner/operator of the mall charges rent from all the store-owners in the mall, so that the stores can sell their products to mall-shoppers. In digital market settings, this model can be very powerful, particularly in the context of digital platforms, which we discuss next.

Generating Revenues on a Digital Platform

One of the most interesting aspects of a multi-sided digital platform is the variety of revenue models that such a digital intermediary can support. Clearly, since the platform attracts multiple types of participants, the default approach would be to generate revenues from all sides. Airbnb is an example of a two-sided digital platform that use this model, since it charges hosts a commission based on the rents they set, while also charging guests a separate service fee. Another example is the Etsy platform for handmade goods, which charges sellers subscription and listing fees, while also charging buyers a commission on their purchases. However, it is not always optimal to try and exact maximum economic surplus from all types of participants, treating each of them as independent customer types. The reason for this goes back to the network externalities realized by each side through participation in the platform.

To see this, consider a social media services platform like Facebook. Consumers who participate in the Facebook platform benefit from both their interactions with other consumers, as well as from the products and services offered by providers, which may include Facebook itself (in the form of Facebook News). However, much of the attraction of Facebook to consumers stems from the same-side reach and network externalities. Even in the extreme situation where there are no independent providers (as was the case when Facebook started), most Facebook members would probably still be members. On the other hand, for third-party providers who participate in the Facebook platform, the primary source of value is the large and potentially lucrative market of consumers that they can access, and the associated cross-side network externalities. Thus, both sides derive value from the size of the consumer base, and thus the platform can benefit by maximizing the size of the base.

Since price usually decreases demand, this implies that the platform may benefit more by lowering prices to consumers,[1] even to the point of making consumer participation free. Not surprisingly, this is precisely what Facebook does. On the other hand, the platform can leverage its large consumer base to charge providers for giving them access to that base, not only for products and services, but also for advertisements and messaging.

A very different situation arises in the case of an operating system (OS) software platform like Microsoft Windows. In that case, the attraction of consumers to the platform largely derives from the broad variety of software applications that can be accessed and utilized through that platform, rather than through same-side network effects due to the presence of other consumers. On the other hand, providers realize both significant same-side effects due to the broad array of standards, tools and software capabilities provided by both Microsoft and other providers, as well as cross-side effects due to the large base of consumers using the platform. Thus, it may be optimal for Microsoft to charge consumers for the use of the OS software and platform, while charging providers less, and possibly nothing at all, to participate in the platform by developing and offering more products and applications.

Thus, a two-sided platform can leverage the power of network effects to structure a revenue-generating model that is more lucrative than linear value system channels. And the history of digital intermediaries that supported platform features illustrates the power of this perspective. As an example, consider the PDF format for document sharing that was developed by Adobe, Inc. Initially, the company tried to charge a fee for a PDF Reader. However, it soon realized that in order to gain market-share, it needed to maximize the penetration of the reader in the market. This led to the current model, in which the company provides the Acrobat PDF Reader at no cost, but then charges a substantial fee for the Acrobat PDF editing software. In fact, now multiple software vendors have included the ability to create PDF documents, and Adobe benefits from those efforts as well, since it creates more demand for its editing software too.

It is also possible to extend the network-effect generating power of user-generated content even further, by actually paying consumers to contribute content, in the form of reviews, opinions, ideas and solutions. This can not only motivate greater participation, but also motivate higher quality participation, which drives greater sharing and therefore positive network effects. In social network platforms, for instance, the proportion of "lurkers" or participants who only consume without contributing, can be quite high. Paying for

---

[1] As exemplified for Uber's context in https://twitter.com/davidsacks/status/475073311383105536?lang=en

content can be a way to convert consumers into contributors. This has been done very effectively by Alphabet, for instance, in its Youtube video platform. People who post popular content are rewarded with money, and even development resources. This approach is likely to become even more powerful with emerging digital technologies such as Web3, for instance (see Chap. 12).

Reflection Questions

- Using the ideas presented in this chapter, can you identify opportunities to generate revenues for your business through the use of digital technologies? How would these new revenue-generating mechanisms affect your current business?
- How can your business use digital technology to generate revenue from consumers, advertisers, and/or suppliers?

Part III

Aligning with Strategy

In Parts I and II of this book, we have discussed the importance and opportunities for competitive digital innovation, and examined the various ways in which business can digitalize their products, processes, business scope and business models. However, the best way to approach competitive digitalization depends on a number of factors, and thus will vary from business to business. These factors include the strategic priorities of the business, its competitive environment and its available resource base.

Following the herd can be a dangerous and expensive approach for strategic innovation in any business, despite the fact that most CEOs are keenly interested in the strategic moves of their competitors, and often justify their strategic initiatives based on their competitors' actions. To see this, consider the example of stock trading systems, which were developed towards the end of the twentieth century by banks and securities trading companies. Over the span of less than a decade, the online trading business became a commodity magnet, with competitors repeatedly undercutting each other in price and profitability. At that time, there was a lot of pressure on Merrill Lynch to augment its investment services with self-directed online investing. However, the firm realized that its competitive advantage was in the investment advisory services that investment managers provided. So while it added online trading for those investors who craved trading independence (thereby keeping them from jumping ship to discount traders), it focused on its advisory services, which proved to be a sustainable advantage.

Thus, understanding what is important for your specific business is an important consideration. In the next few chapters, we will examine some key issues in this regard. We start by examining how strategic priorities can impact prioritization of digitalization initiatives, in Chap. 8. We then discuss in Chap. 9 how a business can plan for digital innovation, and describe some ways in which such initiatives can be evaluated, in Chap. 10. We wrap up the section with a discussion in Chap. 11 of some possible risks that businesses face when considering digital innovation, and some technology trends that are significantly impacting the nature and scope of competitive digital innovation, in Chap. 12.

8

Considering Strategic Priorities

In Part I, we described the various ways in which a business can use digital technologies to innovate its processes and products. In Part II, we considered how a business can redefine its market scope through digital technologies. Using the ideas from these chapters, a business could identify a potentially large number of value-adding digitalization initiatives. While all these initiatives could be valuable, it may not be feasible for the business to pursue them all concurrently. As a result, the business may have to cherry-pick specific initiatives, or at least prioritize the set of possible initiatives.

As digitalization becomes part of the strategic agenda, business executives need to make decisions on what to do and where to start. Furthermore, they need to be careful where to invest as they may find that competitors are quick to emulate their digitalization initiatives at lower cost. This so-called "curse of the bleeding edge" also challenges executives to deal with the paradox that the use of digital technology by firms can be strategic, but firms rarely derive a sustainable competitive advantage from digital technology.

In order to resolve this paradox, it is important for innovators to shift their focus from the digital technology to the information it processes. In other words, when it comes to the use of information technology to gain sustainable competitive advantage, it is not the "technology" part, but rather the "information" part that drives differentiation and lasting value, although the technology is a necessary component. How? By using the technology as an enabler to acquire data, process data to generate useful proprietary information, and learn from this information to enhance knowledge. This information and knowledge can then be used to refine the business's processes and products, and to build new business models such as digital platforms.

Furthermore, the most effective approach to digitalization will differ across different firms, even in the same sector. That is because the key digitalization priorities and choices of each business are shaped by its business and competitive strategy. In this chapter, we connect digitalization to strategy by looking at how strategic planning models can be factored into the choice and prioritization of digitalization initiatives.

Strategic Planning

We view strategic planning as the way in which a business seeks to maximize the value it creates, delivers, and captures through its products, processes and business models. So how can we define value? A simple but elegant view[1] is that the economic value created by a business is the difference between what buyers are willing to pay for the offered product and what suppliers of resources needed to create the product are willing to sell those resources for.

Figure 8.1 below provides a visualization of this perspective. For a given product, the green line represents the maximum amount any buyer would be

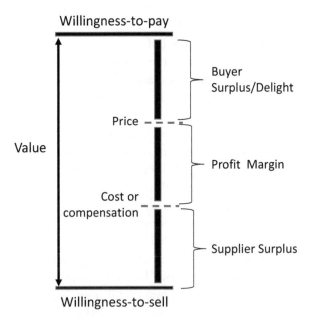

Fig. 8.1   A value perspective on strategic planning

---

[1] Oberholzer-Gee, Felix. Boston, MA. *Better, Simpler Strategy: A Value-Based Guide to Exceptional Performance*, Harvard Business Review Press, Boston, MA.

willing to pay for the product. At that level, the marginal value of the product for the buyer is zero. The business selling the product would typically price the product at a lower level, and the difference between these two levels is the consumer's surplus (or delight). The business has to set its price to achieve profitability while still providing buyers with a positive outcome (surplus/delight). The cost of producing the product then defines the business's profit margin. Finally, the red line represents the lowest price that suppliers of resources, which includes both external suppliers of parts and materials as well as internal suppliers such as employees, are willing to sell to the business. The difference between the business's cost and this willingness to sell level is then the supplier surplus. In the case of employees, it represents their job satisfaction, for instance.

In terms of this view, the goal of strategic planning is to maximize the gap between the green and red lines. Note that raising price or lowering costs can lead to increased profit margin, but that does not change the value created. In the context of digital innovation, much of the internal innovations related to digital transformation are of this type, which is why we don't consider them to be strategic, even though they can be useful for lowering costs, for example. Instead, effective strategic planning should focus on increasing the buyer's willingness-to-pay level and decreasing the supplier's willingness-to-sell level.

How does the business increase the amount that buyers are willing to pay? It does this through product, process and business model innovations that add perceived value, through better product quality, and through positive network effects. On the other hand, the business can lower the level that suppliers are willing to sell at by enhancing the attractiveness of doing business with it (e.g., by improving the work experience of employees, or by providing added value to suppliers through business intelligence services), and by creating switching costs that promote loyalty. In fact, the types of digital innovation we have discussed in this book, in terms of process, product and business model innovations, are very applicable to such value enhancement.

Strategic Priorities

At the business level, a good starting point is to consider its strategic priorities. This is important because different businesses have different priorities, shaped both by their resources and positioning, as well as their leadership and culture. This has been long-recognized in the field. In 1980, Michael Porter[2] proposed

---

[2] Porter, Michael E., 1980, Competitive Strategy, New York: Free Press.

three generic strategies for firms, namely Differentiation, Cost Leadership and Focus. A related framework was proposed a decade later by Treacy and Wiersema (1993), in terms of three value-based disciplines: Operational Excellence, Customer Intimacy, and Product Leadership[3]. The two sets of ideas are relatively similar, and suggest that businesses can benefit by focusing on certain priorities.

In Treacy and Wiersema's model, a business that focuses on operational excellence "provides customers with reliable products or services delivered with minimal difficulty or inconvenience."[4] In other words, a business focusing on operational excellence seeks to compete by being more cost-effective and cost-efficient than its competitors, including those that offer similar products. The cost efficiencies of the business allow it to offer its products at lower cost as well. A good example is Walmart, which offers the same products as its competitors, but at such low costs that they can become the supplier of choice for many products that customers can obtain from a number of suppliers. Interestingly, Walmart traditionally has made very little effort to "know" its customers (individually), and till recently, collected no customer data. Digitalization in such a business is mainly in its processes, both internal—to maximize efficiency and minimize costs, and market-facing—in transaction processes, both with customers and suppliers.

A different approach is taken by a business that focuses on customer intimacy, which competes by building strong relationships with its customers. "Customer Intimacy means segmenting and targeting markets precisely and then tailoring offerings to match exactly the needs of those niches."[5] It involves a deep understanding of customer preferences, adapting market offerings, customer retention, close customer relationships, and focus on the supplier's share of the customer's business. Doing so can result in customers believing that the business understands their needs and preferences and leads to them choosing the business and its products over even lower-priced competitors. A good example of such a business is Amazon. Its customers are very loyal to it, because it seems to understand their needs and priorities. As it turns out, digitalization is at the heart of Amazon's strategy, since it has enormous amounts of data on its customers and their buying behavior, and can thus personalize their shopping experience. This is impressive, particularly in the online

---

[3] Treacy, Michael and Wiersema, Fred, 1993 (Jan–Feb), Customer Intimacy and Other Value Disciplines, Harvard Business Review, pp. 84–93.

[4] Ibid., 2. p. 84.

[5] Ibid., 2, p. 84.

marketplace where customers can easily compare prices and can switch stores at very low cost.

A third approach is taken by a business that focuses on product leadership, which competes by differentiating its products and services from its competitors. "Product Leadership means offering customers leading-edge products and services that consistently enhance the customer's use or application of the product, thereby making rivals' goods obsolete."[6] In other words, such a business focuses primarily on producing the best products in the industry, with the latest technology and the most sophisticated features. A good example is Apple. The company has generally not tried to understand individual customers or build any relationship with them. Rather, it competes by producing high quality products that have a lot of appeal to broad categories of customers. An obvious focus for its digitalization efforts is therefore its products themselves, which are implicitly digitalized, since they are technology products. However, it also designs its market-facing processes to be reliable and accessible, consistent with its strategic priority.

The business needs to focus its digital innovation initiatives on what is important to it, rather than on what is important in general in going digital. For instance, any business that develops an e-commerce initiative needs to deploy digital technologies to support the transaction processes. While it is important to support these processes online, online support for product authentication is relatively more important than online support for customer authentication for a business that focuses on product leadership. Conversely, online support for customer authentication is relatively more important than online support for product authentication for a business that focuses on customer intimacy. Likewise, for a business that touts its low prices, and backs this up through operational excellence, neither product nor customer authentication are relatively more important. Instead, this business needs to prioritize online support for valuation. Thus, the strategic priorities of the business help it to focus its digital innovation initiatives on what is of relative importance to it, while making sure it provides adequate digital support for its other market-facing activities.

To realize its digital ambitions, the business also needs to make sure it has the necessary internal capabilities to support its strategic priorities and capture and leverage the right types of information. For a business focusing on operational excellence, maintenance, repair and operating cost information is key to realize cost efficiencies and effectiveness in its market facing processes. For a business prioritizing product leadership, information that spurs research

---

[6] Ibid., 2, p. 85.

and development, and product design, is crucial to claim superior product performance. For a business concentrating on customer intimacy, customer data sharing and relationship management are vital to personalize its market-facing processes and offerings.

We next identify some focus areas for competitive digital innovation for businesses with each of the three strategic priorities.

Operational Excellence

A business pursuing a competitive strategy that focuses on operational excellence seeks to be the most cost efficient and effective in its operations and processes to be able to have the lowest cost per unit and offer a competitive price to a large set of customers who can easily access its products and services. Clearly, its products and services need to be of acceptable quality, and the customer experience needs to be acceptable too, but its key focus is on bringing cost down and offering competitively priced products to attract customers.

For a business to be operationally excellent, it needs to carefully consider how it can lower its costs and make its products and services easily accessible to customers. Toward that end, standardization is very important. Rather than incurring the added cost and complexity of different processes for serving different customers, the business is better off using standardized processes across its entire market. Likewise, it is hard to justify the added cost and complexity of designing and marketing the best possible products or services. A more effective approach is to reliably and efficiently deliver standardized products and services that cater to a generic customer base. The business can also focus on generating information that allows it to standardize its market-facing processes. Furthermore, it can leverage maintenance, repair and operating cost information to lower product cost for the customer, and potentially engage consumers to improve market-facing processes.

On the other hand, given its strategic focus, the business does not need to invest time and money in collecting data to build customer relationships or develop better products. The key objective for the business is to scale its standardized processes to access a large customer base, with the key appeal being a competitive price and easy to deal with.

Table 8.1 below identifies some key focus areas for businesses seeking operational excellence, laid out in terms of our digitalization framework.

It is important to note that the business does not need to spend time and effort to collect data on the customer. The key thing to do is to make sure prices and ease of doing business are promoted to the customer. Data can be

Table 8.1 Digitalization initiatives aligned with operational excellence

Level	Focus Area	Examples
Transaction processes	Valuation	Promoting low prices in various digital media, including online display ads and electronic marketplaces
		Scanning competitor product prices and enabling the customer to compare prices online
	Payment	Supporting all popular payment instruments
		Negotiating favorable terms with payment processors
	Logistics	Providing cost-efficient delivery options
		Including express delivery and rapid fulfilment
		Improving reverse logistics processes
Decision Support processes	Configuration	Refining product selection capabilities
		Expanding customer self-service capabilities
	Business Intelligence	Emphasizing financial benefits of dealing with the business vs. competitors
		Highlighting operating performance reports
Product Digitalization	Enhancing Existing Products	Focusing on enhancements that exploit and drive cost-efficiencies in production, marketing and service

collected on competitor pricing to back up the business' price claims. However, no data needs to be collected on the customer to engage in dynamic pricing upon customer authentication, and hence prices need not be hidden but can be made fully transparent by posting fixed list prices for easy online retrieval. Also, there is no need to recognize the customer beyond fulfilling the transaction and sending automated order confirmations. After the basic data of the customer has been authenticated once (e.g., name, address, payment details), this data can be used to facilitate repeat transactions and to inform the customer about deals. The focus is on facilitating a large set of transactions, regardless of whether these are from the same or different customers and realizing process efficiencies.

Product Leadership

A business that focuses on product leadership strives to design and market the best possible products or services to customers who value superior product performance and innovation. Its key differentiator is the product or service, not operational processes, or customer relationships. Hence, businesses that have product leadership as their strategic priority need to focus on market-facing processes that highlight their product performance. As to the product, they can focus their product digitalization efforts on continuously improving product performance. This not only enables the business to expand its customer value proposition by adding digital functionalities and capabilities to its products, but it also enables the business to follow its products over their useful lifetime and change its transaction and decision process support accordingly.

Table 8.2 below identifies some key focus areas for businesses seeking product leadership, laid out in terms of our digitalization framework.

Table 8.2 Digitalization initiatives aligned with product leadership

Level	Focus Area	Examples
Transaction Processes	Search	Increasing visibility of the business and its products in premier forums and channels
	Authentication	Promoting distinctive features and quality of products on all channels
		Ensuring inclusion of products in popular review and trustee sites
		Encouraging key influencers on social media to evaluate and promote the products
		Promoting quality features such as warrantees on all channels
Decision Support Processes	Configuration	Highlighting differentiating features and quality attributes in configurators
	Business Intelligence	Sharing reports on performance and quality features relative to competing products
Product Digitalization	Enhancing Existing Products	Digitalizing features and components that provide a competitive edge and differentiation
	New Digital Products	Introducing innovative products that are leading edge and/or clearly ahead of competitors
		Developing products that leverage competitive resources such as proprietary data/knowledge

Customer Intimacy

Businesses that focus on customer intimacy can benefit from both process and product digitalization. In addition to supporting the product search, authentication and valuation processes for customers, digital support for payment, logistics, and after-sales customer support is key to develop the customer relationship. It is also key for the business to offer decision support to customers for personalization. More specifically, digital configuration tools and information sharing help customers to identify the products and services that will meet their needs, while business intelligence helps customers find relevant products and services. To strengthen the customer relationship, the business also needs to integrate its data and applications with its customers' databases and systems.

Customer intimacy through product digitalization can be achieved in two ways: (1) by factoring the preferences of the customers into the products sold to them, and (2) by offering configurable products that customers can customize to their specific (and even evolving) needs and preferences. With respect to consumer products, such features in effect support personalization of the business's products to individual consumers.

The key priority of a business pursuing a competitive strategy that focuses on customer intimacy is to convince each customer that the business understands their needs and preferences better than any of the business's competitors. Clearly, it benefits every business if its customers have a positive impression of the business and its products. Similarly, every business benefits from operational efficiencies and cost management. So what is different about a business that has a customer intimacy focus? In this section, we address this question, and then explore how such a business can leverage digital innovation to effectively support its competitive strategy.

To start with, it is useful to examine what is distinctive about a customer intimacy focus. First, it is important to recognize that the customer experience consists of two parts, the customer's experience with the business, and then the customer's experience with the product. Second, a necessary condition for such a focus is that the business's products and/or customer-facing processes must have attributes that can be differentiated across different customers. In other words, in order for the business to communicate to a customer that it understands and caters to the customer's specific needs, some aspect of that customer experience must be "customizable", or different from that of other customers. Third, it should also be recognized that a business can be a leader with respect to customer intimacy even if its products are not viewed broadly as the best in the market or the business does not have the most cost-efficient operations and processes.

Recognizing that the business can pursue customer intimacy by not only having customizable products but also by designing its customer-facing processes to convince each customer that it understands their preferences and is committed to catering to them is very important. It is easy for businesses that sell commodities or generic products to assume that there is no opportunity for them to achieve a close and "sticky" relationship with their customers. However, even such businesses can build strong customer relationships that lead to customer loyalty. An important factor to consider is that ultimately, many customer relationships are forged at the level of individuals, the representatives of either the selling or buying business who are involved in the business interactions. We will examine below how digital processes can help with this.

The ability of a business to leverage its relationship with customers for competitive advantage depends significantly on the business's ability to obtain knowledge about each customer. For instance, consider a business that has traditional "brick and mortar" stores where customers make cash purchases and the store personnel change frequently. In such a setting, a customer may still be a loyal customer, perhaps because of the convenient location of the stores, the selection and quality of products offered, and maybe even the look and feel of the stores. If each store is designed to capitalize on some specific features of its particular market, such as preferences in a particular ethnic neighborhood, the business is still leveraging knowledge about its customers in designing and stocking each store, which could build customer intimacy. On the other hand, if each store has the same design and stock and each customer is anonymous to the store they frequent, the business clearly cannot claim a customer intimacy focus. Note that by instituting features, processes and mechanisms to capture and use customer information, even small businesses can benefit from customer intimacy. Small 'mom and pop' stores have thrived in many neighborhoods, perhaps because they are run by owners who get to know their customers over time and establish mutual bonds. Unfortunately, this type of close relationship does not scale in the traditional retail setting. However, digital innovations can help achieve customer intimacy even at scale.

Table 8.3 below identifies some key focus areas for businesses seeking customer intimacy, laid out in terms of our digitalization framework.

Finally, note that customer intimacy takes effort and resources on the part of the business. If the products offered by the business are clearly best in class, then it may not be worth the cost of a customer intimacy focus. On the other

Table 8.3 Digitalization initiatives aligned with customer intimacy

Level	Focus Area	Examples
Transaction processes	Search	Using variety of search terms so that shoppers can find highly specific products
		Integrating search based on both products and customer information
		Developing features for recommending relevant products for cross-selling and upselling
	Authentication	Developing sophisticated customer relationship management tools and capabilities
	Valuation	Incorporating customer information into dynamic pricing mechanisms
		Incorporating customer history into dynamic pricing mechanisms
	Payment	Incorporating customer information to streamline payment processes
	Logistics	Personalizing logistics support based on customer preferences and history
	Service	Customizing services to each customer using mechanisms such as dedicated support teams, and information about specific purchases and resolution of past calls.
Decision Support Processes	Configuration	Developing extensive support for customization and personalization of products and services
	Collaboration	Creating rich channels for communication and collaboration with customers to involve them in key processes
	Business Intelligence	Customizing reports factoring in customer priorities and preferences
Product Digitalization	Enhancing Existing Products	Focusing on features that enable personalization
	New Digital Products	Developing personalized products that leverage the business's knowledge of products as well as customer preferences

hand, customer intimacy can help a business win over customers from competitors with better quality products, and even enable the business to command a premium price for its products. This is because customers make buying choices based on a number of factors, some tied to the products themselves and others related to the buying experience. Consider Amazon.com and its book business. Most of the books offered by Amazon are available from other sources as well, and often at even lower prices. In fact, Amazon even informs buyers about such alternative sources. Yet millions of customers still choose to buy from Amazon. While there are several underlying factors, at least one significant factor is that customers appreciate the fact that the company seems to understand them and know their preferences. Furthermore, this knowledge seems to get better over time, and is a classic example of a customer intimacy focus.

Beyond Strategic Priorities

The above discussion illustrates that businesses can differ significantly in terms of their strategic priorities. That does not mean that the three strategic priorities discussed above are mutually exclusive. In fact, when executives are asked to select their priorities, they often identify two, and sometimes even all three options.

Unlike the traditional setting where hard choices have to be made, digitalization makes it easier to pursue multiple strategic objectives at once. If a business chooses to excel on more than one strategic priority, it can consider the above guidelines. Amazon, for instance, can be considered not only to be customer intimate, but also product leading. Its well-known appetite for innovation has led it to launch Amazon Web Services, a leading cloud platform, as a new digital product, which initially served to support its own operations. Likewise, it successfully launched another digital product, Amazon Alexa, a leading virtual assistant AI system, as part of a hybrid digital product, the Amazon Echo smart speakers, after it failed to have the Fire Phone adopted in the market. It also turned Amazon Alexa into a digital platform where developers can access skills to integrate Amazon Alexa in their own products.

Examples: Dow Corning, Philips Lighting and Barco Demetra

The digitalization efforts of Dow Corning, Philips Lighting and Barco, as described in prior chapters, provide interesting insight on the importance of strategic priorities for choosing what to do.

The launch of Xiameter by the Dow Corning Corporation (DCC) was intended to address the long tail of the company's market, namely price-sensitive small customers. Given the company's strategic priorities of product leadership and customer intimacy, it traditionally provided premium services and customized products to large customers, at premium prices. The company's business model was thus infeasible for small price-sensitive customers.

Digitalization through Xiameter enabled the company to expand its market to these smaller customers without disrupting the primary market. It also allowed Xiameter to focus on operational excellence. Hence a large-scale process digitalization effort was put in place, focusing on transaction process support. Interestingly, when Dow later integrated the Xiameter functionality in Dow.com, it adapted and expanded its process digitalization for both transaction and decision support processes, while also expanding its reach for selling its more mature products through online marketplaces such as Alibaba's 1688.com in China. This helped Dow to deliver its reliable products with minimal difficulty or inconvenience to customers. Furthermore, by expanding its support for decision processes through its formulation configuration, collaboration and BI tools, Dow could move towards customer intimacy and develop better online customer relationships, in keeping with its customer experience initiative. The ability to create two distinct operations with different strategic positioning, and then move to converge these priorities in specific segments, is one of the benefits of digitalization. As a next step, Dow could even consider reconstructing its business as a digital platform that leverages its customer base to attract sellers of complimentary products.

Another interesting example is that of Philips Lighting. The launch of the Partner Conversion Program by Philips Lighting in its home market helped the company to become more customer intimate with the electro-technical wholesalers, while its digital outreach to pull installers and customers to its Website and those of its partners drove customer intimacy with them. Its process digitalization effort was consistent with its strategic priority, as the company used digital technologies to enhance the value of its existing customer base. In addition to process digitalization along its value system, Philips Lighting also engaged in product digitalization. Its launch of InterAct Office, a smart connected lighting system for office buildings, was again consistent with its strategic priority, as customers could customize the configurable products to their specific needs.

Finally, the launch of Demetra by Barco, the global technology leader in networked visualization solutions, reinforced the company's traditional product leadership positioning. Through product digitalization, Barco not only developed a better product, it could now also follow the product over its useful lifetime. Furthermore, transaction and decision support process were adapted to the possibilities offered by the hybrid digital product. In a next phase, Barco Demetra could evolve to becoming a leading pure digital product.

Digitalization for Competitive Advantage

Once a digital innovation initiative is aligned with the strategic priorities of the business, it is useful to assess the competitive landscape of the business, and then determine how the initiative would help gain competitive advantage. An excellent tool for the first step is the 5-Forces Model developed by Michael Porter.

Porter's 5-forces Model

Strategic analysis can be done at several levels. At the industry level, several decades ago, Michael Porter developed a model based on 5 competitive forces that has become part of the business strategy lexicon[7]. The model is illustrated in Fig. 8.2 below.

In this model, the competitive threats to a business in a particular industry arise from five sources. Downstream players such as buyers of the business's products and services seek to leverage their bargaining power, as do upstream players such as suppliers. In addition, the landscape of the industry can be threatened by the entry of new competitors, and the industry itself could be redefined by the evolution of substitutes for its products and/or services. All

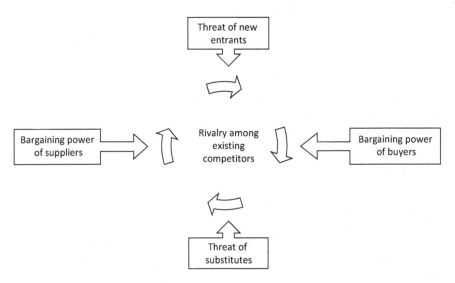

Fig. 8.2 Porter's 5-Forces Model

---

[7] Ibid., 1, p. 4.

these threats come on top of the traditional threat of competition from existing competitors within the industry.

In the context of digitalization, the five sources of threats can be expanded to include the role of the government, especially that of the regulator. In the financial services industry, for instance, the Dodd-Franklin legislation in the US and the Payment Service Directive 2 (PSD2) in Europe require banks to make their consumer data available to third parties in a digital form, given consumer consent, for account information and payment initiation services. These regulations set in motion a move towards so-called "open banking" to stimulate industry competition and FinTech innovation. An example of this is Tink, a Swedish FinTech that makes technology for account aggregation and payment initiation available on a single, cloud-based platform, which can be integrated with banks' systems through an API. It also provides Software Development Kits (SDKs) for accessing the Tink API and acts as a so-called API storefront for financial institutions that want to integrate the building blocks of digital retail banking flexibly and quickly in their offering without having to develop all of the technology themselves or establishing a partnership with traditional software vendors and integrators. BNP Paribas Fortis, a Belgian bank that is part of the European banking group BNP Paribas, enhanced its mobile retail banking applications by integrating the account aggregation, personal finance management, and payment initiation technologies of Tink, making this functionality available to its retail customers.

Given the various competitive forces facing the business, we can examine how a particular digitalization initiative could counter one or more of these forces and yield competitive advantage for the business. Warren McFarlan provided an excellent characterization of five key ways in which business could use information technology for competitive advantage,[8] which we can use for this purpose.

1. *Creating Barriers to Entry*: Digitalizing key processes can be a powerful way to change the competitive arena and reduce the threat of new entrants. A key consideration is the effective use of incumbency. The business can leverage its existing customer base and strengthen its relationship with them by enhancing both transaction and decision processes in ways that capitalize on the knowledge that the business has about them through its past interactions with them. Similarly, the business can also strengthen its

---

[8] E. Warren McFarlan, "Information Technology Changes the Way You Compete", *Harvard Business Review*, May–June 1984.

ties to its supplier base by enhancing the same processes with them. This can be more effective than setting up exclusive contracts, which can back-fire by depriving the business of market efficiencies. And if the business is a platform, it can reinforce these same ties on multiple sides, particularly if participants are inclined to single-home in their platform choices. Such moves raise the cost for new entrants to establish a viable market position by taking away market share. An additional benefit of such innovations is that they can also reduce the threat of existing competitors, since they are "forced" to follow suit or else face more competition from new entrants in their vulnerable situation. An excellent example of this approach is Tesla, the electric vehicle maker. Over the decade or so that the company has been making cars, it has significantly enhanced not only its customer ser-vice support processes, but also its products themselves, through frequent software updates, that constantly raise the stakes for new entrants into the EV space.

2. *Building in Switching Costs*: Switching costs can also be viewed as barriers to exit for external stakeholders such as customers or suppliers. While switching costs can be created through formal contracts, digitalization can be an effective way to create switching costs without restricting stakehold-ers against their will. A powerful way to create such switching costs is by exploiting knowledge about customers and suppliers to build deeper and richer relationships with them. Consider the example of Amazon and its Prime subscription service. Over the years, Amazon has exploited its huge customer knowledge base to keep and build its subscriber base, despite several price increases. The longer a subscriber stays with Prime, the less they are inclined to leave, because the company keeps enriching the value proposition of the service with digital enhancements as well as new ser-vices. As a result, the bargaining power of customers are limited, and these switching costs can also effectively stave off new entrants by limiting their viable markets.

3. *Changing the Competitive Basis*: Markets in many sectors today are charac-terized by intense, even global competition and it is increasingly difficult for any company to differentiate its traditional products and services for very long. As a result, the basis of competition shifts to a race towards com-moditization (the commoditization magnet) and competition on price, resulting in lower profits. Digital innovation can be useful in fighting this vicious cycle, by using data and information to create differentiated value-adding services that change the basis of competition. To see this, consider the example of Barco's Demetra line. While the company initially focused on the physical scanning device, this could easily be emulated by competi-

tors. By recognizing the value of the database of diagnostic data it was obtaining from the scanners, the company was able to create a profitable service offering (a new digital product), even as the device market would be getting more crowded and less profitable. This type of innovation addresses not only the threat of existing competitors, but also reduce the bargaining power of customers and the threat of new entrants.

4. *Changing the Balance of Power in Supplier Relationships*: Can digitalization impact the bargaining power of suppliers? The answer is clearly yes, as we have already suggested, but interestingly, the impact can be positive or negative. For instance, in the early stages of automation in the supply chain space, firms invested in integrated systems (or inter-organizational systems) that enhanced the efficiency of supply chain processes and provided benefits to both buying firms who could operate with leaner inventory and sometimes even less coordination (e.g., through vendor-management inventory systems), as well as suppliers who could better plan production and logistics. However, these systems also locked in the buying and selling firms, thereby reducing bargaining power. On the other hand, more recent trends in supply chain management have benefited from digitalization of transaction processes in the B2B sector that enable firms to reconfigure their supply chains far more easily and quickly. This increases the agility of buying firms, and also decreases the bargaining power of their suppliers. And at the same time, firms that exploit supply chain information to create value-adding business intelligence for their business partners can again create stickiness and reduce the bargaining power of the latter. This is particularly powerful in the case of digital platforms, since the above effects can be magnified when combined with significant cross-side and same-side network effects.

5. *Creating New Products*: As we have discussed in earlier chapters, product digitalization can lead to new and promising market opportunities for many businesses. What is important to remember is that digital products (both new products and digitally enhanced products) may be harder to emulate than physical products, particularly if they exploit proprietary information or knowledge. This in turn means that effective substitutes are harder to create, thereby reducing that threat. An example of this is Netflix's recommendation system. Even though the video streaming space has become increasingly crowded and competitive, Netflix has a very low attrition rate, even though many market pundits wrongly predicted much higher subscriber attrition with each price hike by the company, and after the post-Covid19 correction. We believe that Netflix's service is not just content, but a digitally enhanced, customized entertainment experience.

What is more, digitalization not only impacts the competitive threats to a business, but it can also potentially redefine the industry for the business. As the businesses in an industry or related industries digitalize their processes and products, customer needs can be addressed in novel ways that go beyond traditional industry boundaries. New ecosystems can emerge that span multiple industries and meet a broader set of customer needs, in which firms collaborate with horizontal partners and complementors. Car manufacturers, for instance, now need to involve a partner set that is much broader than before to cater to the customer needs of not just driving, but also entertainment (e.g., music), shopping, and site seeing. Likewise, home construction companies start partnering with tech players to make the transition to smart homes. A case in point was the partnership of Lennar, a large home construction and real estate firm in the US, with Amazon for integrating smart doorbells (Ring), door locks, lighting, and thermostats in new Lennar homes, powered by Amazon Alexa, and showcased in Amazon Experience Centers. As a result of this, the incumbent business needs to make a strategic decision on whether it wants to drive the reshaping of the industry as a first mover or focus on a part of the broader customer need where it can still add and capture value. As part of this, the business also needs to consider whether it seeks to expand its corporate purpose from its traditional product definition to meeting a broader customer need (Porter and Heppelmann 2014)[9].

The net effect of the impact of digitalization varies across industries (Porter and Heppelmann 2014)[10]. A general trend now seems to be that digitalization is increasing industry competition. Especially the threat of new entrants, either posed by big tech or disruptive start-ups, is high on the radar of many executives. As they rethink the strategic position of their businesses, executives need to understand the impact of digitalization on the industry structure and focus on digitalization initiatives that can support or even redirect their strategic priorities.

Example—Eneco Toon Revisited

The Toon smart thermostat introduced by Dutch utility Eneco in 2012 (see Chaps. 3 and 6) was one of several digitalization initiatives identified by the company.

---

[9] Porter, Michael E. and Heppelmann, James E., 2014 (Nov), How Smart Connected Products Are Transforming Competition, Harvard Business Review.
[10] Ibid., 8.

While the strategic priority of Eneco's traditional consumer energy business was operational excellence to compete in the dog-eat-dog Dutch gas and electricity markets, which were characterized by very high customer churn and very low profit margins, Eneco went beyond this strategic priority and strived to become customer intimate, using digital technology to provide consumers with a sense of control over their energy consumption through personalized experiences. Rather than luring consumers with freebies such as digital tablets, it provided them with a smart thermostat that offered real-time insight in energy consumption in Euros through connectivity with Eneco's back-end systems in which the energy contracts were created.

Given its customer intimacy strategic priority, Eneco focused on product digitalization for personalization rather than for cost or performance. This not only helped Eneco to engage consumers in longer term fixed price contracts, reduce churn and enhance operating profit, but also protected it against the curse of the bleeding edge. Indeed, market leader Essent, which in a partnership with Google Nest later introduced the Nest product leading thermostats in the Dutch market, did not succeed in weakening Eneco's competitive advantage. Thanks to its personalization features, Eneco could make consumers who preferred a personalized experience over a product leading thermostat stick with Toon. In addition, Eneco reconstructed Toon as a digital platform business, adding external providers such as Philips and Tesla to connect with its customer base and enriching its personalization value proposition across the smart home. This approach enabled Toon to offer consumers a much broader and richer array of services than it could have developed itself.

The addition of the Toon smart thermostat to a longer term, fixed price, gas and electricity contract encouraged consumers to increasingly rely on Eneco to buy and manage their energy. The mounting of the Toon tablet on a wall in the consumer's living room, as well as its connectivity with the boiler, meter, and the customer contract in the Eneco back-end system, made the initiative stick. Furthermore, Toon reinforced and broadened its value proposition through the development of an ecosystem of complementary partners when it added digital platform features. As it orchestrated the smart home ecosystem for its customers, these customers and the providers in the ecosystem were less likely to switch and stay in a relationship with Eneco. Furthermore, new entrants could not simply replicate this digitalization initiative as customers got hooked to Toon's digital features. What is more, Toon provided Eneco with a valuable image of being innovative and its continued innovations made it a moving target for competitors and new entrants alike.

Thanks to the aggregated insight into real-time energy consumption, production (through solar panels), and storage (in batteries) of its customers,

Toon could also tilt the balance of power in supplier relationships in its favor. Armed with this insight, Eneco could better predict the amount of energy it needed to buy in the market.

Finally, the Toon digitalization initiative also provided Eneco with an opportunity to change the basis of competition as it sought to expand its corporate purpose from its traditional product definition to making sustainable energy available and affordable to all. By aligning the Toon digitalization initiative with this purpose, Eneco expanded the industry definition from energy to the smart home.

Thus, consistent with how digitalization can offer significant competitive advantage, Toon improved its existing product and built both switching costs and barriers to entry, while redistributing the balance of power in supplier relationships, and changing the basis of competition.

Reflection Questions

- Reflecting upon the uses of digital technologies in your business, how do they change the value differential between customers' willingness-to-pay and suppliers' willingness-to-sell?

- What digital innovations can you think of that would significantly support your key strategic focus/priority?

- How could digitalization enable your business to pursue multiple strategic priorities?

- How do your digital innovation initiatives counter the competitive forces facing your business and yield competitive advantage?

9

Planning for Digitalization

In previous chapters, we have covered the various ways in which digital innovations can add competitive value to a business. We now turn to the process view, and examine how the business can pursue competitive digital innovation. In this chapter, we discuss how the business can discover opportunities for such innovation, and then discuss how it can assess its readiness for digitalization. We then discuss alternative approaches for digitalization, and finally overview some approaches for organizing the design and development process for the innovation.

Discovering Innovation Opportunities

The first step in the journey towards a new digitalization initiative is its discovery. How does the business identify a new opportunity for innovation? Inspiration for such innovation can come from various sources, both internal and external. For instance, planning and brainstorming activities within the business can lead to ideas from managers and other employees about digital enhancements of processes and products that can impact competitiveness. Organizing such events is important and often-overlooked in many businesses. Employees who are part of market-facing processes are a valuable source of innovation ideas, but without a conscious effort to identify them, such ideas don't bubble up to management awareness. A good example of institutionalizing such a discovery process is Amazon's 2–4–6 pager approach. Employees can write up their ideas in short 2-page proposals and discuss them with their managers. Ideas that survive these reviews are elaborated with

© The Author(s), under exclusive license to Springer Nature Switzerland AG 2023
A. Basu, S. Muylle, *Competitive Digital Innovation*, Palgrave Executive Essentials,
https://doi.org/10.1007/978-3-031-23440-8_9

additional details and supporting data and then escalated further up the management chain. This process facilitates a progressive development and enrichment of ideas as well as effective management review. Furthermore, the originators of the ideas can stay engaged throughout the discovery process and even later steps.

Another source of discovery is external stakeholders such as customers, suppliers, business partners and even competitors. Useful mechanisms for this include probing on social media (see Chap. 5) as well as traditional mechanisms for obtaining the voice of these stakeholders, such as meetings, surveys, customer service feedback, trade shows and conferences.

In addition to an analysis of the market in terms of the customer, the competition, and the technology landscape, a functional and technical analysis of the digital solution needs to be done to specify its required functionality, while also reviewing existing technology solutions. Mechanisms for such analysis include a feasibility study and even a business case. Here again the viewpoints of various external stakeholders such as customers should be considered.

Assessing Readiness

As the business considers digitalization initiatives in support of its strategic priorities, it needs to keep in mind that whatever it chooses to do, it needs to do it well. In the words of Michael Porter (1996)[1]: "Strategy is wasted without operational effectiveness." Operational effectiveness is about "performing similar activities better than rivals perform them," while "strategy rests on unique activities to deliver a unique mix of value." Digitalization of internal processes can help improve operational effectiveness, by enabling businesses to embrace best practices across the value chain. However, to gain competitive advantage, businesses can go further by identifying externally-facing digitalization initiatives that support their strategic priorities, as we have discussed in Parts I and II, and Chap. 8 in Part III.

Once the business has identified appropriate initiatives, it needs to evaluate whether it is well positioned and has the resources and capabilities to proceed with the implementation of these initiatives. Therefore, it is important for the business to address several next step questions, which are introduced and discussed below.

One key question is: Do we have the necessary digital technologies? As the business engages in digitalization and develops its digital technology

---

[1] Michael Porter, "What is Strategy", Harvard Business Review, November-December, 1996.

infrastructure and applications, it needs to consider what technologies to leverage and what technologies to upgrade or add. This is important, since the process of introducing new technologies can be costly, in terms of both money and time. Thus, in choosing among innovation alternatives, it may be cost-effective to prioritize one that uses familiar technologies, even if others are more exciting. For instance, consider a business for which customer intimacy is a priority. If the business already has the technology to support transaction processes, it can leverage that for implementing an e-commerce initiative that focuses on customer intimacy, at a lower cost than an initiative to enhance digital configuration capabilities using CAD technologies for instance. However, at some point, the business may need to add not only CAD technologies but also technologies to support effective digital collaboration and business intelligence, to support its customer intimacy priorities and develop personalized customer relationships.

Another significant question is: Do we have the right people? Digitalization requires new skillsets for employees in various functional areas of the organization, adds new functions such as data analytics, and changes work practices. Does the business have the right talent base? Does it have the entrepreneurial culture to stimulate digitalization? Does the workforce need to be trained? How and where does the organizational structure need to change? An important consideration is whether digital technology can be used to do some of the work. For instance, could Artificial Intelligence be used to automate some tasks? In order to do this, both AI technologies and people with expertise in AI that work with the business to digitalize the piece of work are needed. As the possibilities of digital technologies continue to expand, especially AI, the business can further reshape its resources and capabilities through redefining work and restructuring the workforce.

The business also needs to ask itself: Do we have the relevant and necessary data? Recall that proprietary information and knowledge from data is a powerful means of creating a sustainable competitive advantage. In order to realize such benefits, the business needs to have the appropriate means for data acquisition, data storage and data management. And these resources in turn are defined by the characteristics of the relevant data. For instance, while many businesses developed robust corporate database systems as part of their digital transformation efforts in recent decades, these are not well-suited for today's "Big Data" environment. The sheer velocity of new data, combined with the complexity and variability can quickly overwhelm traditional relational data management systems. Modern data management technologies, such as federated database systems, data lakes and data ponds are better-suited to such environments. Thus, before embarking on an initiative that will require rapid and even real-time processing of data from sources such as the Web, mobile systems, social media and IoT devices, the requisite data management systems need to be in place.

Furthermore, the business needs to develop a data analytics capability for analyzing and acting on data in a timely fashion. For instance, if the business sets out to enhance an existing product with digital features for product leadership, it not only needs technology to add digital components, connectivity, capabilities, and interfaces, but also to exploit the digital features of the product and enhance its value for the customer. As the digitally enhanced product produces and transfers data on its use and performance over its lifetime, the business, needs to be able to analyse and act on the data. Toward this end, it not only needs the people, but also analytical tools (including AI and machine learning software), and the ability to develop experience and expertise in both people and technology by iterating between them in building the capabilities to have an effective digitalized product.

With regard to the data resource, the business also needs to ensure that its digitalization initiatives comply with the law. Digital applications have enabled businesses to collect vast amounts of rich data about their external stakeholders such as customers and suppliers. In many settings, these data are provided voluntarily by those stakeholders themselves. However, the development of powerful data analytics and data integration methods have created opportunities for businesses to leverage data far beyond the purposes motivating their initial collection. This has in turn triggered significant concerns about possible violation of privacy of data about both individuals and organizations. Thus, in pursuing any digitalization initiative that involves manipulation of external stakeholder data, the business needs to develop expertise in dealing with privacy (e.g., through privacy by design approaches) and security regulation across the different regions in which it operates, while also considering the ethical implications of its digitalization initiatives (see Chap. 11 for further discussion).

Another key next step question is: Do we have the money and time to do this? Each of the resources related to the previous questions can require significant effort and expense. For instance, while a new digital application may promise significant business value, it may require not only application development effort,[2] but also expensive middleware and infrastructure investment. Likewise, the acquisition, development, and retention of people with digital skills is likely to be costly, given the scarcity of expert profiles on the labor market. And putting the systems in place for leveraging data to create a

---

[2] Terms such as "mash-up" and "no-code" are also used to describe such approaches.

competitive advantage can involve significant expense as well. As an example, AI-driven initiatives require algorithms to be trained and outcomes to be validated, and only start to generate relevant results as they improve over time. As Gina Chung, VP of Innovation at DHL, says, "The worst day for AI is the first day, because the algorithm gets better over time."[3]

The business also needs to ask: Do we need to make, buy, or partner? While the business can develop its own resources and capabilities for digitalization, it can also look into the market for solutions that may keep it from reinventing the wheel, or speed up implementation. The increasing availability of pay-per-use, cloud-based solutions from big tech and other players not only give the business easy access to affordable and scalable resources, but also enables it to use the latest technologies. For instance, the process of programming software (coding) itself has evolved from coding from the ground up to a low-code or Lego-block approach, in which programmers can download code snippets from online repositories and adapt them to fit their specific needs. More generally, the business can also choose to formally partner with other organizations to digitalize its processes, products, and business models, and develop this as a capability. A case in point is a digital platform initiative in which the business needs to develop a competency in partnering with complementary providers that drive cross-side network effects with consumers.

Choosing a Digitalization Approach

In deciding on how to digitalize, a business can choose from the following three approaches:

1. Digitalize within the context of the existing business
2. Create a new business
3. Digitalize within and outside the existing business

We look at each of these approaches in turn.

---

[3] S. Ransbotham, S. Khodabandeh, D. Kiron, F. Candelon, M. Chu, and B. LaFountain, "Expanding AI's Impact with Organizational Learning," *MIT Sloan Management Review* and Boston Consulting Group, October 2020 (p. 8).

Digitalizing Within the Context of the Existing Business

This approach by definition impacts the existing business. As the digitalization initiative transforms market-facing processes, products, or even the scope and business model, it also transforms, to a varying degree, the resources and capabilities of the existing business. Hence, its successful implementation hinges on various factors such as the willingness of the workforce to adopt, support and drive the initiative. To enable the implementation of digital initiatives, many organizations are embarking on multi-year digital transformation efforts in which they build new capabilities around digital strategy, technology, data, talent, culture, and governance.

An example of digitalization within the context of the existing business model is the approach of KBC, an integrated bank-insurance group that operates in Belgium, the Czech Republic, Slovakia, Hungary, Bulgaria and Ireland. In 2014, it launched a "Customer 2020" digital transformation program and earmarked 250 million Euros to invest in 250 digital initiatives to become customer centric by 2020. One of the digitalization initiatives involved retail banking consumers using their smartphones instead of their debit cards to withdraw cash from an ATM. The initiative took a few months to take shape, in an end-to-end team with an IT specialist on ATMs, a specialist on mobile, and the involvement of a branch to test a prototype (also known as a minimum viable product), followed by a national roll out.[4] In 2017, the bank increased the budgeted investment in a new program, called C25, with specific focal areas (e.g., instant personal user experience) per year.

Creating a New Business

Instead of digitalizing within the context of the existing business, a new business can be created. So, rather than disrupting the existing business, digitalization can be implemented independently of the existing business. Such an approach also allows the business to avoid the market, organizational and technological legacy that has been built up over time, and instead try new digital initiatives in other markets. This can be done in various ways including building a separate unit, taking an ownership stake in, or acquiring another business, or merging or creating a joint venture with other businesses.

An example of building a separate unit is the launch by JPMorgan Chase, a leading global financial services firm and the biggest US bank by assets, of a

---

[4] https://newsroom.kbc.com/from-now-on-kbccbc-clients-can-withdraw-money-from-atms-in-belgium-using-their-smartphone

digital-only international retail bank, which started operations first in the UK in September 2021, using the Chase brand, and will be expanded to other countries over time. This digital-only bank stands out against the omnichannel approach of the group's retail banking operation in the US, where it has almost 5000 bricks-and-mortar branches, also under the Chase brand. As Jamie Dimon, JPMorgan CEO, says: "There's no chance that JPMorgan will put 100 branches in Mumbai or Hong Kong or London or anywhere and actually compete."[5] To bolster its digital-only proposition, JPMorgan has acquired Nutmeg, which launched in 2012 and quickly became a digital challenger in the British wealth management market, and acquired a 40% ownership stake in C6, one of the fastest growing digital banks in Brazil, launched in 2019. Through its digitalization initiative, JPMorgan Chase seeks to step up its global presence in international retail banking without disrupting its US operation.

Another example of creating a new business is Coca Cola's strategic investment in WoNoLo.[6] WoNoLo is short for Work Now Locally, a 2013 start-up that can be viewed as an Uber for short term gigs (note that Uber incubated Uber Works in October 2019 in Chicago, and expanded it to Miami and Dallas.[7] Uber Works connects workers with businesses to fill shifts, and is no longer operational). Coca Cola turned to WoNoLo to help it address a one billion USD problem, out of stock situations in supermarkets. Through WoNoLo, local workers, vetted by the service, can replenish the shelves with Coca Cola products (which are typically stored in the supermarket) for an hour or two and make some extra money. At the same time, Coca Cola's strategic issue gets addressed through an external digital initiative.

Digitalizing Within and Outside the Existing Business

The two previous approaches can be combined by digitalizing within and outside the existing business and seeking synergies. An interesting perspective on this approach is provided by Clark Gilbert and his colleagues.[8] They distinguish between two types of transformation (A&B) and underscore the importance of a new process for exchanging capabilities between both transformations. Transformation A is about repositioning the core business and

---

[5] FT article, May 23, 2022, JPMorgan estimates overseas digital bank losses could top $1bn in coming years.

[6] https://www.wsj.com/articles/BL-VCDB-17022.

[7] According to its LinkedIn presence: https://www.linkedin.com/company/uberworks/.

[8] Gilbert, Clark, Matthew Eyring, Richard N. Foster, Two Routes to Resilience, Harvard Business Review, pp. 3–9, Dec 2012.

adapting to the altered marketplace (cf. digitalizing with the existing business), whereas Transformation B is about creating a separate, disruptive business to become the next source of growth (cf. creating a new business). The capabilities exchange refers to establishing a new organisational process that allows the two transformation efforts to share resources without intervening with each other's operations.

An example of this approach is Google's acquisition of YouTube through which Google expanded its scope from search advertising to online video entertainment on a social media services platform. While the 2006 SEC press release[9] stated that "Following the acquisition, YouTube will operate independently to preserve its successful brand and passionate community.", Google over time changed its search business by enriching its search results with user generated video content from YouTube such as for instance instructional how-to videos. As a result, the video business started to feed the search business. Likewise, the search business also started to feed the video business by making the videos available in Google's search results.

Developing the Initiative

Once readiness has been assessed and a digitalization approach chosen, the business has to develop an implementation plan and assemble a development and implementation team.

A digitalization initiative typically involves a system based on computer hardware and software. Thus, the development process can leverage established methodologies for systems development. In this section, we briefly review the key methodologies that have been popular over the past few decades, and point out some key advantages and disadvantages of each in the context of competitive digital innovation.

The Waterfall Approach

This is the most popular form of traditional information systems development methodology. It consists of a sequence of well-defined phases, each of which involve distinct tasks and require different expertise. These phases are as follows:

---

[9] https://www.sec.gov/Archives/edgar/data/1288776/000119312506206884/dex991.htm

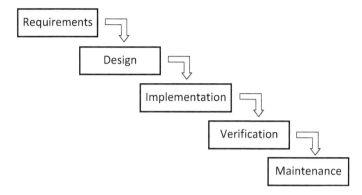

The Waterfall approach

1. *Requirements Determination*: In this initial phase, the technical and functional features needed in the solution are determined by the development team, through communications with the user community and/or analysis of the necessary capabilities and performance requirements. Based on this analysis, a set of specifications are determined for the target solution.
2. *System Design*: In this phase, system designers create one or more designs of systems that satisfy all the requirements and meet all the specifications. They then evaluate the alternative designs based on multidimensional feasibility analysis (including technical, economic/financial, operational and marketing) and select a specific design.
3. *Implementation*: In this phase, the hardware and software components are acquired/developed and assembled. This phase includes the necessary programming and installation tasks for the different components and their synthesis into a working system.
4. *Verification*: During this phase, the implemented system is put through a series of tests to ensure that it meets the relevant specifications and functional requirements of the solution.
5. *Maintenance*: In this phase, the procedures needed to maintain the system during its operating lifetime are determined and implemented.

A key feature of the waterfall methodology is that it is strictly sequential, and the results of each phase are frozen before proceeding to the next phase. It is a highly structured methodology, with established instruments for documenting each phase. This makes it applicable to even large-scale and highly complex systems. Also, the highly structured form allows for project teams and managers that can be replaced relatively easily during the development process.

On the other hand, the strict sequential nature of the methodology assumes that system requirements can be reliably determined and frozen at the outset. Also, the need to satisfactorily complete each phase before moving ahead makes the process rigid and time-consuming, and if changes are needed, they become difficult to accommodate. As a result, the methodology is well-suited to projects with very well-defined and specific objectives and stable requirements such as ERP projects for internal processes.

Rapid Application Development (RAD)

This methodology relaxes the strict sequential feature of the waterfall method, and assumes an iterative, stepwise refinement approach. It consists of four phases:

1. *Requirements Planning*: In this phase, the initial requirements and feasibility analysis of the target system are determined in a collaborative process involving IT staff, managers and users.
2. *User Design*: In this phase, models and designs of the target system are developed, again in a collaborative process involving users and systems analysts, and using a variety of computer-aided software engineering (CASE) tools. Often, prototype designs are also developed in this phase.
3. *Construction*: In this phase, hardware and software engineers work with programmers to implement the designs and models developed in the user design phase.
4. *Cutover*: Once the design and its construction have stabilized, the system is put through a variety of tests to verify functionality and then operationalization is addressed through training and protocol/procedures development.

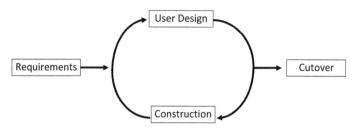

Rapid Application Development (RAD)

A key feature of the RAD methodology is that it enables the team to go through user design and construction rapidly, using multiple iterations and prototypes. This iterative process helps clarify and define the desired functionality and scope of the target system. This approach is not only faster, but provides for more flexibility and the ability to develop effective solutions for novel applications that are not well-understood at the outset.

On the other hand, the RAD methodology relies upon a stable set of domain experts and managers through the various phases of the project. Also, reliance on prototypes can result in significant re-work and even wasted effort, which can be prohibitive for large projects. Thus, this approach is better-suited to small or medium-scale projects such as targeted mobile apps.

Agile Development

The agile development approach is similar to the RAD approach, in that it relies on frequent and multiple iteration through various tasks. Rather than a specific methodology, the term agile is used to characterize a number of methods such as scrum, feature-driven development (FDD) and extreme programming (XP). The approach involves a series of short design-build-review cycles through which the requirements are gradually refined. A key objective is to minimize bugs, cost-overruns and unnecessary features/complexity by limiting the scope of each iteration. Although not every iteration results in a new release of the system, it is suitable for a system that can be released in multiple iterations, which allows for relatively quick deployment and an iterative refinement mindset.

The development process starts with a planning phase, and then iterates through multiple cycles (sprints) through tasks such as design, develop, test, deploy and review, finally leading to the launch of a satisfactory system.

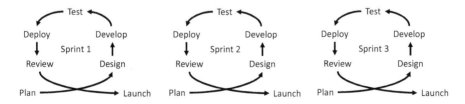

Agile development

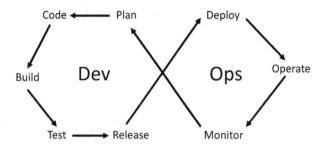

The Dev-Ops approach

As with the RAD approach, agile methods work best for small or medium scale/complexity projects, particularly those intended for novel applications for which the necessary features and specifications are difficult to determine up front. These include social media or mobile device data applications that evolve significantly over time.

The Dev-Ops Approach

This approach also facilitates rapid implementation and deployment of systems that evolve through frequent updates and releases. It focuses on frequent and collaborative interaction between the organizational units involved in the development (Dev) of the target system and the units responsible for using/operating the system in practice (Ops).

As with RAD and Agile, the Dev-Ops approach is well-suited to an environment in which the useful life of any specific system is relatively short, or the features and capabilities of the target system are expected to evolve relatively quickly and frequently. It works best when the dev-ops teams have effective resources for rich and frequent communication and collaboration, and also when updates to target systems can be made easily without significantly disrupting user operations.

Deploying the Initiative

There are three approaches widely accepted as alternatives for the deployment of software or system applications. These are as follows:

1. *Phased Implementation*: In the phased approach, the risk of a new and complex system is mitigated by deploying it in multiple phases, with each

phase adding incremental functionality. Each phase is fully developed before deployment, so the functionality of that phase does not change after deployment. However, feedback from the user experience and performance of that phase can be used to shape subsequent phases. An example of this approach is the initial deployment of a point-of-sale system for handling sales transactions in a store, followed by the deployment of a store management system that includes inventory management.

2. *Pilot Implementation*: In this approach, the entire system is deployed at the same time with all its intended functionality. However, the scale of the deployment is limited to a potentially small part of the business or enterprise. Referring again to the store example, the POS system can be piloted at a single store, and possibly evaluated and refined, before being rolled out to multiple stores.

3. *Big-Bang Implementation*: This is the approach taken for a complete deployment as a single step. In other words, in a big-bang implementation, the entire system with all its functionality is deployed across the entire business at the same time. An example of this is when the POS system is deployed simultaneously across all the stores, or when a new ERP system is deployed for an entire company at a certain cutover date.

In choosing any of these approaches, a business has to consider several factors. First, there is the trade-off between development time/efficiency and risk of failure and redesign. While a big-bang implementation is the most efficient, it is also the most risky. A phased or pilot implementation stretches out the development timeline, but mitigates risk by facilitating adjustments and corrections during the process. Another factor is change management. In a pilot implementation, a small part of the workforce has to be trained on the new system at a time, and as mentioned earlier, learnings from this process can be used to refine the implementation in the rollout to other units. Similarly, in a phased implementation, the workforce has to learn only a (potentially small) part of the new system's functionality at each phase. In contrast, in a big-bang implementation, the entire organization has to adopt the new system simultaneously, which can be done more quickly, but requires adequate scale of resources and a more well-defined and structured procedures in the change management process to succeed.

In the context of digitalization initiatives, the same three alternatives for deployment still apply.

1. *Phased*: For instance, in a first phase, a Website product catalog can be developed using a Product Information Management application. In a

second phase, authentication functionality can be added, including integration with social media platforms. In a third phase, e-commerce can be introduced. Finally, in a fourth phase, e-commerce can be expanded to an e-marketplace in which upstream vendors can cater directly to the consumer base.

2. *Pilot*: An example of a pilot deployment is the implementation of the James initiative by BNP Paribas Fortis Bank in Belgium. The bank rolled out the service initially to its Priority Banking customers, and expanded the service to other customer segments such as Private Banking only after gaining significant experience with the initial rollout and working out a number of operational features.

3. *Big Bang*: In the context of competitive digital innovations, a big-bang implementation is usually feasible only for entirely novel applications. An example is Apple's App Store, which was initially deployed with most of its current functionality available at the outset.

Big-bang deployment is seldom the preferred approach, for several reasons. First, many digitalization initiatives offer novel functionalities and features, and cater to audiences that have no prior experience with such functionalities. Thus, the user reactions to such innovations are difficult to predict, and as a result, the features usually have to be revised or refined over time. Second, rarely can any business sustain competitive advantage from a static digital innovation, since technology innovations can be emulated by competitors, often at relatively low cost. Thus, it becomes necessary for innovators to keep moving the target, by continuous improvement and refinement of their digital initiatives. As Mark Twain said—"Continuous improvement is better than delayed perfection." Digital innovation is a highly dynamic process characterized by intense learning. So a popular mantra for many technology innovators is to "fail fast", which implicitly suggests a phased approach. So for most digitalization initiatives, some combination of a phased and a pilot implementation is the preferred approach. Even in the case of Apple's App Store, while the bulk of its features were available immediately, over the years new features have still been added, such as the Apple Arcade for experiencing interactive games.

Reflection Questions

- Does your business have the necessary technologies, people, data, money, time, and partners, to digitally innovate?
- In digitalizing your business, would you create a new business, or digitalize within and/or outside the existing business?
- What do you see as the pros and cons of the various methodologies for systems development for digital innovation in your business?

10

Evaluating Digitalization Initiatives

How do executives know whether their digitalization initiatives are working? How do they know they are getting it right? In addition to sustaining the competitive advantages of their digitalization initiatives, executives need to identify relevant metrics for evaluating performance.

Apparently, management guru Peter Drucker once said that what gets measured, gets managed. At first glance, this seems reasonable—how could you manage something you cannot measure? However, we know that even on a daily basis, human beings participate in activities for which there are no precise metrics, and this is true of the activities of managers and executives as well. For instance, store managers design store fronts without any reliable metrics for their effectiveness, and companies still struggle with the reliable measurement of customer loyalty and sustainability. That does not mean that efforts have not been made to measure such things, but it is widely recognized that there are intangible aspects to the underlying concepts that are hard to quantify. Furthermore, there are also concerns about what is meant by "managing" something. For instance, there is ample evidence that the presence of metrics can result in managers focusing on optimizing performance with regard to the metrics, even though doing so is counter-productive. For example, efficiency metrics for medical care have resulted in doctors focusing on maximizing the number of patients they treat rather than providing the best care.

Measuring and evaluating digitalization initiatives is particularly complex due to the variety of side-effects and network externalities that can result from such initiatives. With respect to cost-benefit analysis, since digitalization involves the storage, processing, and transfer of data on computers and networks, measurement of the cost of these operations may seem rather

A. Basu, S. Muylle, *Competitive Digital Innovation*, Palgrave Executive Essentials, https://doi.org/10.1007/978-3-031-23440-8_10

straightforward. In other words, it is easy to measure the amount and cost of computer hardware and software, data storage and data communications. However, this is somewhat analogous to measuring the cost of a business in terms of its physical assets and operations only. And the challenges are even greater on the benefit or value side of the equation. Operational metrics (including Website visits and (unique) visitors, visit duration, number of clicks, clickthrough rates, clickstreams, number of requests and downloads, number of likes, comments and post on social media sites, number of mobile app downloads, app functionality use and frequency, app retention, as well as IoT sensor measures) may help managers to closely monitor their digital initiatives. However, this multitude and variety of measures can easily overwhelm managers and detract from the bigger picture. According to Sheila Jordan:[1] "If you try to measure every single thing you are doing, you will manage the ants while the elephants are storming by." Hence, it is important to both choose the right metrics, and to recognize that there may still be elements of value and cost that are difficult to quantify and measure.

Toward that end, three key factors need to be considered: (1) the focus of digitalization, (2) financial performance, and (3) network externalities. We start by considering evaluation mechanisms for process and product digitalization. Then we consider the evaluation of financial performance, which concerns the use of financial metrics to determine the desired outcome and includes measures of cost and revenues. Finally, we discuss the evaluation of network externalities, which focuses on the measurable actual and potential effects (both positive and negative) on different stakeholders and participants of any network-based digitalization initiative.

We also discuss the critical issue of sustaining the value of competitive digital innovations. This is important because technology innovation is not only expensive, but also difficult to leverage as a source of sustained competitive advantage.

Evaluating Process Digitalization

For process digitalization, it is important to define metrics that collect data on the digital mechanisms that support the market-facing processes, and to develop models that analyze the relationships between them. Furthermore, financial metrics need to be defined that connect digital process support to financial performance in the models.

---

[1] Sheila Jordan, in "Social Business: Shifting Out of First Gear", MIT SMR Research Report, 2013.

For transaction processes, metrics that measure the extent of digital support for search, authentication, valuation, payment, logistics, and customer service can be complemented with financial metrics that measure their cost and revenue impact. Furthermore, the sequencing between the processes can be captured by analyzing the conversion or attrition from one process to the next. In so-called attribution models, a key outcome (e.g., an online sale) is defined and the sequence of digital mechanisms that supported the processes and delivered the conversion can be analyzed. Table 10.1 illustrates some of the process mechanisms that lead to an online sale, and the associated operational and financial metrics.

Decision support processes build capabilities that may derive from or lead to enhancements of transaction processes and other decision support processes. We next examine what metrics are important for each type of decision support process.

The evaluation of configuration support requires a focus on the value that is derived by digitalizing configuration of products and services. Appropriate measures should address the extent to which customers use digital media and tools to participate in product configuration, and the extent to which the digital innovations replace or enhance existing mechanisms for customer engagement in product configuration. As discussed in Chap. 2, configuration support can also benefit from digitalization of transaction processes such as search, authentication and valuation. Thus, evaluation of the configuration process can include measures of the effect of enhanced configuration on transaction conversion and sales.

The digitalization of collaboration processes moves communication between internal and external stakeholders to digital media and channels. Thus, appropriate metrics for such digitalization initiatives should address the extent to which these changes are adopted, and the extent to which they add value with respect to the quality and efficiency of the outcomes of such

Table 10.1 Metrics for transaction processes

Process	Mechanism	Operational metric	Financial metric
Search	Google Ads	Ad Clicks	Cost Per Click (CPC)
Authentication	Webpage Content	Webpage Visits	Cost Per Visit (CPV)
Valuation	List price on Webpage		
Payment	Credit Card	Completed Transactions	Revenue
Logistics	Shipping	Product Deliveries	Cost of Delivery
Customer Service	Product Returns	Product Returns	Cost of Returns and Refunds

communications (which include the support of transaction processes), keeping in mind that collaboration can be through both synchronous and asynchronous mechanisms. In the context of asynchronous communications, the measures can address efficiencies gained through the use of technologies such as email, messaging, the Web and social media. On the other hand, synchronous collaboration mechanisms such as virtual meeting technologies can be evaluated in terms of cost and time benefits that they provide, as well as benefits due to the use of rich media, multimedia and shared workspaces and applications.

Finally, business intelligence (BI) processes lead to the utilization of information about products and processes to add value to both internal and external stakeholders. Thus, evaluation of these processes can be in terms of the value that they provide to the recipients. The effort that goes into developing resources such as reports and dashboards can be significant, but are only worthwhile if the resulting resources are used. Thus, measuring the reach and utilization of the outputs of BI digitalization initiatives is key to establishing their business value.

Evaluating Product Digitalization

For product digitalization initiatives, conventional financial metrics for new products can be used, including sales, market share, and margin. Also, these financial metrics can be tied to operational metrics. For instance, for digitally enhanced products that are offered as a service on a subscription basis, the usage of the product's digital features can be monitored remotely. Based on this information, costs can be evaluated but also opportunities for cross-selling to other digital services and up-selling to higher tiers of the service can be identified.

Evaluating Financial Performance

In addition to separating operational and financial metrics, it is also important to separate cost and value metrics, as shown in Fig. 10.1.

Financial metrics can be identified for value and cost, and a traditional Return on Investment (ROI) exercise conducted to evaluate digitalization initiatives. Low value initiatives are considered unattractive by definition, whereas high value initiatives can be classified as either "worth building" or "worth exploring". The former is considered to be low hanging fruit that can deliver high value at low cost. The latter can also deliver high value but at higher cost.

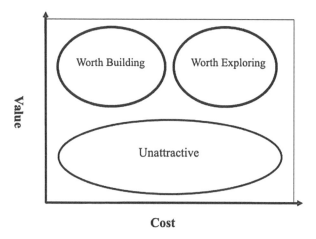

Fig. 10.1   Value/cost

As mentioned earlier, it is important to recognize that there may still be elements of value and cost that are difficult to quantify and measure. In addition to identifying financial metrics, other elements of value can be included. A useful approach is to consider the Triple Bottom Line (TBL) accounting framework. TBL not only incorporates a financial dimension of performance, but also considers social and environmental dimensions. These are commonly referred to as Profit, People, and Planet. For instance, a business can not only consider the financial performance impact of a digitalization initiative but also evaluate how it impacts the experience of frontline staff interacting with the customer, as well as how it impacts the environment in terms of carbon dioxide footprint.

Finally, the organizational change implications of the digitalization initiative and their associated costs and benefits need to be evaluated (see Chap. 9).

Note on profitability. Michael Porter defined sustainable competitive advantage as "above-average performance in the long run."[2] In other words, over time, firms that have a sustainable competitive advantage outperform rivals and earn above-average returns in their industry. It is important to recognize that for many digitalization initiatives, profitability may not always improve immediately, especially when digitalization changes the industry dynamics. Actually, a predominant focus on the bottom line may lead the firm to innovate in place (e.g., by focusing its digitalization initiatives on cost or industry best practices) and forego bigger digitalization opportunities that drive the top line and attract investor money. Rather than focusing on profitability as a key performance measure, other metrics

---

[2] M. Porter, *Competitive Advantage: Creating and Sustaining Superior Performance*, The Free Press, 1985.

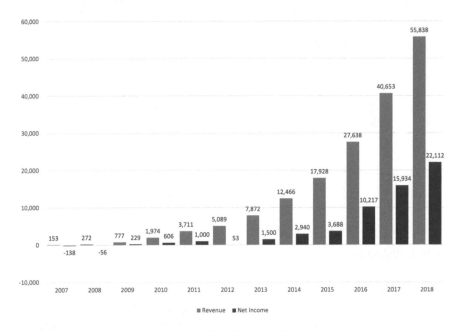

Fig. 10.2   Facebook revenues and profits (2007–2018)

such as number of customers, interactions, and revenues may be better predictors of long term performance. A case in point is Amazon, which got known early on for showing "profits later," and using investor money to build its customer base and expand its activities. Furthermore, as firms evolve their digital businesses into platform businesses, profitability is often not a priority and may come much later, as discussed in Chap. 6. Facebook, for instance, began to generate significant revenues only when it evolved from a closed forum to a two-sided digital platform model in mid-2007 (see Fig. 10.2). However, it had to incur initial losses for a while, and only became profitable once its platform became successful and eventually dominant.

Evaluating Network Externalities

For any network-based digitalization initiative, the actual and potential network externalities, which can be both positive and negative, need to be evaluated to understand how these network externalities impact the different stakeholders and participants.

Network effects are quintessential to digital platform initiatives. When operating such an initiative, a number of metrics should be tracked by managers.[3] These include the number of interaction failures (failed matches between producers and consumers), level of engagement (number of actions such as content sharing and repeat visits of platform participants that enhance network effects), match quality, and activities such as participant misbehavior that create negative network effects. It is also important to understand the financial value of the platform communities and their network effects. In doing this, positive and negative network effects have to be differentiated, and both same-side and cross-side effects.

While network effects are commonly associated with multi-sided digital platforms, these effects are not exclusive to platforms, and can occur in any network-based system. For example, consider the supplier ecosystem of a large auto manufacturer—in Japan, such an ecosystem is known as a keiretsu. The different suppliers in the network can all benefit when any of them negotiates with the manufacturer to add some feature to the processes used in the ecosystem. While they are not restricted to digitalized processes, the network effects are most significant when the change is to a digitalized process, as this can usually be adopted by all participants quicker than changes to physical processes.

Sustaining Competitive Advantage

Digital technology in and of itself rarely provides a sustainable competitive advantage to the business. Technological innovation can be expensive and capital intensive, particularly in the developmental phase. Thus, innovators that are first-movers can face significant up-front costs and risks to bring digital innovations to market, only to have competitors learn from their efforts and emulate successes far more quickly and at lower cost. It is no surprise that the legal specialization of intellectual property protection and patent law has mushroomed in the computer age. While patent and copyright protections are important mechanisms, they are expensive to enforce and increasingly ineffective.

In the technology domain, the problem is exacerbated by the opportunities for disruptive innovation. Unlike traditional competition by improved products and solutions, digital disruption occurs when competitors leverage some features of digital technologies to provide simpler and cheaper solutions to the market, even if the quality and features of these solutions are far inferior to the

---

[3] Marshall W. Van Alstyne, Geoffrey G. Parker, Sangeet Paul Choudary, "Pipelines, Platforms, and the New Rules of Strategy", *Harvard Business Review*, April 2016.

incumbent. A classic example of this is facsimile (fax) technology. Xerox Corporation was a pioneer in that space, and developed high quality fax machines and solutions as early as the 1980s. However, before they could gain a dominant market position, that market was inundated by cheaper and lower quality solutions from Japanese firms such as Ricoh, Panasonic and Canon. Examples of digital disruption abound in the information technology space, ranging from personal computers to music players.

Well, if digital innovations can be so easily emulated and/or disrupted, why should any firm view information technology or digitalization as a strategic resource? Well, digital innovation done right can in fact yield substantial and sustainable competitive advantages. While digital technology itself can be easily emulated, digital initiatives can enable a firm to leverage the data, information, and knowledge in its processes and products, and develop new digital business models, and these innovations are more defensible and potentially provide a sustainable competitive advantage.

Traditionally, sustainable competitive advantages derive from barriers to entry and imitation including market size and scale economies, superior access to resources or customers, and legislation, as well as early mover advantages due to learning costs, established reputation, network externalities, and partner switching costs.[4] Digitalization initiatives can create a variety of competitive barriers too. The following are some key sources of competitive advantage that digitalization can provide:[5]

1. Positive network effects.

A network-based digitalization initiative that provides positive network effects can become more valuable for both existing and new participants, and thereby increase switching costs, as the size of the user network increases. If a business is a first-mover or an early mover in the use of such an initiative, it can leverage the exponential growth rates of the positive network effects to dominate its market, sometimes even to the point of driving out all significant competitors. A good example of this is Google's search business. While the Google Search Engine was not the first search engine, or even one of the early players in that space, its search algorithms were not only better than those of competitors, but they also leveraged usage data to improve performance. As a

---

[4] (Besanko et al., Economics of Strategy, John Wiley, 1999).

[5] A. Basu and S. Muylle, "Planning E-Business Initiatives in Established Companies", Sloan Management Review, vol. 49, no. 1, 2007.

result, the more popular it became, the better it performed. This has significantly raised the bar for any new entrants.

The strategic value of positive network effects is particularly significant in two-sided digital platforms, which can benefit from these effects on both sides. Uber, for instance, grows the value of its ride hailing app for both drivers and passengers every time it adds either one to its network, thereby increasing switching costs. While a variety of competitors have emerged in the ride-sharing market, Uber has continued to benefit from the size of its driver and rider base.

2. Proprietary database.

Digitalization initiatives that acquire and extract stakeholder data ahead of the competition can create switching costs for those stakeholders, provided data protection regulation requirements are not violated. Consumers typically shy away from sharing data with multiple providers, especially when they are satisfied with their current ones. If their provider can demonstrate that the information provided to them is used for the customer's benefit, that can help overcome privacy concerns as well. A digitalization initiative that collects and provides increasing value from proprietary customer data can derive sustainable competitive advantages that are based on such data. When combining the data with positive network externalities, the digitalization initiative can be made "stickier" and hence even more sustainable. Product recommendation systems such as those from Amazon, Netflix, or Spotify are a case in point. By acquiring and leveraging data on the customer's profile and online behavior, and that of many other customers, these AI-driven systems make personal recommendations for products that have a high likelihood of being bought. As the data asset and the network expands, accuracy improves and switching costs increase. In fact, if the patterns derived from the proprietary data are non-obvious even to the customer, the latter can begin to believe that the system knows them better than they know themselves, which can cement customer loyalty.

3. Proprietary knowledge base.

When the digitalization initiative exploits intellectual property, competitors find it much harder to copy it. If the proprietary intellectual assets can be protected or constantly evolved, sustainability of the initiative can be derived. Again, this may be reinforced by positive network externalities as the number of users grows. An example of this is the proprietary matching algorithm used by the eHarmony match-making platform. While it is not the only online match-making platform, it has been able to sustain its market due to the quality of matches that its algorithm can generate. To the extent that the firm can improve its algorithm's performance through AI-based learning features, the competitive advantage of the proprietary knowledge can be further enhanced.

4. Proprietary hardware and/or software.

When it is possible to embed domain expertise in specific hardware or software, the digitalization initiative can be protected from emulation, even if it is accessible through a public user interface. A case in point is IBM Quantum Experience,[6] which allows outside users to develop and deploy quantum applications in diverse areas such as AI, chemistry, and finance, with a simple graphical interface.

Note that this source of competitive advantage is based on the technology itself, rather than on data. Consequently, it is one of the hardest to sustain, without legal and regulatory protections.

5. Personalization.

By providing a personalized user experience through the exploitation of the user's personal data, a digitalization initiative can be protected from emulation. GeneInformed, for example, provides evidence-based advice reports on diet, fitness, skin care, and risk of exposure to environmental toxins, which are tailored to a person's genetic profile based on their DNA test results, from the company's DNA kits and analyses or those of others such as 23andMe.

While personalization can benefit a broad variety of products and services, it is particularly effective in the context of digital products and services. Conversely, it is often prohibitively expensive for traditional physical products, without significant digital enhancement. In recent years, manufacturing systems for physical products have moved from large-scale production of standard/generic products to flexible, and even mass-customizable production systems. In most such cases, the basis for the transition has been the adoption of digitally enhanced production resources, such as computer-controlled machinery and robotics.

---

[6] https://quantum-computing.ibm.com/.

6. **Exclusive partnerships.**

By involving exclusive partners, a digitalization initiative can create customer switching costs and competitor entry barriers, making it more sustainable. An example is Verizon's partnership with Riot Games, which is owned by Tencent, to collaborate on content and demonstrate its terrestrial fibre-optic as well as 5G wireless and network services to millions of players and viewers of the League of Legends Championship Series in North America, as their esports matches get streamed on LoL,[7] Twitch, and YouTube. The partnership can also involve multiple players such as in the case of TrustChain™, the consortium of diamond and precious metals companies that, together with IBM, develop a blockchain network to trace the origin of precious stones (see also Chap. 4).

By carefully considering the above features of digitalization initiatives, a business can not only identify information-driven ways of getting ahead but also staying ahead. Clearly, these features can be combined to expand and reinforce the sustainability of the competitive advantage that is derived from them.

Reflection Questions

- In what ways could your digital innovation initiatives provide sustainable competitive advantage?
- What types of metrics would you use to evaluate your market-facing process digitalization initiatives?
- What types of metrics would you use to evaluate your product digitalization initiatives?

---

[7] (https://lolesports.com/).

11

Risks of Digitalization

So far, we have examined the benefits of digital innovation in the interactions of a business with its external stakeholders. We have demonstrated that competitive digital innovation can significantly redraw the competitive landscape and position a business for sustained competitive advantage. We now turn to the other side, and examine the potential risks that executives need to consider regarding digitalization initiatives. We also discuss how these risks can be mitigated.

Technological Risk

Since digitalization involves the development and use of novel digital applications, there is always the risk that the desired functionalities with respect to computer hardware and software cannot be achieved with the necessary levels of reliability and performance. It is common knowledge that most information technology fail, even for traditional applications where the goal is to automate a well-understood process or task. Given that most competitive digitalization initiatives involve applications that are not only novel (which makes it difficult to prespecify all aspects of the target system's functionality, user interface, etc.), but also likely to have users who are outside the business (external stakeholders such as customers, suppliers and business partners), failure can have severe business consequences. In addition, many such initiatives are championed by functional managers in marketing, sales, business development and procurement, rather than the IT unit which may have to manage the development and implementation. So the business has to be very

A. Basu, S. Muylle, *Competitive Digital Innovation*, Palgrave Executive Essentials,
https://doi.org/10.1007/978-3-031-23440-8_11

diligent in assessing and monitoring the technological risk in developing and implementing any digitalization initiative. As part of this, the business needs to make sure it has proper backend systems in place when scaling a digital initiative. For instance, when ramping up an e-commerce pilot, integration with an Enterprise Resource Planning (ERP) system can link customer, product, order, inventory, shipping, and other information.

The business can also consider third party cloud solutions. To provide compelling user experiences, big tech companies now customdesign computer chips and combine their hardware with their software for superior performance. Amazon Web Services (AWS), for instance, custom designs its Trainium™ and Inferentia™ chips for providing its customers with the fastest and best price performance machine learning applications in the cloud. Likewise, Meta is developing custom chips to power the so-called metaverse (see Chap. 12), while it is also partnering with Qualcomm to produce custom chipsets for its Quest™ Virtual Reality devices to deal with heavy hardware and software requirements for spatial computing, given specific cost and form factors. While big tech players are pushing the envelope on information technology development, the business can turn to cloud solutions for reliable, performant and up-to-date applications. For instance, for training and inference of deep learning models, the business can turn to AWS (see above). This again goes to show that technology in and of itself is not a sustainable differentiator. Instead, it is the information that is stored, processed, and transferred through digital applications that can yield a sustainable competitive advantage for the business.

The successful deployment of a digital initiative can also be hampered by a lack of infrastructure. For instance, at the start of the commercial Internet in the early nineteen nineties, there was hardly any infrastructure for digital authentication or payment, which led many Web retailers to failure due to inadequate payment support. Two decades into the twenty-first century, the essential infrastructure for most basic market processes is now in place. However, information technology is constantly evolving, and the emergence of new technologies such as quantum computing and Web3 (see Chap. 12) again generates technological risk.

Dealing with technological risk involves effective design of the development team, good planning, leadership buy-in and effective project management. Given the nature of market-facing initiatives, including relevant players from functional areas such as marketing, sales and business development in the project team can be critical from the outset of the effort. Also, given that unpredictable changes can occur in novel applications, using development methods such as agile and Dev-Ops can be helpful, at least for initial versions of applications such as prototypes and pilots. And with change comes unpredictable costs, so having an executive champion who can help sustain the project with necessary resources is essential. And finally, as with most IT projects dealing with the complex digital marketplace, good project management can keep a development effort going through turbulence and change.

Competitive Risk

Given that the goal of most competitive digital innovation is to help the business compete more effectively, it might seem odd to consider downside competitive risk in that context. However, there are a number of ways in which digitalization can actually hurt the business in its ability to gain and sustain competitive advantage (see Chap. 8). For instance, it is widely known that information technology can lower entry barriers, by lowering various costs. For instance, digitalization can reduce personnel costs, by automating functions that were manual in the past. The use of software can also reduce certain capital costs, such as those associated with facilities and physical machinery/equipment.

In some situations, digitalization can have a disruptive effect, by enabling the business to use relatively inexpensive and simple technological innovations to replace or compete with expensive legacy technologies.

The lower entry barriers and potential disruptions can lead to new entrants in the market that operate very differently from incumbents. Competing against these upstarts can be very expensive and difficult. For instance, large businesses with significant legacy assets can find that their fixed costs are significantly higher, and the costs of maintaining and using the legacy assets are also uncompetitive.

The key defense against competitive risk is to focus on digital innovations that create sustainable competitive advantage. As we have discussed in earlier chapters, competitive levers such as switching costs for external stakeholders, proprietary information and knowledge resources that accumulate value over time, and defensible intellectual property should be the key drivers, rather than technological sophistication, automation and cost savings. Since the latter factors are often significant drivers of digital transformation (i.e., internally focused digitalization), it is therefore important to recognize the difference between internal innovation and competitive innovation.

Information Risk

As we have maintained throughout this book, digitalization is about unleashing the power of data, information and knowledge through the effective use of digital assets. However, data and information are assets that are not always easy to manage. For instance, data about individuals and even businesses can be private and proprietary. Thus, the business has to assess the risks associated with the security and privacy of its data assets.

There are two key aspects of data security and privacy that have to be considered. First, the business has to ensure that its use of customer and consumer data is consistent with the expectations of the data sources. In other words, data that is acquired for one purpose but then deployed to other purposes can expose the business to significant risk of litigation and loss of reputation and goodwill. Second, the business has to ensure the security of the data it acquires, and prevent it from getting into the wrong hands. Most organizations focus on what is known as perimeter defense with respect to data security, ensuring that external players cannot access its proprietary and competitive data. However, there could be risks even within the business, given that violations of data security tend to be far more often within the business itself.

The way the business uses customer data can also be a source of competitive advantage. Instead of merely complying with legislation (e.g., the General Data Protection Regulation (GDPR) in Europe, the California Consumer Privacy Act (CCPA) for California residents, and the Personal Information Protection Law (PIPL) in China), the business can actively promote its data ethics to its customers. A case in point is Apple who makes data privacy an integral part of its product design and gives users control over the way their data is collected, used, and shared. A counterexample is Facebook, whose data practices have been questioned in terms of ethics, as evidenced by the whistleblower testimony of Frances Haugen, former data scientist at the company, stating that Facebook "chooses profits over safety" and incentives "angry, polarizing, divisive content."[1]

For each of the digital technologies the business uses in its digital innovation initiatives, it needs to consider specific information risks. For instance, when using AI/ML in its digital applications, biases could occur from the data sources and the way the system is programmed. Again, the business can go beyond legal requirements and promote responsible AI. Philips, for instance,

---

[1] https://www.cbsnews.com/news/facebook-whistleblower-frances-haugen-misinformation-public-60-minutes-2021-10-03/.

commits to ethical use of AI through its Philips Data Principles on privacy, security, and beneficial use of data.[2] Likewise, for the Internet of Things, sensor data that is collected through third party components in the product may be at risk of being compromised.

Information risk can also be due to geopolitics. For instance, uncertainty exists about whether Chinese Internet companies such as IoT component providers and social media platforms share data with their government. ByteDance, for instance, the Chinese owner of popular social media video hosting platform TikTok, is being suspected of spreading disinformation to manipulate public opinion to subvert democracies, while it claims it stores international user data in the US and Singapore, and from 2023, in Ireland.

Dealing with the above-mentioned types of information risk starts with building awareness of the risks and factoring this awareness into the planning and design of digitalization initiatives. In particular, the implementation process for any initiatives that imply the collection and use of customer data should include robust data stewardship procedures that are recognized early in the process and considered at every stage. Thoughtful design of the planning and development teams can also help avoid nasty surprises in later stages when unforeseen events occur.

Rigidity Risk

Another inherent feature of digital innovation is that it is never a static, one-time change. Most software and hardware innovations can be emulated by competitors over time, sometimes at much lower costs than the business that introduces the innovations (on what is ironically called the "bleeding edge" rather than the "leading edge"). Thus, in order to sustain competitive advantage, a business that pursues competitive digital innovation has to be prepared to continue to innovate and evolve.

Even when rigidity protects your business' competitive advantage, regulation may challenge it. An example is the Dodd-Franklin legislation in the US and the Payment Service Directive 2 (PSD2) in Europe that require banks to share their consumer data with competitors and new entrants, given user content (see Chap. 8). Likewise, in China, digital businesses need to consider the risk of the regulatory crackdown on their operations. A case in point is Ant Group, whose $37 billion initial public offering to fuel its growth was scrapped in November 2020 by Chinese regulators.

---

[2] https://www.philips.com/a-w/about/artificial-intelligence/philips-ai-principles.html.

Another risk factor is sustainability, given mounting environmental concerns around digitalization, ranging from climate change due to carbon dioxide emissions to natural resource use and waste production. Distributed ledger technologies (DLT) such as the blockchain and cryptocurrencies, for instance, are very energy intense given the large amount of computing power needed to execute transactions, and the associated costs are hence referred to as "gas" fees. In response, DLT developers are exploring new ways to cut back on energy use while remaining secure. As case in point is Ethereum's The Merge initiative, which was executed on September 15, 2022, in which it moved from a proof-of-work to a proof-of-stake mechanism to verify transactions, which essentially eliminates the need for Ethereum mining and reduces its energy consumption by 99.95%.[3]

Likewise, e-commerce ventures can also pose risks for the environment. China's Shein, for instance, is a fast fashion business that challenges Zara and H&M by using machine learning technology in a visual search engine to scan trending fashions online and matching them to product design and inventory across its network of over 6000 Chinese suppliers, which then manufacture and mail the new item directly to international customers in less than ten days (generating carbon dioxide emissions). Its design-driven software, which is claimed to violate the intellectual property rights of fashion designers, its agile network of Chinese suppliers, which it is claimed to pressure its workers to fill orders fast, and its enlisting of social media influencers to promote its very cheap, immediate fashion items, make Shein's products easily disposable, which adds to the growing piles of fast fashion waste, and raises concerns about labor ethics.[4] Given the concerns for the environment, some digital platforms are launching sustainability training initiatives for their producers. For instance, online fashion retailers About You, YOOX Net-A-Porter, and Zalando have launched an online learning portal for brand partners to reduce carbon dioxide emissions in their operations and supply chains, in alignment with Science Based Targets initiative (SBTi) guidance and criteria, in a co-opetition model.[5]

As is clear from the above, sustainability also involves social risk. A potential risk is for people not to have Internet access, and hence being excluded from the digital economy, which is referred to as the digital divide (or gap between those who have access to digital technology and those without it),

---

[3] https://ethereum.org/en/upgrades/merge/ accessed Sep 19, 2022.

[4] Lau, Yvonne, China's Shein: Fast Fashion, Made Even Faster. Fortune, June/July 2022, pp. 32–35.

[5] https://corporate.zalando.com/en/newsroom/news-stories/about-you-yoox-net-porter-and-zalando-join-forces-launch-new-climate-action.

such that the business needs to make sure it is not excluding certain demographic clusters. Even when universal basic access is provided, social risks remain. A potential risk is Internet addiction, exacerbated by AI algorithms that serve to maximize user engagement. Pew Research Center, for instance, finds in a 2022 survey that about one-in-five American teenagers visit or use YouTube almost constantly, while almost one-in-six do so for TikTok, and 54% of American teens say it would be hard to give up social media.[6] Another risk relates to the mental health impact of social media use. For instance, Frances Haugen, whom we introduced earlier in this chapter, accused Facebook of not doing enough about how Instagram worsens body image issues among teenage girls, while making it hard for them to stop using the service. Furthermore, the human moderators who are tasked with evaluating user generated content on social media platforms have reported mental health problems due to their constant exposure to toxic content.[7]

While no amount of planning can prevent the occurrence of unforeseen events, and few strategic innovations have guaranteed outcomes, it is important to recognize that competitive digitalization can have major consequences for the business. The above discussion illustrates the importance of broad and comprehensive risk assessment and risk management in the planning and implementation processes, not just as a one-time task, but as an ongoing concern, due to the inherently dynamic and evolving nature of digitalization initiatives.

Challenges for Digital Platforms

So far we have discussed the various types of risk facing any business as it pursues competitive digital innovation. We now examine some additional challenges that face businesses that position themselves as multi-sided digital platforms. For instance, such businesses have to deal with the possibility that changes on each side can impact not only the participants on that side but also those on the other sides of the platform. A change that benefits consumers, for instance, can have negative effects on providers. And due to the presence of network effects and their exponential effect on the platform, small mistakes can quickly become crises.

A first challenge that a platform has to face is the management of the growth of the community on each side. Here, authentication of participants,

---

[6] https://www.pewresearch.org/internet/2022/08/10/teens-social-media-and-technology-2022/.

[7] https://www.bbc.com/news/technology-57088382.

which includes both identity and quality verification, is very important but often overlooked. For instance, MySpace, an early social media platform, failed to recognize the importance of user authentication features that are needed to sustain the community it was trying to build. As a growing number of undesirable and potentially malicious participants joined the one-sided platform and alienated users, it did not manage to build a community, let alone attract new sides.

A second challenge facing a platform is management of the growth of content. Platform operators can lose control of core features when the community on one or more sides grows very quickly. Striking examples of this are Facebook's inability to control fake news due to the participation of unprincipled and malicious providers, and Amazon Marketplace's issues in dealing with counterfeit and/or dangerous products bolstered by manipulated fake reviews and even fake transactions.

A third challenge facing platforms is the management of its reputation and liability. It is key to really think through the core functionality of the platform in terms of what it is offering and what it is responsible for versus what upstream providers and developers are doing. For instance, Uber riders can perceive the drivers to be part of Uber, such that what they do impacts Uber's reputation. Likewise, the regulator can classify the drivers as employees rather than contractors, and force Uber to treat them as such and pay out a minimum wage and sick days. The European Commission is currently working on a proposal for a Directive, which aims to improve working conditions in platform work.[8] Another regulatory development with respect to liability is the introduction of the Digital Services Act (DSA) and the Digital Markets Act (DMA) by the European Commission.

A fourth challenge for any platform is to motivate continued engagement and participation on all sides. Since, as in traditional markets, customer acquisition is more expensive than customer retention, relational engagement of participants can lead to more successful platforms. If a platform has low repeat business and the benefits are transactional, a relationship-oriented platform can enter and sway the participant base. For example, Monster was successful as an online job search intermediary but largely ignored mechanisms for same-side interactions among job-seekers, or among businesses seeking employees. As a result, individuals (and many businesses) used the site transactionally. On the other hand, LinkedIn not only filled vacancies but also

---

[8] European Commission proposals to improve the working conditions of people working through digital labor forms. Press release dd. 9-12-2021 (https://ec.europa.eu/commission/presscorner/detail/en/ip_21_6605).

engaged applicants to update their LinkedIn profiles and share their new positions, thus maintaining long-term relationships on the platform.

A fifth challenge for a multi-sided platform is to evolve without alienating incumbent participants. For instance, social media platforms such as Facebook and Twitter that offer individuals the ability to communicate within their social networks, have to be careful when they introduce other players such as merchants and advertisers. In other words, as a business builds out a platform, it has to do so in a way that does not diminish value for the users on existing sides. This is particularly challenging when the platform operator offers products or services that directly compete with those provided by external producers. For instance, Amazon and Netflix are increasingly facing this challenge as they have introduced their own content on their media platforms.

Finally, monetization is no easy feat. The race for winner-take all-or-most markets can be long and full of obstacles, and may necessitate postponement of monetization and profitability. This is compounded by the fact that premature attempts to monetize a platform can suppress critical positive network effects and stymie growth, as in the case of WhatsApp when it merely proposed the initiation of modest user fees. The long gestation of digital native platforms such as Amazon, Facebook and Twitter before they achieved profitability is worth noting for established companies considering platforms. It underscores the importance of patience and the likely need for sustained investment for some time before seeing significant returns. In other words, platforms should be viewed as strategic investments, rather than tactical opportunities.

Value creation in a platform is not limited by internal assets and brain trust, as in a traditional enterprise. Rather, the core capabilities of the platform operator are significantly complemented by input from participants on one or more sides. As a result, network size and engagement become key in driving growth and superior performance. As positive network effects amplify on different sides, the value and market power of a digital platform can grow exponentially, creating significant and sustainable competitive advantages for the platform business.

As with all competitive digitalization initiatives, effective risk management of digital platform initiatives is critical to their success. As the above discussion illustrates, the potentially explosive growth of platforms due to the network effects on each side, and the fact that the defining features of a platform are often dependent on the actions of stakeholders other than the platform operator make it particularly important to recognize and respond to risks and adverse events promptly and decisively, and to ensure that the business has the risk mitigation and remediation resources in place to make that feasible.

Reflection Questions

- What are the key types of risk facing your digital innovation initiatives?
- Which potential challenges are key to your digital platform initiatives?
- Do you have a risk management strategy in place to recognize and respond to risks promptly, with the necessary recourses and capabilities?

12

Broadening the Lens

We have discussed a number of popular and important digital technologies as we have gone through the book so far, including the Web, social media, mobile apps, big data, blockchain and IoT. These technologies will be integral to competitive digital innovation for the foreseeable future. However, the concepts and ideas we have presented are not technology-specific and thus will help businesses continue to leverage digitalization for competitive advantage, even as new digital technologies emerge. So we would like to end with a brief look at a few new technologies that could offer exciting opportunities for digitalizing processes, products and business models in new and creative ways.

Artificial Intelligence

Artificial Intelligence (AI) can be defined as technologies that enable computer systems to perform tasks normally requiring human intelligence. The latter refers to the ability of humans to acquire and apply knowledge and skills, which involves learning and putting the learning into operation.

AI applications can be organized around three sets of human activities: sense, think, act.

- Sense refers to technologies that enable computer systems to allow what humans do in terms of sensing. Well-developed applications for hearing are speech recognition and natural language interfaces, such that humans can talk to the system rather than having to program it. Likewise computer vision enables seeing.

A. Basu, S. Muylle, *Competitive Digital Innovation*, Palgrave Executive Essentials,
https://doi.org/10.1007/978-3-031-23440-8_12

- Think involves applications such as expert systems that can exhibit human expert levels of problem solving capabilities or virtual agents to which reasoning tasks can be assigned that otherwise would be assigned to humans (e.g., bank tellers, customer service representatives).
- Act refers to applications that generate an output. These include robots and autonomous, mechanical devices, as well as voice interfaces.

To understand where AI can be applied in a system, it is useful to start by considering a closed-loop system. Such a system consists of an input, a process, an output, and a feedback loop (See Fig. 12.1).

As an example, consider an operator who needs to separate synthetic bottle corks from natural ones on a conveyer belt that gathers bottle corks for recycling. The input involves the operator monitoring all the corks, both synthetic and naturals ones, on the belt. The processing concerns the operator spotting the synthetic corks. The output is the operator removing the corks he or she identified as synthetic from the belt. Finally, the feedback loop is about a quality inspector verifying whether the removed corks were indeed synthetic in nature, and whether the corks that went into recycling were all natural. Based on the feedback of the quality inspector, the operator can increase his/her processing accuracy in separating the synthetic from the natural corks on the conveyer belt, and the performance of the closed-loop system would improve.

AI can be applied to all elements of the closed-loop system. Continuing the example, computer vision could be used to monitor all the corks on the conveyer belt and an algorithm developed to analyze the computer images for recognizing the synthetic corks. A robotic arm could be built to pick and remove the identified corks from the belt. The quality inspection of the corks could be used as feedback to improve the accuracy of the processing algorithm.

An interesting question that arises is whether AI needs to have human-like capabilities for it to be effective. When AI is used on the input or output side, the interface and the interaction preferably needs to be human like. Consider a chatbot as an example. Here, the interface and interaction can be enabled

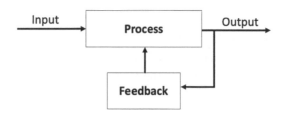

Fig. 12.1 A closed-loop system

through the use of natural language processing and voice simulation. However, for other applications, especially in processing, AI does not necessarily need to be human-like.

An AI system can be represented as shown in Fig. 12.2 below.

In addition to the application of AI in the input and output elements of the system, the thinking element can consist of machine reasoning mechanisms and a knowledge base. One example of this is an inference engine that applies logical rules to the domain knowledge base to deduce new information. Alternatively, a set of heuristics (rules-of-thumb) can be applied in a trial-and-error set-up using large amounts of computing power, connecting the input to the output. The rules or heuristics are separated from the domain knowledge. Instead of writing a traditional software program in which the domain knowledge is embedded, the domain knowledge is separated such that it can evolve and get added, while the rules or heuristics do not change. Another important component is learning, which can involve algorithms to locate patterns in the output, and add to the domain knowledge base. Anytime anyone of these AI components can be incorporated into a system, it becomes an AI system.

Some AI systems can start off without any domain knowledge and hence generate output that would be inacceptable according to human standards. However, if it has a learning mechanism, then this mechanism can learn relevant domain knowledge over time from feedback data. As a result, the system may over time produce human-level output or even surpass that. In other words, the ability of such an AI system typically improves over time.

At some point then, can the AI system replace the human?

The extent to which the inference engine captures all required inputs to arrive at meaningful outputs is key for developing an effective AI system, as is

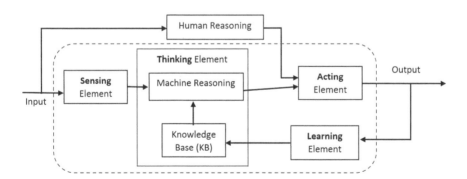

Fig. 12.2 An AI-enhanced system

the ability to perform all the necessary reasoning. For most complex activities performed by humans, factors other than those considered in existing AI systems come into play. In order to successfully complete such activities, the reasoning performed by the AI system has to be combined with human reasoning. Thus, in Fig. 12.2, the actions of the AI system are the result of the combination of human reasoning and machine reasoning.

The structure of an AI system also depends upon the type of task or activity that it is applied to. For tasks that require physical actions as outputs, the actions of the system are implemented through robotic or other mechanical actuators and devices. On the other hand, for information processing tasks, the actions and outputs can be decisions or information flows.

AI methods can be categorized as being either knowledge-based or data-based. Early AI research methods tried to emulate human behavior, attempting to solve a problem like a human expert would. They were top-down, axiomatic and prescriptive, like doctors' rules for patient diagnosis. The primary focus of these early AI systems was to capture human expertise in appropriate machine interpretable forms in knowledge bases, and then apply this expertise using suitable deductive reasoning in inference engines. Much of the effort in designing such systems was to emulate how humans might reason about a problem. In other words, these systems sought to emulate human behaviour (or reasoning). The focus today has shifted. Current AI research methods attempt to emulate human performance, rather than human behaviour. In other words, the emphasis in system design has shifted from effective knowledge representation and inference engine design to the design of sophisticated learning mechanisms. These newer systems are bottom-up and inductive, and their key resource is large amounts of relevant domain data, rather than domain experts. What is more, they can behave in ways that are completely different from how humans would behave and even outperform humans. However, this performance comes at a price, since the most powerful machine learning methods lead to AI systems that are opaque "black boxes", whose behavior and workings cannot be explained, which can in turn limit their applicability to certain problems and tasks. This is also true of emerging Generative AI (GAI) systems such as ChatGPT (from OpenAI), which exploit large language models (LLM) to address very broad varieties of queries and tasks, as well as generating creative output in various media.

Where can AI play a role in competitive digital innovation? Simply put, it can play a role in pretty much all the types of innovations we have discussed in this book. In other words, it can be used to digitalize processes, products and even refine the implementation of digitalized business models. The extent to which AI can be applied to any initiative is determined by the key driver of AI, which is data. In any initiative in which a business collects data on the process or product involved, machine learning algorithms can be potentially applied to refine the process or product respectively. Ideally, this results in an artifact (process or product) that is not static, but rather one that learns and improves over time, such as the Eneco Toon smart thermostat and the Barco Demetra skin imaging solution. Similarly, data that is collected as part of a digitalized business model can be applied to improve the implementation of the model by leveraging appropriate AI and machine learning algorithms, like Amazon's use of AI to render personalized Web pages to online shoppers. We expect to see such applications in increasing number and variety of settings over the foreseeable future.

The Metaverse

As "digital native" younger people become a larger segment of online markets, the role of technology is clearly becoming more significant. One important trend in this move towards technology-enabled commerce is the convergence of Web, mobile and gaming technologies (including augmented reality, virtual reality and artificial intelligence). And a fascinating and potentially significant outcome of this convergence is a phenomenon that is described as the Metaverse.

So what exactly is the Metaverse? It is the use of digital technologies to create virtual environments that are flexible, fluid and possibly decoupled from physical reality with respect to spatial, social and possibly even temporal attributes. In other words, the Metaverse allows people and organizations to represent themselves in multiple stylized ways, and supports interactions and processes that are different from those in the real world. More specifically, instances of the Metaverse allow stylized representations of people and organizations to immerse themselves and interact in artificial settings, with artificial products and artificial processes, artificial money and even artificial laws and norms.

One early manifestation of some of the features of the Metaverse was the Second Life virtual World created by Linden Lab in the beginning of the Millenium. It allowed participants to create avatars of themselves with aliases, and then interact with others in virtual settings that were created by both the company and also by the participants themselves. It had its own currency, mechanisms for property purchase and ownership, mechanisms for creating buildings, businesses and institutions, and therefore a host of artificial social and commercial systems. Many real businesses created virtual representations of themselves in Second Life, and conducted business there. For instance, some schools and colleges used Second Life to conduct information sessions that could be attended by prospective students from around the world, who could also explore the virtual campus to find information about the school's programs and services.

Businesses such as Meta (the parent of Facebook, Whatsapp and Instagram), Roblox Corporation (a leading digital gaming company), Epic Games' Fortnite, Alphabet (the parent of Google and Youtube), and Microsoft are among the frontrunners in developing Metaverse initiatives. In Asia, new instances of the Metaverse are emerging that quickly amass large user bases. ZEPETO, for instance, is a metaverse initiative of South-Korean tech group Naver that has attracted over 300 million users since its launch in 2018, mostly in South-Korea, Japan, and China, while it is expanding to Europe, the Middle East, and the Americas. It is geared towards mostly female teenagers who can create their own virtual worlds and represent themselves through 3D avatars in their own fashion designs, which they can also trade. Through licensing partnerships, ZEPETO lets brands engage with users such that they can drive a virtual Hyundai car, have virtual Samsung appliances, wear digital Bulgari, Gucci and Ralph Lauren luxury fashion, and gear up with digital Adidas and Nike sportswear.

How can businesses use the Metaverse? Consider the fact that just as social media enabled businesses to be represented in public forums based on inputs not only from themselves but also external stakeholders such as consumers, suppliers and even competitors, the Metaverse enables even more creative and powerful representations of businesses and their products and services. Thus, in addition to using the new channels that the Metaverse creates for business transactions of both existing and new products, businesses can also leverage this new environment in the following ways:

- **Better understand the needs of Customers**: By letting customers engage with simulations of new products and services in the virtual setting, businesses can learn what works (or not), in far more dynamic and at much greater scale than existing product and marketing research mechanisms.
- **Discover new Customers and Markets**: By putting simulated products and services out on the Metaverse (and leveraging the social engagement there), businesses can expose their products to new customers and even new markets.
- **Scope out the Competition**: In public Metaverse settings, businesses can visit, discover and engage with the offerings of competitors (as well as players in non-competing markets) to better track trends in innovation and competitor innovations. Of course, since these are virtual settings, they also provide ample opportunities for businesses to "game" the market and their

competition, far more effectively than businesses announcing vaporware and non-existent products in traditional settings.

Web3

As the World Wide Web evolves, it keeps offering new opportunities for businesses to transform their processes, products, and business models. Currently, the term Web3 is attracting a lot of attention as it could potentially disrupt established ways of doing business in the digital economy.

The basic World Wide Web, invented by Tim Berners-Lee in 1989 at CERN (the European Organization for Nuclear Research), which made the Web protocol and code royalty free in 1993, is about the sharing of static content. Anyone can put up content on a Website and add hyperlinks to connect with other Websites. The content on the basic Web is decentralized across many Websites and users can share and browse text and images globally. Web 2.0, a term coined by Web designer Darcy DiNucci in 1999 and popularized by O'Reilly Media corporation in 2004, is about the sharing of rich content. Users cannot only generate and share static content like text and images but also rich content such as multimedia and social media. However, this is done in a way that the basic functionality is centralized. For instance, on Facebook users can share rich content but the particular type of content they can share is determined by Facebook. Hence, the dominant providers of social media services and multimedia content platforms exert control over the functionality of how content can be shared. Web3,[1] a term coined by Ethereum co-founder Gavin Wood in 2014, which became popular in 2021, is about the packaging of basic and rich content *and* application functionality in sharable bundles, which can be developed by anybody and shared, using protocols for sharing and established approaches like object identification. If the functionality can be decentralized, the hope is that it becomes a more democratic and equitable system, rather than a system controlled by a small number of big tech companies. For example, Facebook can no longer control what can be done with the content in Web3 environments.

Decentralized applications, called dApps, can be used to achieve this level of decentralization. These apps build on the standard telecom protocols for low level communication, and adopt application level protocols for rich content and functionality, which are controlled by whoever builds them. DApps

---

[1] Web3 is distinct from Web 3.0, which is sometimes used to refer to the Semantic Web, a term coined by Tim Berners-Lee in 1999 to describe a web of data that can be processed by machines.

bring development down to the level of exchanging and sharing objects and applications that have functionality built into them. This allows for a more decentralized environment, with data being stored in either peer-to-peer storage networks such as the InterPlanetary File System (IPFS) or distributed digital ledgers like blockchains with smart contracts. Since not only functionality, but also content and data are being obtained in a more decentralized way, interesting revenue models are possible in which content and ideas can get crowdsourced. Users can get rewarded with digital tokens for the content they generate, and protocol changes can only be adopted by a majority of users with voting rights in a decentralized autonomous organization (DAO). Use cases are emerging in decentralized finance, referred to as DeFi (e.g., lending, trading, derivatives, and insurance), gaming (e.g., Decentraland), and social media (e.g., Mastodon), as well as other sectors. The Metaverse-oriented initiatives that businesses are pursuing today can also leverage Web3 ideas like DeFi mechanisms such as blockchain and cryptocurrencies to implement transaction processes which are different from and decoupled from the financial processes used in traditional commerce.

Notwithstanding the promise of having democratic groups of open-source developers build Web3 applications to the benefit of their users, this approach can also lead things to go wrong. When content and functionality are decentralized, security, control and reliability become more complicated. Indeed, if code and functionality can be embedded in sharable objects, then those objects can be harmful as well. Hence, it becomes key to maintain accountability and keep malicious actors from exploiting vulnerabilities overlooked by developers. As a result, regulatory oversight is increasingly needed to protect consumers against fraud and implement robust know-your-customer (KYC) and anti-money laundering (AML) procedures. Other factors that are blocking widespread adoption include poor user experiences, transaction costs (so-called "gas fees" on blockchains to execute transactions), and privacy concerns.

So what is the role of Web3 in competitive digital innovation? Essentially, it will hopefully spur more creativity and innovation at small scale since it is decentralized and will lead to new ways of developing innovations that could leverage the wisdom of crowds and benefits from a broader base of resources like developers, and can create an infrastructure for distributed exchange of ideas and value. An example of an organization that is using Web3 features is Opolis, a cooperative that provides independent workers with group employment benefits such as automated payroll (which can be partially in cryptocurrencies), health, dental and vision insurance, retirement plans, and short- and long-term disability policies. Every member also earns rewards ($Work digital tokens) for utilizing its services and referring friends, which can be used to earn enhanced voting power, get discounts, or claim profits.

Reflection Questions

- In what ways are the three trends that we discuss in this chapter significant for your business? Can you identify any opportunities to exploit them to become more competitive?
- Which emerging digital technologies could you leverage to transform your products, processes, and business models for sustained competitive advantage?

Index

© The Author(s), under exclusive license to Springer Nature Switzerland AG 2023
A. Basu, S. Muylle, *Competitive Digital Innovation*, Palgrave Executive Essentials,
https://doi.org/10.1007/978-3-031-23440-8